ok may be kep
W9-BWI-640

A MIRROR FOR PRINCES

A MIRROR FOR PRINCES

THE QĀBŪS NĀMA

by

KAI KĀ'ŪS IBN ISKANDAR
PRINCE OF GURGĀN

Translated from the Persian by

REUBEN LEVY

Professor of Persian in the University of Cambridge and Fellow of Christ's College

LONDON
THE CRESSET PRESS
MCMLI

First published in 1951 by
The Cresset Press Ltd., 11 Fitzroy Square, London, W.1,
and printed in Great Britain by J. W. Arrowsmith Ltd., Bristol 1.

CONTENTS

INTRODUCTION

THE *Qābūs-nāma* is described by its author as a guide intended to warn his favourite son and destined successor against the pitfalls on life's journey and to direct him in the path likely to lead to the greatest benefits. In essence it combines the functions of popular educator, manual of political conduct and text book of ethics, with expediency as its motto. The author declares at the outset that it contains the distilled essence of his own life's experience, set down when he was sixty-three years of age; if his advice does not receive the attention it deserves from the beloved son to whom it is addressed—and the author is not sanguine that it will—someone destined for felicity in this world and the next will doubtless be found to take advantage of it. In any event he himself will have fulfilled his duty as a father in proffering it. He gives the date of composition as the year 475 of the Hijra, corresponding to A.D. 1082.

Kai Kā'ūs ibn Iskandar ibn Qābūs ibn Washmgīr, the author, belonged to the princely dynasty of the Ziyārids, who held sway in the South Caspian provinces of Gīlān, Tabaristān (Māzandarān) and Jurjān (or Gurgān). The first member of the dynasty to gain power was a certain Mardāwīj ibn Ziyār, whose name is said to be an arabicised form of the Persian *mard-āwīz*, *i.e.* "The Man-hanger". The biographer Yāqūt (A.D. 1179–1229), a Greek by birth, who in his childhood was sold as slave to a Baghdad merchant, tells how Mardāwīj, on attaining to the kingship, had a throne of pure gold constructed for himself, upon which he seated himself with the declaration that he was another King Solomon and that his Turkish slaves, of whom he had purchased a great horde, were the demons, over whom he held mastery. His treatment of them was in fact so brutal as to goad them into secret revolt, and they did him to death on an occasion when he was taking his ease in the hammam.

His most influential subjects, members of the Dailamite tribe, chose his brother Washmgīr to succeed him; but his reign was disturbed by twenty years of war against the neighbouring Buwaihid princes, at one time Ziyārid vassals. Peace was declared in the reign of his son Behistūn, who gave one of his daughters in marriage to a Buwaihid princeling. Washmgīr himself, like his brother before him, met a violent end, and for the same reasons, his cruelty and harshness having driven his slave-soldiery to conspire against him. They one day, in the depth of winter, compelled his son Minuchihr to seize and imprison him in a fortress, where they left him to freeze to death, without clothes or other covering.

To him there succeeded his son Qābūs, a famous character whom the author of the present work, his grandson, appears to have venerated and from whom, seemingly, the work derives its title. This Qābūs, we are informed by Yāqūt, was a mixture of fierce and cruel warrior and accomplished man of letters. He was a skilled Arabist, well-read in philosophy and astronomy, a poet and patron of poets, a prolific correspondent and generally well-versed in the arts of his time.

Yet he displayed his inherited traits by putting to death the officers of his bodyguard one by one until hardly any were left. A conspiracy among his troops drove him into exile for a period of eighteen years, after which he managed to collect a force strong enough to regain possession of the throne for him. Finally, however, he was assassinated and his body carried to Jurjān. His coffin was placed in a lofty tower-tomb which he had himself erected and which is still standing.

Robert Byron, in his *Road to Oxiana*, repeats a legend that Qābūs was placed in a crystal coffin which was suspended by chains midway between roof and floor of the tomb. That legend, however, is merely a repetition of one originally told of the Prophet Daniel's tomb by Rabbi Benjamin of Tudela, who travelled in the lands of the Eastern Mediterranean in the years between A.D. 1166 and 1171. When speaking of Khūzistān the Rabbi says:[1] "In the midst of its ruins is Shushan the capital, the site of the palace of King Ahasuerus. The river Tigris divides the city and the bridge connects the two parts . . . On the one side where the Jews dwell is the sepulchre of Daniel . . . In the course of time [the Sultan] Sinjar Shah came to this place and [seeing the rivalry between the Jews and the other inhabitants for the possession of the Prophet's coffin, which brought prosperity] he said, 'I command you to take the coffin of Daniel and place it inside another coffin of crystal and to suspend this from the middle of the bridge by a chain of iron'."

Kai Kā'ūs clearly admired his grandfather despite the very obvious defects in his character, which he does not attempt to extenuate and some of which it is quite possible that he shared himself; for in view of his gospel of expediency, he is unlikely to have had any scruples about removing from his path anyone who stood in his way. He says as much in Chapter XX, where he urges his son not to neglect his duty

[1] *Benjamin of Tudela*, ed. M. N. Adler, Oxford 1907, pp. 51f. I am indebted for the reference to Professor V. Minorsky.

when the "general welfare" demands the shedding of blood.

And here a word of caution may not be out of place. With expediency always his first consideration, his words cannot be regarded as containing the ideals or ideas of all Persians, still less of all Muslims. Indeed, they no more reflect official Islamic doctrine and ethical theory than Machiavelli's *Prince* or Lord Chesterfield's *Letters* those of Christianity. Yet the normal and customary exhortations are not lacking in the work, and in the passage describing his views of *noblesse oblige*, the author rises to a very great height. And, in general, he appears anxious to impress upon his son the necessity for living the life of a good Muslim.

In its mixture of the ideal and the practical the *Qābus-nāma* reflects standards prevailing in official life in the East to this day, the essence being succinctly stated in a passage in Sir Charles Lyall's *Life of Warren Hastings*, published in 1889. "There is no such school for practical politics", says he, "as Asia, where the good old rule of taking and keeping still prevails side by side with the most solemn and laudable precepts of justice and virtue; and where inconsistencies between acts and axioms trouble no one." It may not be devoid of significance that the India Office Library's manuscript copy of the *Qābūs-nāma* bears the autograph signature of Warren Hastings.

Although the author of that work urges his son to be observant in his faith, his family had probably not long been converted to it, the provinces bordering on the Caspian Sea having been among the last in Persia to accept Islam. As late as A.D. 912 we read how Ḥasan ibn 'Alī, the "Great Missioner", invited the inhabitants of Tabaristān and Dailam, of whom some were idolaters, others Magians, to become Muslims. By no means all responded, and records of the year 394/1003 show that the poet Abu'l-Hasan, a native of the Dailamite province who had been a fire-worshipper, was only then received into the new faith. In the early stages of the Muslim conquest, it would appear that it was chiefly the members of noble families who accepted the religion of the invaders, for material as well as other reasons. A good example is that of the Barmecides (Barmakids). The name Barmak was originally, says the traveller and historian Mas'ūdī[1], a title borne by the High Priest of the great Magian fire-temple at Naw Bahār in Bactria. But his descendants, down to the destruction of the family by Hārūn al-Rashīd, proudly retained the name of Barmecides.

The spirit of ancient Iran refused to die with the coming of Islam; it merely took on the colouring of the new faith and its observances. In a land where life was, and is, particularly full of uncertainties, the doctrines preached by Muhammad did not to everyone's satisfaction solve the problem of good and evil which had long been argued there. Professor E. G. Browne, in one of his lectures, declared that Pessimism had been one of the chief influences in the evolution of most of the religions and philosophies of Persia and that hardly anywhere had so much thought been devoted to the problem of the nature and origin of Evil. "The old dilemma that the Creator, if He could have prevented the appearance of Evil in the universe, and did not do so, cannot be All-Good, while if He wished to prevent it, but could not, He cannot be All-Powerful, has troubled the Persian more than it troubles the European mind."

The two pre-Muhammadan religions which originated or developed in Iran, namely Zoroastrianism and Manichaeism, certainly recognise two independent and hostile powers in

[1] *Murūj al-Dhahab*, "Prairies d'Or", ed. Barbier de Meynard, iv, pp. 47f.

the universe, struggling for supremacy; whereas primitive Islam hardly regarded it as a problem, since Allah was All-Knowing as well as All-Powerful. In the utterances of Kai Kā'ūs there is neither speculation nor judgment about good or evil. He shows himself influenced by the feeling pervading all Persian literature that life is transitory and that "the end and aim of all human activity is death and departure from the world". There is also present the old Iranian conception of an inexorable fate ruling the world. But it is incalculable as well as inexorable, and brings good as well as evil. The wise man therefore will suffer its decrees passively and with equanimity. The author advises his son to await what the heavens may send with shoulders braced and mouth open, and so be ready either for blows or titbits.

It is here if anywhere that some parallel is to be found with Lord Chesterfield's counsels to his son, although the polished Englishman's lucubrations were characterised by Dr Johnson as teaching the morals of a whore and the manners of a dancing-master, while there is a good deal that is genuine in the medieval Persian warrior, who advised what he thought good for success in living regardless of conventional ethics.

The world in which he existed was politically in a state of flux, with life uncertain and hard. Some of his territory, sloping northwards down to the Caspian Sea, was fertile, but much was covered with forest, while most of the eastern part was barren desert. All was liable to Turcoman invasions, which have been endemic throughout Persian history, and he himself, as a vassal of the Seljuq Turkish Sultans, was burdened by payment of tribute. These Seljuqs were a restless marauding family of warriors, who appeared on the Persian scene from Central Asia at a time when the Abbasid Caliphate, with its capital at Baghdad, had lost all temporal power. They had themselves been newly converted to Islam and by over-running Persia, Mesopotamia, Syria and Asia Minor, they gave unity to a great stretch of territory which had long been without it. With the zeal of converts they stiffened the wavering faith of the original inhabitants of those lands and so combined them that they were able to drive back the Byzantines, who had been creeping back on to their ancient territories and were in part recovering them. The Seljuq efforts "bred up a generation of fanatical Muhammadan warriors, to whom, more than to anything else, the Crusades owed their repeated failure".[1] Gibbon describes with apparent satisfaction the overthrow, in A.D. 1071 at Malazkerd or Manzikert, of the Byzantine forces, which were made up "of the subjects and allies of Europe . . . and, above all, the mercenary and adventurous bands of French and Normans. Their lances were commanded by the valiant Ursel of Baliol, the kinsman or father of the Scottish kings".

Socially, the world which the book describes was a man's world and the general picture of life in it that of a small town lying in the midst of agricultural land, on which many of the town's inhabitants were employed and from which they returned to sleep at home in the evening. Distinctions of class were recognised, but the divisions between them were extremely tenuous and easily broken through. Indeed the social circumstances revealed in the book do not greatly differ from those described in James Morier's *Adventures of Hajji Baba of Ispahan*, where a man might by his efforts raise himself from slavery to princedom and be cast by his evil

[1] S. Lane-Poole: *Muhammadan Dynasties*, *s.v.* Seljuks.

star from the height of prosperity into the depths of penury and ignominy, and where all things were possible.

This is not to say that all achieved equality or had the same kind of privileges open to them. Only men belonging to princely families, for example, or men destined for the learned professions, received or attained by their own efforts any formal education. Our author for one appears to have been instructed in the arts regarded as suitable for acquisition by a man of good family in his time, and almost certainly acquired others by himself. Although it is unlikely that he would have burdened himself with the task of setting down his work in writing, for which he probably employed a scribe, the consistent style of the whole indicates the hand of a single accomplished author, with possibly some additions in the way of anecdotes borrowed from other sources, whether Persian or foreign.

In the course of his reading and instruction, or in conversation with *savants* who resided at his father's court, he doubtless learnt much of the religious and philosophical lore of his land and faith, and since Islamic tradition is filled with reminiscences of the stories in the Old and New Testaments, it need not surprise us to come across such a story as that of the youth Fatḥ, who found loaves floating down to him on the Tigris. It is a characteristically naïve illustration of the behest to "Cast thy bread upon the waters" (Ecclesiastes, xi, 1).

It is similarly at second hand that the author would have had any knowledge of the Greek classics, which some of his instructors might well have read in translation. Not all the Greek classics, it must however be said, but rather the works of the philosophers and doctors. Among the lands of the Near East, Syria and Mesopotamia had come under the influence of Greek learning and science in the days of Alexander the Great and his successors. Propagation of such learning was encouraged still further by the Byzantine rulers, whose efforts were greatly helped by Christianity. Monks in Syrian monasteries engaged in translating sacred books from Greek to Syriac, but did not confine themselves merely to works of ecclesiastical interest; philosophy and science in all its branches also engaged their minds. When, in the fifth century, the Nestorians expelled from the Byzantine empire took refuge in scattered communities in Mesopotamia and Iran, they founded special schools in which Greek medicine and other sides of "philosophy" were taught. The most famous of these schools was one, established at Gunday Shāpūr, some little distance to the north of Ahwaz, which was in existence as late as the time of the Caliph Mansūr (A.D. 754–775), grandfather of Hārūn al-Rashīd.

The work of propagating Greek science was carried a stage further when Christians and Jews engaged in translating texts from the intermediate Syriac form into Arabic. With the establishment of the Caliphate at Baghdad, such learning and activity was greatly encouraged, so that Greek philosophy and science became widespread wherever Muslim *savants* were to be found. And, in this context, it is to be borne in mind that Arabic was as much the language of learning in the Muhammadan world as Latin that of learning in medieval Europe. Men of Persian culture, though not always of Iranian stock, eagerly absorbed the new learning, and the names of Rhazes and al-Fārābī, who flourished in the ninth century A.D., and Avicenna, who died in A.D. 1037, bear witness to the competency with which they handled it.

Avicenna at one period of his career had Qābūs ibn Washmgīr as his patron and would have remained with him had not the prince been exiled. There were numerous similar courts of the kind, which sprang up all over Persia as the Caliphate declined and local spirit and patriotism began to assert itself. The most famous, perhaps, was that of Maḥmūd of Ghazna, where many a poet and learned scholar was kept as a guest, honoured but often unwilling, to add lustre to the monarch's name. Had the poet Firdawsi not escaped this would-be patron's clutches in time, his great epic recounting the legends of Iran's pre-Muslim heroes and heroines would probably never have survived, at least in its present form.

It was the work of such men as these, locally encouraged, which achieved national fame. What commanded a market best, however, was laudatory verse, much of which, perhaps too much, has survived. Essays and *belles lettres* were a comparatively late development, and not having a specifically personal appeal were always of rare occurrence. In the period more or less contemporary with our author, only three works in that class having any merit are known, the *Qābūs-nāma* being the earliest. Of the others, one is the *Siyāsat-nāma*, or "Treatise on Government", of the Niẓām al-Mulk, the famous vizier of the Great Seljuqs whom legend connects with Omar Khayyam and who died by the hand of an Assassin envoy in 485/1092–3. The second was the "Four Discourses" (on Secretaries, Poets, Astrologers and Physicians) of Niẓāmī 'the Samarqandī Prosodist', who flourished in the first half of the twelfth century A.D. and was personally acquainted with Omar Khayyam.

Manuscripts of the original Persian text of all three works are rare, but Charles Schefer published the text of the *Siyāsat-nāma*, with a French translation, in 1891, and Mirza Muhammad Qazwini and Professor Browne respectively the text and English translation of the "Four Discourses", under the auspices of the E. J. W. Gibb Memorial (1910, 1921). The Trustees of the same Memorial in the early part of the present century entrusted the work of editing the Persian text of the *Qābūs-nāma* to the late Mr Edward Edwards of the Oriental Department of the British Museum, but he was prevented from making any more than a beginning by pressure of other work and the onset of serious illness.

It may be asked why such works as these are not better, and more generally, known. Pure chance may have been one reason, rarity of texts—due to destruction wrought by the Tartar hordes under Chingiz Khan's subordinates—another (preferred by Persians), and still another that between the seventeenth century, when Persian studies are first heard of in this country, and the beginning of the nineteenth, the main concern of scholars was with Biblical literature. With the more secular outlook of the nineteenth century, when Persian literature began to be studied for its own sake, in the first instance by men who were, or had been, in contact with the Mogul Empire or its successors, the first task of scholars was seen to be the deliverance from obscurity or oblivion of the great numbers of works which lay buried in manuscript.

Scholars therefore devoted themselves to cataloguing the accumulations in European and Asiatic libraries and only very slowly began to engage in the arduous, and, from the point of view of earning a living, unremunerative task of editing and publishing the texts that were being demanded. Since these were for the benefit of learned fellow-workers in the same field, translations were deemed unnecessary—possibly even inexpedient sometimes. Ordinarily too, it was the poetical literature, steeped in mysticism, which attracted, rather than the prose, much of which dates from times when Mongol, Turkish and Indian authors were imposing their own intricate and flowery patterns on the basic simplicity of Persian.

It remains to say that the princeling Gīlānshāh, for whom the *Qābūs-nāma* was composed, was the last ruling member of his line. After a reign of seven years he was overthrown by Hasan-i Sabbāḥ (the Old Man of the Mountains of whom, and of whose successors, the Crusaders stood later so much in dread) in the year 483 of the Hijra, i.e. A.D. 1090–1.

REUBEN LEVY

ACKNOWLEDGMENT

I wish to thank Mr. John Hayward for helping me with the translation of some of the verses quoted in the text.

R.L.

BIBLIOGRAPHICAL NOTE

THE TRANSLATOR HAS made the present version from a Persian text edited by him, and to be published by the Trustees of the E. J. W. Gibb Memorial, on the basis mainly of the following manuscripts:
India Office Library: Ethé no. 2153; undated, but probably of the seventeenth century A.D.,
British Museum: Cod. Or. 3252; dated 861/1457,
Paris (Bibliothèque Nationale): Ancien fonds 138; dated 879/1474, and
Leiden: Cod. 449 Warn. (Catalogue IV, p. 207); dated 719/1319.

The Persian text has been twice printed:
1. A "bazaar" text, with an introduction by Riḍā Qulī Khān "Hidāyat", Tihrān, 1285/1868, and
2. An edition with good notes by Sa'īd Nafīsī, Tihrān 1312/1934. An expurgated edition for school use has been made from the latter.

At various periods the work was translated from Persian into Turkish and of these versions two are extant, one made for the Sultan Murād II (A.D. 1421–1443) and the second for Hasan Pasha, Governor of Baghdad in 1117/1705–06. Manuscripts of the Turkish translation appear to be commoner than those of the Persian original.

The work was twice translated into a European language in the nineteenth century:
1. Buch des Kabus, oder Lehren des persischen Königs Kjekjawus für seinen Sohn Ghilan Schach . . . aus dem Türkisch-Persisch-Arabischen übersetzt und durch Abhandlungen und Anmerkungen erläutert von H. F. von Diez.

Berlin, 1811. (This appears to have been made from one of the Turkish versions.)

2. Le Cabous Namè, ou Livre de Cabous, de Cabous Onsor el Moali, souverain du Djordjan et du Guilan, traduit . . . en français avec des notes par A. Querry. (Bibliothèque Orientale Elzévirienne, xlviii). Paris, 1886.

A MIRROR FOR PRINCES

AUTHOR'S PREFACE

PRAISE BE TO God, Lord of the worlds, and blessings and peace upon Muhammad and his kinsmen, all of them. These are the words of counsel given to his son Gilānshāh by their compiler 'Unṣur al-Ma'ālī Kai Kā'ūs ibn Iskandar ibn Qābūs ibn Washmgīr, Client of the Commander of Believers:

Know, my son, that I have become old and that feebleness has taken possession of me: from [the colour of][1] my hair I see, as it were written in my appearance, the proclamation of my dismissal from life. Seek as he may no man's hand can annul it. Therefore, my son, since I find my name in the company of them that are about to pass away, I deem it fitting, before the intimation of my dismissal arrives, to record in writing my views on showing a proper indifference to destiny's decrees and on the advantages to be acquired from possessing a good repute. I impart this to you out of paternal affection, so that before you are crushed by the hand of fate you may read these words of mine with an understanding eye and, benefiting from my counsel, gain repute which shall be good both in this world and the next.

Let your mind not hesitate to receive my counsels, although, in any event, I shall have discharged my fatherly

[1] Words in square brackets are additions by the translator. Words in round brackets are the author's.

duty. If you do not wish to profit by what I say, there are others who will regard it as a boon to hearken to it and apply it to use. But the fashion of the time insists that no son will take his father's advice, because there is a burning ardour in the hearts of young men which through folly persuades their intellects that their own knowledge is superior to that of their elders. I am aware of all this, yet my paternal affection would not allow me to remain silent and I have therefore searched my mind for every kind of topic and collected some matter upon each, setting down what is most appropriate and beneficial in this record. If you decide to use it, all is well; if not, at least I shall have done my duty as a father. There is a saying that the function of the speaker is no more than to speak; there is no cause for grievance if the hearer is not receptive.

Be aware, my son, that men are so constituted that they are ever in a fever about the transmission to those dearest to them of the fortune allotted them in this world. My fortune consists of these words of mine and you are the one dearest to me. Since, now, I have begun my journey onwards, I transmit to you the fortune which has come to me, to enable you to avoid becoming self-willed and refrain from what is unfitting, so ordering your life that it may be worthy of your unsullied origin. Your origin indeed is lofty, noble on both sides, your ancestors having ever been world-dominating monarchs. For example, your grandfather was King Shams al-Ma'ālī Qābūs ibn Washmgīr, grandson of Arghish son of Farhādān who in the time of Chosroes ruled over Gīlān and of whom Abu'l-Mu'aiyad Balkhī gave an account in his *Book of Kings*.

The kingdom of Gīlān remained after him the inheritance of your ancestors, and your grandmother, my mother, was the daughter of Prince Marzubān son of Rustam son of Sharwīn, author of the *Marzubān-nāma*, whose ancestor thirteen generations earlier was Kā'ūs ibn Qubād, brother of Nūshīrwān the Just, while your mother was the daughter of that royal protagonist in holy wars Mahmūd ibn Nāsir al-Dīn. Further, one of my ancestors was Hasani Fīrūzān, king of the Dailamites. Be quick of understanding therefore, my son, to appreciate the value of your birth and not to disgrace it. Although I perceive in you the marks of goodness and virtue, yet I regard it as my duty to repeat what I have said.

You must realise, my son, that the day of my departure approaches and the day when you will succeed me is near. Know then that this world is ploughland; as you sow, be it good or ill, you reap. Yet no man enjoys on his own ground what he has reaped there. It is in the place of Delight that he enjoys it, and that is the Everlasting Abode. Now in this present world virtuous men are imbued with the spirit of lions, whereas wicked men have the spirit of dogs, for while the dog consumes his prey where he seizes it the lion takes it elsewhere. Your hunting-ground is this fleeting world and your quarry is knowledge and virtuous conduct. Carry through your pursuit to the end here, so that when the time comes for enjoyment in the Everlasting Abode it may be with the greatest degree of pleasure. The one way to achieve it is by submission to God Almighty. The parallel to the man who seeks after God is fire, which strives to ever greater height and volume the more it is suppressed; whereas the man from whom the path of God (and of obedience to Him) is remote is like water, which, however high you may carry it, seeks ever to run downwards.

I have put this book into forty-four chapters which I set down as follows here:

I. Knowledge of God.
II. The creation of the prophets.
III. Gratitude to the Giver of bounty.
IV. The performance of religious duties to the best of one's abilities.
V. Acknowledgment of the debt owed to parents.
VI. Enrichment of personality by acquisition of talents.
VII. Speech; the good and the evil.
VIII. The counsels of Nūshīrwān the Just.
IX. Old age and youth.
X. The etiquette of eating.
XI. The etiquette of wine-drinking.
XII. The practice of hospitality and providing entertainment.
XIII. On playing backgammon and chess.
XIV. The art of love.
XV. Sexual enjoyment.
XVI. On going to the warm baths.
XVII. Sleep and repose.
XVIII. The chase.
XIX. Polo.
XX. War.
XXI. The accumulation of wealth.
XXII. Loyalty to trusts.
XXIII. Buying slaves.
XXIV. Buying houses and estates.
XXV. Buying horses.
XXVI. Seeking for a wife.

XXVII. Duties towards children.
XXVIII. Choosing friends.
XXIX. Precautions against enemies.
XXX. Pardon and punishment.
XXXI. Study of religious doctrine; the office of qadi.
XXXII. The practice of commerce.
XXXIII. The study of medicine.
XXXIV. Astronomy and geometry.
XXXV. The art of versification.
XXXVI. The minstrel's art.
XXXVII. The service of the king.
XXXVIII. Companionship with the king.
XXXIX. The functions of scribes and the conditions they fulfil.
XL. The Vizierate.
XLI. The command of troops.
XLII. Kingship.
XLIII. The Peasantry.
XLIV. Knight-errantry.

CHAPTER I

On Knowing God

MY SON, THERE is nothing, existing or non-existent or capable of existence, the nature of which cannot be comprehended by men. But when you come to understanding the Creator, you fail, since there is no medium by which such an understanding can be attained. With the exception of him all has become knowable, and you will become a knower of God only when you acknowledge yourself without knowledge. Knowing is like a blank surface to be engraved, the knower resembling the engraver; unless the blank surface is capable of being engraved no one can carve a legend in it. It is evident that seals are made with wax rather than stone because it is more susceptible of taking an impression. With all knowing, therefore, there is knowability, but the Creator is unknowable.

In your thinking, therefore, direct your mind to yourself and not to the Creator;[1] reflect on what he made and so recognise the Maker. And take heed lest delay snatch from your hand [deprive you of] the knowledge of the Way to the Maker, for delay is concerned with time, which is transitory and as such has a beginning and an end. So far as concerns this world, which you regard as barred [so that you cannot advance on the Way], do not regard the barrier it forms as an impassable one. Have no misgivings, for the barrier will not remain shut [against you].

Think about the benefactions and blessings of the

[1] "Know then thyself, presume not God to scan." Pope, *Essay on Man*.

Creator, but not about the Creator himself: is there anyone so utterly lost as he that seeks a way where there is no way? As the Prophet said, "Think on the benefactions of God and not on what he is". If the Lord, speaking by the tongue of the lawgiver [Muhammad], refused to permit men such presumption, then no one can have the temerity to speak of knowing the Way of God. Whatever name or attribute you may employ to designate God originates in your own helplessness and your lack of capacity to conceive of anything nobler—it cannot accord with his Godhead or sovereignty. You cannot praise God in terms worthy of him. If you cannot even praise him worthily, how can you know him?

If you desire the truth about [God's] oneness, you must realise that any metaphor possesses some reality in God's sovereignty, but even he who realises that oneness achieves no more than either innocence or polytheism. The One, in verity, is God Almighty; all else is dual. The reason is that the mark of duality appears upon everything which becomes two through an attribute or through being compounded of two (or more) things, for example the body, or becomes two by division like a number, or becomes two by combination as with [the employment of] adjectives, or is two in outline like plane surfaces, or in conjunction is two like quiddity and form, or by contrast is two like essence and attribute, or by generation is two like root and branch, or in space is two like model and copy, or as when one thing is the product of another like matter and element, or in dimensions is two like an area, or in extension is two like time, or in limitation is two like idea and proof, or is two by potentiality like a personal character, or which may be two in the mind's eye like a thing doubtful as to its existence and non-existence; or finally, is two in itself, like a thing and its converse.

The distinctions in all these examples are the sign of duality; the exception is God, who is without parallel. The true course is for you to realise that, whatever the idea which you may conceive of him, it will not be God; but God, free of all association and likeness, will have been its creator.

CHAPTER II

Concerning the Creation of the Apostles and their Mission

YOU MUST UNDERSTAND, my son, that God did not create this world through any need of his own, nor yet idly, but he created it in accordance with his justice and equipped it in accordance with wisdom, since he knew that existence is preferable to non-existence, life better than annihilation, increase better than decline and the beautiful better than the ugly. He possessed the power and the knowledge to create either alternative, but he made nothing that was unworthy and nothing that was opposed to his understanding. He worked in a fashion appropriate to him and what he did was in accordance with justice—it could not have been done out of nescience.

The structure of the universe, therefore, is based upon wisdom, and God designed it as was most becoming. Thus he might have provided light without the sun, rain without clouds, temperaments without the humours and good or evil influences in the world without the stars. Since, however, his work was based upon wisdom, he produced nothing except through a medium (making such medium the instrument of creation or annihilation), and the greater its importance the greater the glory and dignity of the plan [of the universe]. Further, were it not for the plan there would be no order, and for [God's] working there is essential need of order. The medium too is essential, and he therefore so contrived that one thing might be predominant and another subordinate, one a consumer and another a provider, such duality being testimony to the oneness of God (May he be glorified!).

Since, therefore, you can perceive the medium but not its further purpose, beware lest you pay regard merely to the medium. Never look upon anything great or small as having its origin in the medium, but only as due to the Master of the medium. If the earth yields no produce, lay no blame upon the earth; and if the stars give no justice, lay no blame on the stars; for the stars are as little conscious of justice or injustice as the earth of being fruitful. When you scatter wholesome seed upon the earth, it has no power to bring forth venom, nor can the stars, following the same law, of themselves produce either good or evil. Since the world was constructed in wisdom, that which was so constructed was inevitably provided with equipment. Look then upon the world and behold its equipment, plant and animal, food and raiment and all kinds of goodness; for all these are useful appointments created in accordance with wisdom, as God says in his own book: "We created not the heavens and the earth and what lies between as a diversion. It was in a spirit of reality, and nought else, that we created them" (Koran 44, vv. 38 f.).

Now that you understand that God created no blessing in the world without purpose, it would be futile conduct to leave the just aims of his beneficence and providence unfulfilled. The just aims of his providence are that you should give to the man that consumes; and, that being so, he created men in order that they may eat. Since he originated mankind, all his bounty was designed for mankind. Now, man has need of government and regulation; without direction he is brutal [uncivilized] in the respect that he eats his daily bread without regard to order and justice and fails to render due thanks to the Giver. This implies a defect in the Provider of daily bread, insomuch as he has granted their sustenance to ignorant and ungrateful men. Now, since the Provider is without flaw, he has not left the consumer without knowledge, as he indicates in his book ("I created neither spirits nor men save that they should worship me" (Koran 51, v. 56)).

Moreover, he sent apostles amongst men to teach them the way of knowledge and the rules regulating the eating of one's daily bread and of rendering thanks for it, so that the structure of the world might be based upon justice. Now the achievement of the aims of justice rests with wisdom, that of wisdom with bounty, that of bounty with the consumer of daily bread and that of the consumer with the apostles who give guidance, there being no break possible in this sequence if true guidance is to be achieved. Philosophically regarded, the honour and graciousness accorded to the consumer by God's bounty and providence make it inevitable that God should recognize his own guidance and have a claim on the gratitude of the consumer. He in his turn should declare his indebtedness to the apostles, accord them his loyalty and acknowledge the truth of the messages brought by all the prophets from Adam to Muhammad. Further, he should be obedient to [the laws of] his faith, never fail in his gratitude to his Benefactor or in the proper observance of the duties imposed by his religion. Thereby he may gain goodly repute and the praise of his fellowmen.

CHAPTER III

On Gratitude to the Lord of Bounty

KNOW, MY SON, that it is the fixed duty of all men to give thanks to the Lord of Bounty in accordance with his command, though they cannot be according to the measure of his deserts, because even if all men converted themselves entirely into thankfulness it would not suffice as gratitude for one thousandth part of what was due. Understand then that the full extent of submission to God consists, in the faith of Islam, of five acts, of which two are demanded exclusively of wealthy men and three of the generality of mankind. First of the three is the oral confession of faith and inward belief, second is performance of the ceremonial of worship five times daily and the third is the thirty days' fast.

The attestation [of the unity of God] is proof of the negation of the reality of anything but God, worship is proof of the oral acknowledgment of submission to God and the thirty-day fast is confirmation of the oral confession of faith and acknowledgment of the divinity of God. When you say that you are his servant, you must be truly submissive. If you wish your own servant to be obedient to you, do not refuse obedience to your own Master; if you do, expect nothing of your own servant, for, however good your treatment of him, it is no better than God's treatment of you. Further, do not be a rebellious servant; for such a one ever seeks to be master and is speedily destroyed.

'Tis well to cut the throat of any slave
That for the place of mastery may crave.

You must be aware that worship and fasting are for the especial behoof of God. Do not therefore be remiss in carrying them out, for if you are remiss in your performance of what is God's prerogative, you will fail in your duty towards ordinary men. Understand, too, that the lawgiver [Muhammad] made worship equal to the whole of belief, so that you must regard the man who abstains from worship as one who abstains from performance of all the duties of the faith; and the penalty for irreligion is death and ill-fame in this world and God's punishment in the next.

Do not permit the thought to enter your head that any neglect in your devotions is permissible, for whether you regard it from the point of view of religion or of philosophy there are several advantages to be derived from worship. The first is that he who performs the obligatory ritual of worship has body and garments clean, and cleanliness is ever preferable to defilement. Secondly, the worshipper is free from vainglory, for the reason that the principle of worship is based upon self-abasement. If your spirit has accustomed itself to submission, your body follows; and it is well-known to understanding people that if one wishes to become a member of a particular group one must consort with it. If a man consorts with an unfortunate group, he becomes unfortunate; if he seeks happiness and fortune he must ally himself with those possessed of good fortune. Now the collective opinion of the wise is that there is no greater blessing than that of the faith of Islam, and no authority greater than that of Islam. If, therefore, you wish constantly to be endowed with good fortune and prosperity, seek out those possessed of fortune and make yourself their servant, avoiding anything to the contrary, lest misfortune overtake you. And, my son, beware of behaving with levity or frivolity during worship, by omitting to bow down and prostrate yourself completely or by jesting; such practices are not those characteristic of religious people.

Realise, my son, that fasting is a duty to be performed once a year. To be remiss therein would be ignoble, nor would understanding people regard any neglect as permissible. Yet see to it that you do not indulge in over-zealousness, for the month of fasting is not without its acts of fanaticism. Do not display fanaticism over the beginning and ending of the Fast. When you have ascertained that five learned and reasonable men have begun the Fast, begin it with them; and end it with them, paying no heed to what ignorant people say. You must appreciate that God needs neither your satiety nor your hunger. What is significant in the fasting is the consideration which God as owner feels for his possessions; and this not merely for a particular part of them but for the whole of the body—hand, foot, eye, mouth, ear, belly and sexual organs. All these must be sealed, so that, in appropriate fashion, they are kept free of pollution.

Therefore, keep these parts of the body clear of transgression and sin, that you may observe the Fast with due reverence. Remember, further, that the greatest act of piety during the Fast is that, having postponed your day's meal to the evening, you shall bestow on the needy the portion of food you had set aside for the daytime. In that manner the practical aim of your suffering will become apparent and the kindliness and benefit deriving from it will accrue to some deserving person. Take heed that you permit yourself no shortcoming in these three acts of piety which have been prescribed for the generality of mankind, for there is no forgiveness for shortcomings. In the two duties more especially assigned to the wealthy, excuses for failure are possible. But on that score arguments are plentiful; I have said what is indispensable.

CHAPTER IV

Acts of Piety to be increased with Increase of Wealth

YOU MUST BE aware, my son, that God imposed two religious duties more particularly upon men of wealth and of ample means. They are: alms and the pilgrimage to Mecca. He commanded that all who could make due provision should visit his house, but did not enjoin the pilgrimage on those not possessed of sufficient means. (Surely you realize that in worldly matters also, those capable of undertaking the ceremonial of royal courts are the wealthy?) Moreover, the onerous part of the pilgrimage is the journey, which it would not be an act of wisdom to enjoin on them that could not equip themselves for it, for to undertake the journey without proper equipment would be [to invite] destruction.

Yet if you have the means and fail to make the journey,

you have not attained completely the happiness and pleasure of worldly riches; indeed, the perfection of pleasure lies in seeing what you have not already seen, eating what you have not hitherto eaten and experiencing what you have not yet experienced. Only by travel can this be achieved, seeing that it is travellers who have seen the world and been tried in active affairs who become prosperous and wise through having seen what [others] have not seen and heard what [others] have not heard. The Arabs say: "Hearsay does not equal seeing".

God, therefore, prescribed the journey for them possessed of wealth that they might discharge the duty of worthily employing his bounty and carrying out the Lord's command to visit his house. He did not impose it on the poor, who are portionless and without means, as I have said in my quatrain:

The friend who fails to place me at his side,
But leaves me in my misery to abide,
Forgiveness finds, since all creation's Lord,
Would leave a pauper languishing outside.

You must understand, my son, that if the impecunious man undertakes the pilgrimage, he casts himself into peril; the pauper who apes the wealthy resembles the cripple who attempts tasks only feasible by the able-bodied, as instance the pilgrim in the following story. I have been told how a certain chieftain of Bukhara once set out to make the pilgrimage. He was a man of wealth; indeed nobody in the caravan was better provided, more than a hundred camels being laden with his baggage, while he himself rode in a litter with stately luxury. With him was a mixed company of people both poor and rich. As he was approaching

Arafat,[1] a beggar approached barefooted and thirsty, his feet blistered. Catching sight of the chieftain in all his luxury and ease he looked up at him and said, "When the time for requital comes, my reward and yours will be the same, though you now progress in plentiful ease and I am in sore straits". The chieftain replied, "God forbid that at the time of requital he should make my reward equal to yours. Had I known that your position and mine would be the same, I should never have ventured into the wilderness." "Why so?" asked the dervish. The rich man replied, "I came by God's command, but you came in opposition to it: I was invited as a guest, but you are an intruder. How can the attention paid to an intruder be the equal of that given to a guest? God enjoined the pilgrimage on people of means, but said to the poor, 'Cast not yourselves of your own accord into peril' (Koran 2, v. 191). You ventured into the wilderness against God's command, unprovided and hungry, and cast yourself into danger. How can you claim equality with obedient men? He that undertakes the pilgrimage having the capacity to do so, does justice to God's bounty and fulfils his command."

When, therefore, you possess the requirements for the pilgrimage, let there be no shortcoming in your [discharge] of the obligation. The requirements are five:—ability, time, dignity, freedom from care and easy circumstances. If you have secured any of these, endeavour to complete them; and be aware that the duty of pilgrimage is one from which there is no exemption where the means for discharging it are present.

Further, God has called them who bestow charity his

[1] A hill to the East of Mecca, on which an oration is delivered on the ninth day of the month of pilgrimage (Dhu'l-Hijjah). See Burton, *Pilgrimage to Al-Madinah and Maccah* (London, 1893), II, p. 289.

intimates; they stand amongst other men as a king amongst his subjects, whose provider he is, while they are the consumers of his bounty. God had power, truth to tell, to make all men rich; but in his wisdom he decreed that some should be rich and others poor, that the rank and honour due to different men might be clearly shown and the more noble of them be distinguished. Thus, for example, there is the king, who appoints a servant to be the provisioner of the people. If the servant so appointed consumes the allotted provision, failing to distribute it, he cannot be secure against the king's wrath. Similarly, if the man of wealth himself consumes all his riches and gives no alms, he is not proof against the wrath of God.

The giving of alms is a religious duty once a year, but munificence in the giving of charity is a pious act; it is not imposed as a bounden duty but it is looked upon as noble and virtuous conduct. Give as you wish, but without grudging; men of charity dwell in God's protection, which is something to be treasured. Have a care that doubts shall not enter your mind concerning the laws of pilgrimage and of alms-giving. Do not ask the reason for the running, stripping naked and the cutting of hair and nails,[1] nor why half a dinar must be given out of every twenty, nor a fixed levy raised upon [property like] oxen, sheep and camels, nor the reason for sacrificing.

Clear your heart of all such [doubts] and never fancy that what you may not understand is of no value, for the good is something which neither you nor we may understand. Busy yourself with fulfilment of God's commands; your concern is not with "How?" or "Why?". Then, when you have executed God's command, recognise your duty towards

[1] Various rites of the pilgrimage.

your mother and father, for that is also part of God's command.

CHAPTER V

On Showing Gratitude to Parents

UNDERSTAND, MY SON, that when the Creator desired to make the world a place worthy of habitation, he produced the means by which men are begotten and made the procreative desires of fathers and mothers the instrument whereby children are brought into existence. For that existence it behoves children to be grateful to parents. Beware against saying: "What claim have my parents on me? Their desire was for their own pleasure and they had not me in view." Leaving aside the question of their pleasure, they showed you much kindliness and had much to endure. The smallest debt due to your parents is that of having been the intermediary between you and your Creator. Inasmuch, therefore, as you hold your Creator in honour, you must for consistency hold the intermediary in honour.

As long as a child is young he cannot but be indebted to his father and mother for their guidance and affection. God calls them "Those in authority" (Koran 4, v. 62), and I have read in a commentary the opinion that the intention of the phrase is mothers and fathers, the meaning of the Arabic word *amr* ["authority"] being properly a double one, "command" and "affair(s)". Consequently, "those in authority" are the people endowed both with command and power, and parents have the power to rear you and [are given] the command to teach you what is good.

My son, do not despise the anxieties suffered by your parents, for God insists upon recognition of the obligations they created. The story is told that when the Commander of the Faithful, 'Alī, was questioned on the subject of showing gratitude to parents, he replied, "It was a practice inaugurated by God at the death of the Prophet's parents". When asked how that came about, he replied: "If they had survived into the Prophet's time, it would have been his duty to place them above himself and humble himself before them out of filial piety. Had he done so, his [well-known] declaration: 'I am lord of the children of men, and [I say] that without sense of pride', would have ceased to be true."

If, therefore, you do not respect your parents on religious grounds, do so from your own sense of honour, for they are the source of all kindliness to you and the well-spring of your nurture. If you fail in your duty towards them, it would appear as though you were unworthy of any kindliness, for he who fails in his comprehension of what he owes to the root cannot appreciate the goodness [required] of the branch. Of what advantage is it to show kindliness towards those who are themselves ungrateful? Do not then look merely to the blessings you have yourself received but let your conduct towards your parents be such as you desire from your own children; for the child begotten by you will expect from you what you expected from your father.

A man may be compared to the fruit and his parents to the tree; the greater the care you give to the tree, the better will be the fruit. If you hold your parents in great honour, their prayers for your well-being will be swiftly answered and you will be brought near to God's favour. Guard against wishing for your father's death merely for the sake of the inheritance; your allotted portion will come to you irrespective of your parents' death. Each man's allotted portion is pre-ordained and to each there comes that which in past eternity was decreed to be his fate. Do not, therefore, burden yourself with overmuch anxiety; your fortune is not improved by your endeavours. It has been said: "Your daily bread depends on your earning, not on your fretting."

If you desire to have satisfaction from God in the matter of your fortunes, each dawn look for someone in worse case than yourself and you will ever receive contentment from God. If you are poor in material goods, strive to be rich in wisdom, for wisdom is better than riches. By it you may gain wealth, though by wealth you do not acquire wisdom. The fool is soon bankrupt of possessions but no thief can deprive the wise man of his store, which cannot be destroyed either by fire or water. If you have wisdom, therefore, acquire virtue, for wisdom without virtue is like a man without clothes or a person without a face or a body without a soul. Indeed there is a proverb to the effect that "virtue is the visage of the mind".

CHAPTER VI

Natural Qualities Heightened by Increase of Accomplishments

UNDERSTAND, MY SON, that as long as a man lacks accomplishments he remains without value (then resembling the Arabian thorn-tree, which, though possessing a trunk, casts no shade) and is of use neither to himself nor to others. It is true that men of lofty descent and noble origin, even if deficient in accomplishments, do not remain without a measure of respect from other men. (Worse off are they who have neither birth nor talents.) Yet there is need to exert oneself, for even though it happens that your birth and quality are noble, you possess a certain quality in your own person. Such quality in the individual is nobler than that of descent, as is illustrated by the [Arabic] proverb which says "Honour lies in the mind and in acquired worth, not in origins and noble birth" (that is: greatness lies in wisdom and knowledge, not in lineage and descent).

Be not self-satisfied over the name with which your parents endow you, for that name is a mere indicator. True fame is what you acquire for yourself by merit, so that to the proper name "Ahmad", "Muhammad", "Musa" or "Ja'far" you may attach the title "Learned Master" or "The Perfect Sage". If the man of noble birth be not endowed with the quality acquired through attainments, he is worthy of no man's society; and if you find a man with the double qualification, grapple him to yourself and do not let him escape from your hands; he will be of value to everyone. Best of all accomplishments is that of eloquence. The Creator made man chief of all his works, and man acquired supremacy over other living creatures by reason of ten qualities contained within his person, five being internal and five external. The five hidden ones are: thought, memory, observation, imagination and speech; the five external ones: hearing, sight, smell, touch and taste. Of this total, those possessed by the remainder of the animal world do not include the qualities whereby man became absolute sovereign over other living beings.

In view of this knowledge, you must acquire skill in the arts. Practise [especially] the art of speech; your tongue will ever speak as you direct it and there is a proverb that "The sweeter the tongue the greater the talent". With all your skill contrive that your words shall be timely; however subtle they may be in themselves, if they are inappropriate they appear coarse. Yet prefer silence to over-abundant loquacity; useless words are entirely harmful and words from which no fragrance of good taste is perceptible are better left unspoken. The wise have likened speech to wine, which produces not only intoxication and mirth but also headaches. Beware against speaking unasked and refrain from uttering frivolities. However, when asked a question, answer nothing but the truth, and give no one advice unless he desires it. Admonish no one and especially no person who refuses to listen; in any event give no counsel in public, for there is an [Arabic] proverb that "Exhortation given before all men is a reproof".

If a person has grown up in crookedness, do not undertake to straighten him; you will be unsuccessful. A tree which has grown crooked, put forth its branches and come to full height, can only be made straight by felling or by lopping.

Much as you would not be parsimonious over kindly words, so also, if you have the means, do not begrudge your material largesse; men are more often beguiled by money than by words. Be on your guard against places of doubtful repute and flee from a companion who sets an evil example in conduct and thought. Do not of your own accord venture into dubious situations, and go only to places where, being sought, you may be discovered without shame. In the position in which you have established your character there seek it, in order to be sure of finding it.

Never rejoice at other men's griefs, to ensure that they will not rejoice at yours; grant justice, that you may receive it, and utter kindly words that you may hear them. Sow no seed on barren ground, for it will yield no produce; to bestow good on worthless men is merely to sow seed on barren ground. But do not grudge your kindness to them that are deserving. Set an example of goodness, for there is an [Arabic] proverb that "He that shows the way to goodness is equal to him that practises it". The man that practises good and he that ordains it are brothers, between whom the bond is never broken by time.

Never regret your kindnesses; repayment whether for good or for ill reaches you even in this world. If you ever do anyone a kindness, observe how at the very moment of your action there is created in your own heart as much solace and happiness as in the heart of your beneficiary. If, on the other hand, you do another man a wrong, there enter into your heart anguish and oppression as great as the pain suffered by him.

Thus, truly regarded, without suffering anguish yourself you can do no ill to others and no comfort is brought by you to others without happiness for yourself. It is therefore correct to say that you will receive your reward for good and evil even in this world, before you reach the next. No one can deny these words, for anyone who has in the course of his life done good or evil to another knows that in this matter I speak the truth. While you have the ability, therefore, do not begrudge a benefaction, for it will one day produce fruit.

I have heard it said that during the period when Mutawakkil was Caliph at Baghdad, he had a slave called Fatḥ, a happy and well-omened [youth] who had acquired arts and learning and whom he had adopted as a son. On Fatḥ's desiring to learn swimming, boatmen taught him the various branches of the art. Now although he was not yet competent to swim in the Tigris, yet, as is the habit with children, he wished to show that he had learnt. One day when he was alone, his teachers not having arrived, he went swimming, and the river, which was running strongly, tossed him about. Realising that he could not return against the current, he reconciled himself to going with it and allowed himself to relax and float away on the surface until he disappeared from men's sight.

Some way downstream there were holes in the bank, eaten out by the water, and suddenly the current brought him within reach of them. With an effort he threw himself into one, and there he remained resting, at a loss to understand God's purpose in all this but [knowing] that for the time he had saved his life. In that hole he remained for seven nights and days.

On the first day Mutawakkil, on being informed that Fatḥ had been drowned, descended from his throne and seated himself on the ground. Then, summoning the boatmen, he proclaimed that he would give a thousand dinars to anyone who brought Fatḥ to him, either dead or alive, and he swore solemn oaths that until they brought Fatḥ, whatever his condition, for him to see, he would eat no food.

The boatmen flung themselves into the Tigris, dived and sought about until, after seven days, one of them chanced upon the hole and to his joy beheld Fatḥ, whom he told to wait until he went and brought a boat. Coming into the presence of Mutawakkil, he said, "Commander of the Faithful, if I bring Fatḥ to you alive, what will you give me?" He replied, "I will give you five thousand dinars in coin''; on hearing which the boatman declared that he had found him and would restore him alive.

So a boat was taken and Fatḥ brought back alive. Mutawakkil gave the boatman what he had assured him and said to the vizier, ''Go to the treasury and give to the poor one-half of all that is there''. Then he said, ''Bring food, for he has been hungry for seven whole days''. Fatḥ, however, replied, ''I have had enough to eat'', and on Mutawakkil's asking whether he had satisfied his hunger on river-water, he said, ''Every day during this past week ten cakes of bread came laid on a tray. By making an effort I got two or three of them and so kept alive. On each there was written, 'Muhammad ibn al-Hasan the Shoemaker'.''

Mutawakkil thereupon gave orders that proclamation should be made [to discover] who it was that had cast the bread on to the Tigris, and that whoever it was should be brought and informed that the Commander of the Faithful wished to reward him. Next day a man presented himself who declared that it was he who had cast the bread on to the Tigris. When Mutawakkil asked what proof he adduced, he replied, ''This, that on each loaf was written my name, Muhammad ibn al-Hasan the Shoemaker''. He was told that his evidence was confirmed. Being then asked how long he had been thus casting bread on the Tigris, he replied, ''A year''. ''What was your purpose'', he was then asked, ''in so doing?'' He answered, ''I had heard it said, Do good and cast upon the waters, for some day it will yield fruit''. Mutawakkil remarked, ''What you were bidden you have done and you now receive the reward for your action''. He gave him five villages at the gates of Baghdad for his own possession, and to them the man departed. There he became greatly honoured, [his fame lasting] till the time of [the

Caliph] al-Qā'im bi-Amr Allah, when I went on pilgrimage and God granted me the felicity of visiting His house. I then saw the man's grandchildren at Baghdad and heard this anecdote from some old men there.

Never, therefore, as long as you have the ability, cease from doing good, but make yourself an exemplar of beneficence and charitable conduct. Once having made a profession of your beneficence, however, let not your actions contradict it. Do not say one thing with your tongue and harbour a contrary thought in your heart, lest you reveal yourself to be one who displays wheat but sells barley. In all your behaviour do justice of your own accord, for he that is just of his own accord requires no lawgiver [to direct him].

When either joy or sorrow befalls you, speak of it [only] to him who has some concern for your joy or sorrow; do not reveal your pains and sorrows, your griefs and joys to everyone. Do not permit yourself to be completely overwhelmed by joy or sorrow at any and every piece of good or ill, for such is the behaviour of children, but so conduct yourself as not to lose self-possession at every trivial occurrence. Men of wisdom are not disturbed by all [they hear], whether true or false. If the consequence of any pleasure is pain, refuse to regard it as a pleasure; but at a time of discouragement be the more hopeful, knowing that despair is linked with hope and hope with despair. The consummation of all activity is departure from the world.

Do not reject the truth. If a man quarrels with you, still his anger by your silence; remember that silence is the answer to fools. Let no man's toil go unrewarded; recognise what is due to all men according to their deserts, especially if they are of your own kin. Also hold in honour the elders of your clan, for the Prophet said, "The elder is to the clan as the prophet to the nation". Yet be not over fond of them, so that you may be able to perceive their faults as well as their merits. If you find yourself insecure against external foes make yourself secure against them according to the measure of your insecurity, and do not reassure yourself in thought against what is dangerous, for it is unwisdom to take poison in the faith that it is wholesome medicine.

Inquire into the nature of mankind's wisdom and virtues. If you are persuaded that you can secure name and fame without wisdom or merit, then remain without them; but, otherwise, acquire merit. Never be ashamed to learn or listen, that you may be delivered from shame. Study the faults and merits of the virtuous and see where their good and evil and their successes and failures lie. Then, from the midst of it all, seek out what will benefit you, yet avoid those things which will bring other men to harm. Accustom yourself to acquiring wisdom and merit and learn those useful arts of which you are ignorant. Socrates says that there is no treasure better than virtue, no honour more glorious than knowledge, no ornament more beautiful than modesty and no enemy worse than an evil disposition.

Do not, therefore, appoint any particular time for learning; whatever the time or the circumstances, not a moment should be allowed to lapse without your learning something. If, at any time, a learned person should not be available, then it is possible to learn from an ignorant one; for whenever you study the ignoramus with the eye of understanding and apply the mind's vision to him, you realise what conduct in him you disapprove of and is not to be imitated. On this principle Alexander said, "I have derived advantage not so much from my friends as from my enemies, because, if I commit a fault, my friends cover it up, so that I am unaware of it. The man who is hostile to me, however, informs me of it because of his enmity, and thereafter I avoid that improper course of conduct. Thus I profit by my enemy."

Do you similarly acquire knowledge from fools as well as from wise men. Indeed it is the duty of all men, whether noble or humble, to acquire skill and learning, for by their means you may achieve superiority over your fellows. Discovering in yourself a quality which you do not see in your fellow men, you will ever regard yourself as superior to them, and other men likewise will realise that you are superior to your fellows by reason of your learning and talents. When a clever man realises that he is accorded distinction, he strives to become even more learned and talented. Men who so conduct themselves are not long in becoming superior to all others. Indeed, to seek knowledge is to seek preferment over one's fellows and equals.

To refrain from striving after merit is a proof that one is satisfied with ignorance and inferiority, but the acquisition of virtue and control of the body are of great profit. As has been said, sloth is the body's ruin. If your body will not obey you, you cannot prosper, and it is only through your slothfulness and love of ease that it will not obey you. The reason is that movement is not spontaneous in us; every motion made by the body is the effect of a command and not voluntary, so that unless you exercise your will and command it, the body has no inclination to act. Render your body submissive, therefore, by compulsion, and force it to obedience, for he that cannot make his body obedient will never be endowed with virtue. Once you have subjugated your body to the task of acquiring skill, you will assure yourself of welfare in both worlds by virtue of it.

The basis of all virtues consists of knowledge, discipline of the flesh, piety, truth, pure faith, innocuity, sympathy and modesty. As for modesty, although it is said [in Arabic], "Modesty is part of faith", yet it may frequently happen that bashfulness is a misfortune to men. Do not therefore be so shamefaced as to cause failure or injury to your own interests. There are many occasions when boldness must be exercised to ensure that your purposes may be achieved. Be ashamed of obscene talk, of ignoble or improper conduct and of falsehood, but do not be ashamed of straightforward speech and conduct.

Now, since modesty is the product of religion [morality] and indigence the product of modesty, the place of shame and unashamedness must be understood and that course followed which is most proper, seeing that, as men say, modesty is the antecedent to goodness and immodest conduct to evil.

Regard no foolish man as cultured, though you may reckon a gifted man as wise; and esteem no ignorant abstainer a true ascetic. Do not consort with fools, especially those who consider themselves wise. And be not self-satisfied with your own ignorance. Let your intercourse be only with men of good repute; for it is by such association that men themselves attain to good repute. Do you not observe how sesame-oil is mingled with roses or violets and how, when it has been for some time in association with roses or violets, it ceases to be sesame-oil and is called oil of roses or oil of violets?

Through the blessedness of such goodly men never cease to appreciate goodly conduct, nor forget it. Do not turn your face away from the man who makes petition to you in his need, for that very necessity is to him an utter affliction. Be benevolent in spirit and of generous conduct, and keep yourself aloof from unworthy feelings. Never be malicious, for the fruit of malice is impoverishment and the fruit of impoverishment humiliation. Strive to earn the praise of understanding men but not to become an object of commendation to fools, for he that is praised by commonplace and ignorant people is scorned by men of distinction, as is shown in the following story.

It is related that while Iflātūn [Plato] was one day in session, one of the city's dignitaries came and seated himself by him. He conversed about this and that, and at one point said, "O sage, I have seen a man who spoke of you and blessed and praised you exceedingly, saying that Iflātūn was a man of pre-eminence whose like there has never been nor can be, and I wished to convey to you his gratitude". Iflātūn was thrown into distress at these words and shed tears. Whereupon the man asked, "O sage, what sorrow have these words brought you that they cause you to weep thus?" Iflātūn replied, "It is not you who have caused me distress, my master; but what misfortune could befall me worse than this, that I should be praised by a fool and my work be approved by him? Would that I knew what act of folly I have committed which is thus appropriate to his taste and pleases him; so that I may do penance for it! My grief is brought about through my becoming the object of praise to fools."

I remember also another anecdote on the same theme: Once when Muhammad son of Zakarīyā al-Rāzī [Rhazes] entered a certain place with a group of disciples, a lunatic presented himself and smiled in his face. Immediately on his reaching home he ordered an infusion of epithymon, which he drank. When his disciples asked why he took this infusion, he replied, "It is because of that lunatic's smile. If he had not perceived some of his own dementia in me, he would not have smiled in my face. There is a proverb that birds of a feather flock together."

To continue, be neither harsh nor sharp-tempered nor devoid of clemency (yet be not so entirely yielding as to be swallowed up on account of your softness) and never be so morose that you are not to be won over. Adapt yourself to every society; by making yourself agreeable you can attain your purpose with any man, whether friend or enemy. Set no one an evil example, for to do so is double wickedness. If anyone innocently does you an injury, strive never to injure him; the house of Little-hurt lies in Generosity Lane. Indeed, clemency is the very root of generosity, so that if you are a generous man you will do little hurt to others.

A man should ever regard himself in the mirror. If his face is handsome, his deeds should be as handsome; if it is ugly, he should do more good. For if his conduct is ugly, one ugliness is piled upon another, and it is very grievous to have two uglinesses in one place. Take advice from congenial friends and ever admit your counsellors to your intimate conclaves.

When you read the words that I record, do not be puffed up with your own learning and virtue, nor think that you already know everything. Account yourself rather as being of the company of the foolish, for you only become wise when you realise your own unwisdom, as may be seen in this story which I have heard. In the time of Khusraw Parwīz, when Buzurjmihr was vizier, an envoy arrived from

[Eastern] Rome. As was the custom of the Persian kings, Khusraw seated himself upon the throne and, while giving audience to the envoy, was desirous of displaying his pride in having so wise a vizier in his service. But the envoy, addressing the vizier, demanded "Oh, Thus-and-thus, do you know everything in the world?" Buzurjmihr replied, "I do not, O Lord of the world." Enraged at the reply and abashed before the envoy, Khusraw enquired, "Who is it then that knows all?" Buzurjmihr answered, "It is the whole of mankind that knows everything, and the whole of mankind has not yet been born".

You, therefore, place yourself in the category of the less wise, for when you have recognised yourself as foolish you have attained wisdom, a wise man being one who recognises that he is foolish and incapable. Socrates, with all his wisdom, says, "If I were not afraid that after my death the greater men amongst the philosophers would pass censure on me, saying that I laid claim at one blow to all the knowledge in the world, I would assert that I knew absolutely nothing and was completely powerless. But I cannot assert that because it would be too great a claim."

Abu Shukūr Balkhī[1] says in his own praise:

> *To such a pitch has my wisdom come, that now I know how much I know not.*

Therefore, be not puffed up with your own learning, however learned you may be. And if any task befalls you, even if you have the capacity to perform it, do not rely entirely on your own judgment, for he who relies entirely on his own judgment ever regrets it. Never be ashamed of

[1] A poet of the Sāmānid period who was alive in 336/947-8 (*Cf. Lubāb al-albāb* (ed. E. G. Browne), II, p. 21).

asking advice, consulting old men of understanding and well-disposed friends. Even Muhammad, despite his wisdom and his prophethood, after becoming the exemplifier and agent of God's work, was told by him, "Consult them in the matter, O Muhammad" (Koran 3, v. 153). ("Take counsel with persons of approved quality and with your own friends. It is for you to propose and for me, who am the Lord, to grant aid.")

Understand that the opinion of two men is not the same as that of a single individual and one eye cannot see what two eyes see. Do you not observe how, when a physician falls ill and his illness becomes acute, he does not trust himself in his own treatment but brings another physician? It is only after he has enquired his opinion, that he proceeds to the medical treatment of himself, even though the other may be a lesser physician than himself.

If an emergency should arise affecting a person of your own status, you must not, whatever the cost, begrudge him your effort, personal toil and resources, even though he is your enemy and rival. Should it become possible for him to take suitable action through your coming to his assistance, he may find deliverance from his difficulty and thus his enmity may be converted into friendship.

If men of eloquence, understanding in the power of expression, come to salute you, treat them with regard and grant them largesse, so that they may remain eager for your welfare. The least respected of human beings is he for whose welfare men fail to pray. In addressing other men be not over-mild; for even if a man be wise, his wisdom does not bear the appearance of wisdom if he is too mild. His words then lack distinction. Consider, therefore, the rules of speech and what they betoken.

CHAPTER VII

The Good and Bad in Speech

BE OF READY speech, my son, yet never tell lies and do not gain the reputation of being a liar. Rather become known for veracity, so that if ever in an emergency you utter a lie it will be believed. Whatever you say must be the truth, but never utter a truth which has the appearance of a lie; for a lie which has the air of truth is preferable to an accurate statement which seems to be false, and this kind of lie will be believed where that kind of true statement is not.

Avoid the kind of incident which befell me with the Amir Abu'l-Aswār. In the time of that Amir, Abu'l-Aswār, Shāwir b. al-Faḍl,[1] in the year in which I returned from the Pilgrimage, I went on a holy war against Ganja. I had frequently been on such wars against Hindustan and desired that such wars should also be prosecuted against Eastern Rome. Now Abu'l-Aswār was a sedate and wise man, a great prince, full of laudable qualities, just, courageous, eloquent and far-sighted, fully possessed of the characteristics of noble princes. He was entirely serious, without any frivolity in his nature. When he beheld me, he received me with great honour, entered into conversation with me and in the course of discussion of topics of every kind asked me numerous questions, to which I duly replied.

So pleased was he by what I said, that he loaded me with

[1] Governor of Armenia under the Seljuq Sultan Alp Arslān; d. 459/1067. *Cf.* Zambaur, *Généalogie de l'Islam*, pp. 184 f.

honours and refused to let me return home, and, from the abundant favour which he showed me, I for my part conceived a liking for him and for several years made my residence at Ganja, where I always formed one of his company at food and wine. At all times it was his custom to discuss topics of every kind with me. One day the subject was the marvels that occur in countries everywhere. I recalled that in the countryside of Gurgān there was a village whose well lay at some distance away from it and when the women set out to fetch water they collected in a group. In front of them scanning the road one went carrying an empty pitcher, for the reason that there are certain green worms in the fields about that village. Whenever the woman leading sees one, she leaves the pathway to prevent any of the women who are carrying the water from stepping on one. If a worm should by chance be trodden on and die under her foot, the water in her pitcher immediately turns fetid, making it necessary for it to be poured away and a return made to the well, where the pitcher is washed out and fresh water drawn.

When I had related this anecdote, the Amir Abu'l-Aswār frowned in displeasure and turned his face away, and for several days he was on less agreeable terms with me than he had previously been. Finally Pīrūzān the Dailamite said to me, "The Amir was annoyed at your story and said, 'So-and-so is a man of well-established position; what induced him to speak to me as one does to children?'." At that I promptly sent a messenger from Ganja to Gurgān and ordered an attestation to be written and witnessed by the qadi, the public orator, the [regional] headman and the learned doctors of the district to the effect that the village existed and that the existence of the worm was similarly well-established.

It required four months for me to have the attestation properly prepared. When, on its arrival, I laid it before Abu'l-Aswār and read it, he smiled, saying, "I myself know that no lie would be told by a man like you, particularly to me. But why make a statement, even though it is true, which demands four months' time and an attestation witnessed by persons of distinction belonging to that region before it can be accepted as veracious?"

Understand, my son, that words are of four classes. They are:—those neither to be understood nor uttered, those to be both understood and uttered, those to be uttered though not understood and those to be understood though not uttered. Those which are neither to be uttered nor understood are they that contain some peril to the faith. Those to be both understood and uttered are those which contain something beneficial to the faith and the world, of value both in the hereafter and in this life, yielding profit both to the utterer and the hearer.

Those to be understood but not uttered are such that concern a blunder (which has come to your knowledge) committed by a public personage or by a friend, or such that concern something which either reason or experience of affairs declares to be contrary to the law. Or else they are such things which, if discussed, will expose you to the anger of that personage or bring down harm upon a friend or create the possibility of uproar and disturbance. Such words may be understood but not uttered.

Lastly those words which may be uttered though they may not be understood are those which occur in the Book of God, in the Traditions of the Prophet and in the books of the various sciences, over whose interpretation the learned display fanaticism and differences of opinion, and failure to comprehend which does not incur God's displeasure.

Of these four categories, the most noble contains those words which can be both understood and uttered. Each of the four categories has two aspects, one good and the other evil; when you have occasion to address men, have recourse to the better aspect, to ensure your words being more acceptable and your own quality being recognised. Man is, indeed, concealed behind his speech; as the Arabic phrase says, "A man is hidden underneath his tongue". There are matters which darken the spirit to hear them, yet the same matters can be so differently expressed as to refresh the spirit.

I have been told a story relating how Hārūn al-Rashīd dreamt that all his teeth had fallen out of his mouth. In the morning he summoned an interpreter, from whom he demanded an explanation of the dream. The interpreter replied, "May the life of the Commander of the Faithful be long! All thy kinsmen will die before thee, so that after thee none will survive." Hārūn ordered the interpreter to be beaten a hundred blows, saying to him, "You such-and-such, that is for the cruel way in which you have informed me of this matter. If all my kinsmen die before me, whom shall I have to associate with me?"

He then ordered another interpreter to be brought to whom he related his dream. The second man said, "The dream which the Commander of the Faithful has dreamt is an indication that Your Majesty's life will be longer than that of any of his kinsmen". Hārūn remarked, "So far as meaning goes, this is the same thing. This interpretation goes no further than the other, but there is a difference in the way the two things are told." And to this man he gave a hundred dinars.

I have also heard another story, unsuitable for this book—and yet, "Nothing witty should be wasted". A man, lying with his page, said to him, "Turn your bottom this way". The youth replied, "Master, that could be better expressed". "How should I say it?" asked the master. "Say, turn your face the other way", replied the page. "The meaning of both phrases is the same, and thus you avoid uttering what is ugly." To that the man replied, "I agree with your remark and, furthermore, I grant you your freedom".

Both the obverse and the reverse of words, therefore, should be known, and what you say should present the best aspect. Thereby you will ensure being not only capable of uttering speech but of understanding it. Otherwise, if you speak words without understanding them, what difference is there between you and the bird called the parrot, which too is capable of utterance but not of understanding? If a man has the gift of speech, he should have the capacity to make all that he says comprehensible by others. Thus only can he be reckoned amongst persons of intelligence, and, if he has not the capacity, he is merely an animal in human form.

Pay great regard to speech, for it originated in Heaven; if you know a word, do not withhold it in its season, but do not waste it where it is untimely, and thus avoid any outrage to understanding. Let what you say be veracious; make no baseless assertions. In any assertion that you make, let argument form the greater part and your own proposition the lesser, and do not pretend to a science which you do not possess. If you have acquired a certain science, do not seek your bread by it, even if you realise your ambitions by your knowledge. On the other hand, you will attain nothing by ignorance of a subject.

There is a story of how during Chosroes' reign a woman

presented herself before Buzurjmihr [the vizier] and asked him a question. His thoughts being elsewhere at the moment, he replied that he did not know, whereat the woman remarked, "If you do not know, why do you enjoy your master's bounty?" "It is for what I know", replied he. "The king gives me nothing for what I do not know, and if you do not understand that, come and enquire of the king."

Do not go to excess in anything that you do, recognising excess as dishonourable. In all your affairs take the middle course, for the author of our laws [Muhammad] says, "Of all things those in the middle are best". Both in speech and action be weighty as a matter of course; if you are blamed for being weighty and deliberate, regard it as preferable to being praised for hastiness and uncertain action. Curb any desire you may have to learn secrets which do not in any way concern you, and utter your own secret to no one other than yourself. If you do so utter it, cease to regard it as a secret. Do not exchange confidences in the presence of third parties, for, however good the actual intention of your words may be, men will draw evil conclusions from their mere external utterance, since human beings are ever ready to suspect each other.

In all your deeds and words let your generosity be as large as your means will permit, and in whatever you say let your words be witness to your veracity in such fashion that you may be held by others to be a man of his word and truthful. Then, if you dislike being accused of dishonesty, never give evidence in any cause. But, if you do so, then at the time of giving your testimony throw hesitation aside. Listen to the words men utter, but when it comes to applying them to action do not be over-hasty. Say nothing without consideration, making thought the advance-guard of your words. Thus you will never repent of what you say, because forethought provides a double safeguard.

Never weary of hearing what men have to say, whether it be of [immediate] use or not, so that no gates of information may be barred to you. For your own part, do not give utterance to unpleasant remarks, for they are the seed from which enmity grows. If you are wise, you will reckon yourself as being without knowledge, in order that the gates of instruction shall remain open to you. Neither trample down the words of others nor overpraise them, until their faults or merits are understood by you. Let your address be the same whether it be to noble or humble persons: thereby you will save transgressing the bounds of wisdom and your speech will not be distressing to your hearer. However, in circumstances where your words will not be accepted in evidence and argument, speak as your hearers would wish; thus you may emerge with impunity from any assembly. However well informed you may be, behave as though you were less competent than you are in fact, so that when the time comes for speech and action you may not be left standing helpless.

Be one who knows much but speaks little rather than one who talks much though knowing little, for there is a saying that silence is double security and loquacity double folly. The reason for this is that the generality of mankind regard a man who is much given to speech, however wise he may be, as numbering among the foolish; whereas though a man be deprived of wisdom, if he maintains silence the common run of men will reckon that silence as cleverness. However moral and pious you may be, do not praise yourself, for no one will listen to your evidence in your own favour. Strive to become the object of other men's praise rather than of your own. Further, however much you may know, say only what is to the point, so that your power of speech may not become your undoing. Apropos of this there is the story of what the 'Alawid said to the man of Zinjān:

I have been told that in the days of the Sahib Ismā'īl[1] there lived in Zinjān, as the town's Mufti and preacher, an old scholar learned in the law and held in great esteem, who was an adherent of the Shāfi'ī[2] rite. There was also a young 'Alawid [descendant of 'Ali, the Prophet's son-in-law], son of the headman of Zinjān, who practised the profession of preacher. Now between these two great rivalry existed, each casting aspersions on the other from the pulpit. One day the younger man while in the pulpit called the other an unbeliever, whereat, on report of it reaching the elder man, he retaliated in the pulpit by calling him a bastard.

Immediately on news of this being brought him, the young 'Alawid set out for Rayy [Rhages] where he lodged a complaint about the old man before the Sahib, saying with tears, "In the time of a great man like yourself there are those who call the descendant of the Prophet a bastard".

The Sahib was stirred to anger. He despatched a messenger to summon the old man and seated himself in company with the doctors of the law and the Saiyids to hear grievances. Addressing the defendant he said, "Shaikh, you are one of the Shāfi'ī imāms, a man of learning and one who has reached the brink of the grave. It is improper for you to call a descendant of the Prophet a bastard. Either, therefore,

[1] The Sahib Ismā'īl ibn 'Abbād, a vizier famous for his learning, who flourished under the North Persian dynasty of warrior princes known as the Buwayhids. He was the patron of many men of letters. He died at Rayy in A.H. 385 (A.D. 995).

[2] One of the four main divisions of the Sunni ("Orthodox") community.

justify your words or I will sentence you to the sharpest penalties, as a warning to all men not to commit this offence. This is as the law ordains."

The old man replied, "The evidence for the truth of my words is what this 'Alawid provides against himself. You can require none better. According to my statement he was born in lawful wedlock and is hence pure, whereas according to his own statement he is illegitimate." "By what reasoning?" asked the Sahib. "Everyone in Zinjān", said the old man, "knows that it was I who celebrated the marriage of his parents. He now denounces me from the pulpit as an unbeliever. Consequently, if he utters the words in good faith, he must have been born out of wedlock, since the marriage celebrated by an unbeliever is invalid. If, on the other hand, he uttered the words without believing them, he must be a liar; and, as no descendant of the Prophet can be a liar, you may call him what you will. He has no alternative but to stand by one or other of these two things."

The 'Alawid was shamed and unable to reply; his thoughtless words thus leading to misfortune for him.

Do you therefore acquire command of words, but not for the purpose of uttering falsehood, since lying is a form of madness. When you are addressing someone, whoever it may be, look whether there is a willing recipient for your words or not. If you find an approving hearer, proceed with what you are saying; otherwise, adapt your words in a fashion to make them accord with the hearer's pleasure and so to gain his approval. With civilised men be a civilised man and with the common order of men behave like them, for civilised men are one thing and the common order of men another. Anyone who has been awakened out of the sleep of indifference will regulate his life in society in the way I have described.

To the best of your powers overcome any unwillingness to listen to oratory, for a mastery of words is gained by listening. It is an argument for this that if a child on being born were transported below ground and there reared, without its parents or nurse ever speaking a word to it and without its hearing a word spoken, it would grow up dumb and incapable of uttering a word, though in course of time it would hear speech and then learn it. Another argument is that a child at birth is incapable of speech, and, further, that all dumb persons are deaf.

Philosophers declare that kings acquire lustre of the eye by hearkening to the counsel of the wise, and that philosophy is the antimony and collyrium of the eye of the mind. The words of such men, therefore, should be listened to with the ear of the mind and confidence should be placed in them. A number of the best of their sayings have been recorded as the utterances of Nūshīrwān the Just and set down in this work so that you may put them to practical application. Indeed, putting the counsels of that king into practice is a bounden duty.

I have read in the annals of bygone Caliphs that the Caliph Māmūn once visited the tomb of Nūshīrwān the Just and found his body reposing on a throne which had crumbled to dust. Round the wall of the building there was an inscription in gold ink written in the Pehlevi character. Māmūn gave orders that scribes with a knowledge of Pehlevi should be summoned to translate the inscription into Arabic, which in its turn was made comprehensible in Persian. It began as follows: "Throughout my lifetime, all God's creatures enjoyed my justice and no one came into my presence but received mercy from me. When the time came for me to be reduced to helplessness I saw that the only charity I could bestow was to have these sentiments inscribed upon these walls. Then, if anyone should visit me, he could read the words, understand, remember and apply them, and so not depart from me empty-handed.''

CHAPTER VIII

The Counsels of Nūshīrwān the Just to his Son

NŪSHĪRWĀN BEGAN BY saying: As long as day and night come and go, never marvel at the vicissitudes of [human] affairs. Then he said: How is it that men commit actions of which they afterwards repent, although others before them have done them and repented?

How can a man who has acquaintance with kings lay himself down to sleep free of care?

How can a man count himself happy whose life has not gone according to his desires?

Why not account that man your enemy who secretly knows his generosity to be to the detriment of mankind?

Do not call him your friend who is the enemy of one of your well-wishers.

Form no friendship with men lacking merit, for such men are worthy neither of friendship nor of enmity.

Beware of the man who deems himself wise but is in actual fact a fool.

Do good of your own accord, thus may you be free of the [compulsion of the] lawgiver.

Speak the truth though it be bitter, and if you desire your enemy not to become possessed of your secret do not reveal it to your friend.

The great man who looks upon himself as small is indeed the great man of his age.

Do not regard as living creatures men who lack all value.

If you desire to be rich without unhappiness, let all your actions be worthy of praise.

Do not buy at any price, so that you may not be compelled to sell at any price.

Better die of hunger than be sated with the bread of ignoble men.

Place no reliance, for some fancy you may conceive, upon untrustworthy men, nor cease your reliance upon them you can trust.

Regard it as a great misfortune to stand in need of kinsmen humbler than oneself, for it is better to die in the water than to beg help of a frog.

The sinner who is a humble seeker after the next world is better than the devout but self-important man who is a seeker after this world.

There is no fool greater than he who sees a man of lowly state risen to greatness and yet continues to regard him as lowly.

There is no fault greater than for a man to lay claim to knowledge which he does not possess and then to resort to lying.

Be not misled by him that gives something which he has picked up in exchange for something not so [easily] acquired.

There is no meaner person in the world than he to whom appeal is made for help and though able to grant it refuses.

Regard him that speaks ill of you, when you are innocent, more worthy of forgiveness than him who carried the report of it to you.

He that is stricken by the misfortune of one dear to him suffers less grievously than he that hears of it and is helpless [to succour].

He that is afflicted by what his eyes behold suffers far more than he who himself suffers affliction.

Reckon any slave that is bought and sold freer than the man who is slave to his gullet.

No wise man should undertake the task of instructing him that has not been given understanding by the experience of time.

It is easier to guard a fool against anything rather than his own body.

If you desire men to speak well of you, then do you speak well of your fellow-men.

If you desire your efforts on behalf of other men not to be wasted, then do not permit others' efforts on your behalf to be wasted.

If you desire to remain free of unhappiness, be not envious.

If you do not wish to be reckoned insane, do not seek to discover the undiscoverable.

If you desire to command men's respect, then exercise justice.

If you wish not to be disillusioned, do not regard an undone task as having been done.

If you do not wish to be stricken with shame, do not remove what you have not yourself deposited; and if you desire not to be mocked behind your back, respect them that are subordinate to you.

If you wish to be saved long-lasting regret, do not indulge in the desires of your heart.

If you desire to be amongst the great, then see yourself in the mirror of other men.

If you desire to be included in the number of honourable men, give covetousness no place in your heart.

If you desire to be a man of justice, be generous as far as lies in your power towards them that are subordinate to you; and if you desire your heart never to be stricken a blow which no remedy can heal, never engage in argument with fools.

If you wish to retain men's esteem, learn how to esteem other men.

If you desire to be the most lauded of men, never reveal your secret to one who has no discretion.

If you wish to be superior to other men, be lavish of bread and salt [*i.e.* hospitable].

If you desire to be untouched by other men's disapprobation, then be ever laudatory of their works.

If you wish to remain beloved in the hearts of men and never to incur their dislike, then speak of them in the fashion that pleases them.

If you wish for effectiveness in your tongue, then restrain the rapacity of your hand.

These were the sayings of Nūshīrwān the Just. If you read these words, do not hold them in contempt, for there is exhaled from them the fragrance of wisdom and kingly dignity in that they are the utterances of sages and kings. Master them now while you are young: once you are old you will have no need to hear and acquire instructive counsel and wise saws, for time itself will have taught those who reach old age.

CHAPTER IX

Age and Youth

ALTHOUGH YOU ARE young, my son, be old in understanding. I do not demand that you shall not behave as a young man, but be a young man governed by self-restraint. Yet neither be a lack-lustre young man; it is well for a young man to be spirited for, as Aristotle says, "Youth is a species of madness". Be not foolhardy; no harm can come out of high spirits, but misfortune can come from foolhardy conduct. To the full extent of your powers enjoy the period of your youth, for when you reach old age you will be unable to achieve much. An old man once said, "For so many years I was grieved and tormented by the thought that when I was old the fair would have no desire for me. Now that I have reached old age, I do not desire them, and, if I did so, it would be unbecoming."

Even though you are young do not forget God and never feel secure against death, for death makes no distinction between young and old. Thus 'Asjadī says: "If death came not both in old age and in youth, the old would always die but the young would live".

The story is told that there was once a tailor in the city of Rayy who had a shop near the gate leading to the burial-ground. He kept a jar hung upon a nail and conceived the fancy of casting a stone into the jar whenever a funeral emerged from the gate. Each month he counted how many had died during the time and emptied the jar, then again beginning to throw in stones until the end of the month. In the course of time the tailor himself died. Now it happened that a man came in search of him unaware of his death, and seeing the shop-door closed made inquiry of the neighbours about the tailor's whereabouts. One of the neighbours replied, "He has fallen into the jar in his own turn".

Be prudent, my son, and be not led astray by your youth. Whether it be during pious exercises or in the act of transgression and whatever the circumstances in which you find yourself, be mindful of God and fear death, lest you fall into the jar without warning, laden with sin. Do not always consort with youths, but associate with older men also and let your friends and companions be mingled of young and old. If a young man in drunkenness utters an indiscretion, an older man may warn you of it, for older men have knowledge which young men do not possess. Yet most young men ridicule older ones, seeing them as lacking in youthfulness, for which reason also they seek to take advantage of them and act disrespectfully towards them.

Though it may be the case that old men sigh for youth, yet doubtless also young men hunger after old age, to which they may or may not attain; and, if you observe carefully, each is envious of the other, despite the fact that the young believe themselves the wisest of all beings. Have a care; do not range yourself with that kind of youth. Treat old men with respect and do not address them frivolously, because their retort, like that of clever persons, may be sharp. I have heard that a very old man was going along with bowed back and leaning on a stick when a youth mockingly said to him, "Grandfather, what did you pay for that bow? I should like to buy one, too". He replied, "If you live long enough and exercise patience, you will be given one free, even though you do not deserve one".

Yet you need not consort with old men who are fools. The society of clever young men is preferable. Be young while you may, but when you reach old age act like an old man, for then youthful conduct is undignified. He that acts the young man in his older years is like the man who sounds the trumpet for the advance in the midst of retreat. The poet has said:

> *'Twould be to sound the charge in full retreat*
> *For one far gone in years to ape the youth.*

In old age do not become a babbler, and shun old men who are improper and unjust. But grant full justice rather to old age than to youth, for youth still has hope of growing old, whereas old age has nothing to expect but death. When the corn is ripe to whiteness, if it is not reaped, it sheds its grain; and fruit once ripened, if it be not gathered, will fall to the ground.

Rubā'ī:

> *Above the moon on high exalt your Throne,*
> *Or Solomon-like for Wealth and Pow'r be known;*
> *Yet when your Life's matured, prepare to fall.*
> *The Fruit once ripened from the Tree is strown.*

[The Arab poet says:]

> *When the climax is reached, the descent approaches;*
> *Look for the waning when men say, "It is full".*

Be conscious also that you will not be allowed to remain as you are. When your youth fails, the gates of speech, sight, hearing, touch and taste will all be closed to you. No longer will you find pleasure in being alive, nor will anyone delight in you. You will become a burden to other men. Death therefore is preferable to such existence. Man's life resembles the sun; in youth it is in the quarter of the heavens where it rises, in old age in the quarter where it sets. As I say in my verse:

Kai Kā'ūs by old age gripped is helpless now.
Prepare to leave, your years are three score three.

The day has reached the hour of evening prayer;
That prayer once past, the night you'll swiftly see.

That being so, an old man must be youthful neither in thought nor in action.

Be ever compassionate towards the aged, for an old man is an invalid to whom nobody pays visits and old age a disease for which nobody knows any cure but death; from the malady of old age the aged find no relief until they die. Usually, when illness befalls a man, if he does not die of it he recovers; the exception is the illness of old age, which worsens every day and from which there is no hope of recovery. I have read in some book that man up to the age of thirty-four increases in strength and bodily structure. Thereafter until the age of forty he remains unchanged, without either increase or reduction, thus resembling the sun, which, having reached the middle of the heavens, is at the solstice until the moment of decline. Between the ages of forty and fifty years, he experiences each year a progressive enfeeblement which he had not perceived in the years before. Between fifty and sixty he sees each month a certain failure that he had not perceived the month before, and between sixty and seventy a certain failure each week.

Between seventy and eighty he sees some failure in himself that he had not seen the day before, and if he passes eighty he finds some pain or affliction that he had not perceived the hour before.

The limit of pleasure in life is reached at the age of forty, and when forty is reached on the ladder, it is the highest rung; once you have passed it you indubitably descend. Can anyone be happy who each hour experiences some pain or affliction not experienced the hour before?

And now, my son, my heart's solace, I have made a long lament to you over old age because I am a sufferer from it. And indeed there is nothing there to wonder at, for old age is my enemy and there is room for complaint against one's enemy, as I have said in my verse:

If I lament it, wonder not at me;
It is my tragedy and therefore cause for grief.

Also it is to one's dearest friends that one makes complaint about one's enemies—I pray God you will have occasion to make this complaint to your own son. I have composed two bayts[1] on this theme:

Alas! to whom, I ask, shall I complain?
Only repentance now my sickness eases;
Draw near, old man, and let me speak my heart,
Youth's blissfully unaware of such diseases.

Nobody, indeed, knows the troubles of old age better than one who has reached it. One of my father's chamberlains

[1] The Persian (following the Arabic) *bayt* consists of two hemistichs, each of which is conveniently represented by an English line. The rhyme thus comes at the end of every second line of the English.

was an old man called Mujāhid, the Perfect Chamberlain. Once, when he had passed the age of eighty years, he wished to buy a horse, and a horse-breaker brought one which was well-fed, of good colour and straight-legged. He approved of it when he saw it and agreed to the price, but on looking at its teeth and finding that it was old, he refused to complete the purchase and the horse was bought by someone else. When I said to him, "Chamberlain, so-and-so bought the horse. Why did you refuse it?" he answered, "So-and-so is a young man, whereas I have experience of the troubles of old age, its weakness and misfortunes. If, possessed of that knowledge, I had bought an old horse, how should I ever be excused?"

Once you have reached old age, endeavour to remain settled in one place. Travel in old age is unwisdom, especially if one is not well endowed; for old age is one enemy and lack of means another. To go journeying with two enemies is hardly sagacity. Yet if you are compelled to travel and find yourself far from home, and if, God having been merciful to you on that journey, there accrue to you from your sojourning in foreign lands and from your travelling benefits greater than those you would have got from remaining at home, then cherish no longings for your own place but settle yourself where your interests lie, recognising that place as your fatherland and the country in which your profit lies. Although the saying goes that one's homeland is a second mother, do not be over-concerned with that. Pay heed to where success in your fortunes is to be found, for there is another saying that what rouses longings in the fortunate is more good fortune while in the unfortunate it is their homeland. When you have found success for yourself and found profitable employment, then work to give permanence to your employ and be assured that it is firmly established.

When you have found that permanence, seek no further, for in that search after increase you will fall into loss. Once a thing is well established, strive no further to improve it, lest in your eagerness for the impossible you lose what you have already achieved. Do not let the way in which you spend your life be devoid of method.

If you wish to find honour in the eyes of friend and foe, your character and dignity must be patent to mankind in general.

CHAPTER X

The Etiquette of Eating

YOU MUST BE aware, my son, that the common run of men observe neither seasons nor order in their occupations and pay no regard to what is timely or untimely. The great and wise, on the other hand, clearly indicate times for what they do and allot the twenty-four hours of the night and day to their various occupations. For each task they appoint a limit and for each period a measure, so that their different affairs are not confused. It is understood by their servants also in what task they are to be employed at each hour, and thus all their tasks have a due system.

First, then, on the question of meal-times. You know that men occupied in the bazaar have the habit of eating at night. It is conducive to great harm and they constantly suffer from dyspepsia. As for soldiers, their practice is to disregard fixed times and to eat a meal whenever there is one to hand. That is the way of animals, which eat whenever they find fodder. Men of quality, however, and those held in esteem, eat no more than once [in the day]. Such self-restraint is good but leads to debility of the body, with the consequence that the persons concerned are frequently lacking in efficacy. The best course, therefore, for men of importance, is for them to make a light meal in private and then to engage in the business required by their personal economy until the time for mid-day prayers, when the usual meal is brought in and those who eat with them are summoned.

Then, let them not eat hurriedly, but let them be deliberate. It is fitting to converse over the food, for that is the rule in Islam, but keep your head forward so that you may not observe what the others are eating. I have been told that once, when the Sahib Ismā'īl ibn 'Abbād was at table with his retinue, one of them drew out of the dish a morsel to which a hair was clinging. The man did not see it and the Sahib said, "So-and-so, remove the hair from that piece of food". Thereupon the man put down the food in his hand, arose and departed. The Sahib ordered him to be brought back and questioned him as to why, with the meal only half eaten, he had left the table. The man replied, "It is not for me to eat the bread of a man who sees a hair in the mouthful I take up". The Sahib was abashed.

For your part, concern yourself with the business in hand. First, at meal-times, contrive some delay and after a period order the various dishes to be served. The practice of men of distinction is of two kinds; some have each dish set first before themselves and then before their guests, while others first place the dish before their guests. The second is the better custom because it is induced by generosity, whereas the other is suggested by self-importance. Insist that when the dishes are brought in they should be served quickly; all bellies are not alike, and when [the guests] arise from the table he that eats little and he that eats a great deal should have been satisfied equally.

If you have food before you and others have none, you should give some portion to them. Do not sit with a sour visage at your meals, and do not wrangle with your butler while at table; it is a vicious practice, which is discussed in another chapter.

Now that you have learnt the orderly disposal of meals, learn how to conduct your drinking.

CHAPTER XI

The Regulation of your Wine-drinking

WHILE DISCUSSING wine-drinking, I neither urge you to drink wine nor can I tell you not to drink, since young men never refrain from action at anyone's bidding. Many persons spoke to me but I did not listen, until, when I was past fifty years of age, God's mercy granted me repentance. Should it happen that you do not drink, you will not only earn rewards in both worlds and win divine favour but also you will be saved public disapprobation, the society of witless companions and senseless conduct. Moreover, there will be great saving to your economy.

For these several reasons I should prefer you not to drink.

Yet you are young and your friends will not let you go without drinking, whence [the Arabs] say, "Solitude is better than an evil companion". If, then, you drink, set your mind on repentance, pray to God for the blessing of repentance and be ever regretful for your misdeeds, that perchance he may by his grace vouchsafe you a favourable answer to your penitence.

Be that as it may, if you indulge in wine, you must know how to drink, for it is poison if you do not know how it should be drunk whereas it is a physic against poison if you do know. In truth, everything consumed, whether it be food or drink, becomes poison if taken in excess. That is what the poet meant when he said:

Your antidote for thirst is none the less
A poison when you use it to excess.

When you have eaten food, it is inadvisable to drink wine immediately afterwards. Wait until you have felt thirsty three times and drunk water or beer. If you do not feel thirsty, delay for a period of three hours after eating, for although the stomach may be in sound condition, yet if it has taken several courses of food and drink, seven hours are required for digestion. Of these, three hours are needed for the maturing in the stomach, three for the strength of the food to be absorbed and passed to the liver for distribution to the members—its function being that of distributor—and one hour more to pass the residue into the intestine. By the eighth hour the stomach should be empty, and any stomach unable to function in this wise is no more than a gourd; it is not a stomach.

It is for this reason, therefore, that I say, Drink wine when three hours have passed after eating food and thereby derive benefit both from your food and your wine. Begin your drinking after your recitation of the afternoon prayers, so that by the time that you are intoxicated the night will have fallen and nobody will perceive your drunken condition. When you are drunk, do not travel; for that is a reprehensible practice, and the [Arabic] proverb says,

"Journeys are a trial".

Never drink wine in the open or in an orchard; but, if you do, then return within doors before reaching intoxication and be drunk in your own home, for what is proper within your own dwelling is intolerable under the open sky. And the cover provided by your own roof is preferable to that of a tree, for a man within his own four walls is a monarch in his kingdom whereas a man in the open is no more than an exile, and it is well known how poor he is.

On all occasions rise from your wine while you still have room for two glasses more, and guard yourself against both that last morsel of food which brings over-satiety and the cup which brings drunkenness, for over-satiety and drunkenness are not the results of the sum total that one eats and drinks; but the one comes from the last morsel and the other from the last cup. Accordingly, take one morsel of food and one cup of wine the less, in order that you may be saved from excess in all. Endeavour not always to be in a state of intoxication. The consequences for wine-drinkers are twofold—illness and madness; for the wine-bibber is either always drunk or suffering from crapulence. In the state of drunkenness he is a madman and when suffering from crapulence he is sick. Those consequences, therefore, are a kind of disease. Why indulge in a practice of which the fruits are either sickness or madness?

Howbeit, I know that you will not withhold your hand from wine because of these words, nor will you welcome my advice. Yet, as far as possible do not drink wine in the morning, for the custom of drinking early has been held by men of wisdom as one to be condemned. Its first reprehensible sequel is that the dawn prayers are omitted; the second that before the effects of the previous night's drunkenness have worn off that day's fumes are added to them, with the inevitable consequence of melancholia. Further, while others are asleep you will be awake, so that you must of necessity sleep when all other men are awake; thus, being asleep the whole day you will undoubtedly be awake the whole night and every part of your body will be weary and aching.

There is seldom any early drinking without some show of quarrelsomeness or the commission of some act which brings cause for regret or unnecessary expenditure. If from time to time, however, the occasion arises when wine is drunk early, it is lawful to do so; but a practice should not be made of it, for that is reprehensible. Then again, however much you may indulge in wine, make it a rule never to drink on the night preceding Friday, for although Friday and Saturday are both sacred days, yet Friday has an especial sanctity because of the assembly for worship. And if you refrain from drinking wine on Friday, you will reconcile men to your drinking all the rest of the week and people will refrain from comment about your doings. Thus you will achieve reward in the next world and good report will be yours in this world. And a good name, once acquired, should be cherished; it becomes even better if one's behaviour remains impeccable.

CHAPTER XII

Hospitality and the Duties of a Host

MY SON, DO not offer hospitality to strangers every day, for you cannot constantly provide it in worthy fashion. Observe on how many occasions each month you have guests at your table, then reduce them from five to one, expending on that one occasion what previously you have spent on five. Thereby your table will be freed from defects and the tongues of cavillers will be stilled.

When guests come to visit you, go out to welcome each one and pay him your respects, giving them severally the honours which are their due. The [poet] Abu Shukūr[1] of Balkh says:

To every guest, be he friend or foe,
Night and day thou must honour show.

If it is the season for fruit, present your fruits to them to eat before the meal. Let there be an interval of an hour and then order the food to be brought in for the company, but do not yourself sit down until your guests invite you to do so; having done so, pay them compliments and say "Allow me to serve you". When they repeat their invitation, sit and eat with them, but take a place lower than the rest. If there is a guest of great importance, do not sit at all.

Do not apologise to your guests (it is the habit of tradesmen), and do not continually be saying, "Eat well" or

[1] See p. 33.

"You are eating nothing; I pray you not to be modest", or "I, for my part, cannot provide you with anything worthy of you, but next time something better will be provided". Expressions of that kind are not used by persons of distinction. They are the words of men who only entertain once in a matter of years; they cause such embarrassment to the company that they are prevented from enjoying their food and rise from your table only half-satisfied.

Now we in Gīlān have a very excellent custom. When the guests are summoned to the table, flagons of drinking-water are placed in the midst of it and the host and his servants retire, a single person being stationed at some little distance to serve the dishes. In that manner the guests are left to eat as pleases them.

When the guests have washed their hands [after the meal], call for rose-water and perfume. And pay proper attention to your guests' servants, for it is they who will spread good report of you abroad.

In the room where you assemble, have herbs in abundance and engage sweet-voiced and expert minstrels to be present. Unless the wine is good, do not place it before your guests; it is a daily experience for men to eat, and in consequence the wine and music should be good, so that if there are any shortcomings at table or in the dishes provided, they will be covered by the wine and the music. Furthermore, wine-drinking is a transgression; if you wish to commit a transgression it should at least not be a flavourless one. If you drink wine, let it be the finest; if you listen to music let it be the sweetest and if you commit a forbidden act, let it be with a beautiful partner, so that even though you may be convicted of sin in the next world, you will at any rate not be branded a fool in this.

Even if you have performed towards your guests all the duties I have mentioned, do not regard them as being under any obligation to you, considering, rather, that they have many claims upon you. I have been told how Ibn Muqlah gave the office of tax-gatherer at Basrah to Nasr ibn Mansūr Tamīmī, whom the next year he recalled for a reckoning. Now Nasr was a man of wealth and the Caliph had been stirred to cupidity by him, so that at the reckoning a large additional sum was demanded from him, which, said Ibn Muqlah, he must either pay down or go to prison. Nasr replied that although he possessed the money it was not there with him, and he asked for a month's respite to save him from going to prison [while waiting] for the sum in question.

Ibn Muqlah was well aware that it was not difficult for Nasr to provide the money and that he spoke the truth; he therefore replied, "There are no orders from the Commander of the Faithful permitting you to return to your home. Until you have delivered the money you may remain in a room in my house and be my guest for this month". Nasr's answer was that he obeyed the command, and so settled himself as a prisoner in the house of Ibn Muqlah. It happened that the day was the first of the month of Ramaḍān and, when night fell, Ibn Muqlah gave orders that So-and-so [naming the prisoner] was to be brought in and was to break his fast with him every evening.

For the whole month therefore, Nasr broke fast with him, and at last, when the Feast of Breakfasting had been celebrated and a few days more had gone by, Ibn Muqlah sent a servant to him with the message that the money was a long time being brought. "How", he inquired, "was the matter to be settled?" To this Nasr answered that he had paid the money. "To whom did you give it?", asked Ibn Muqlah. "I gave it to you", said he.

At that Ibn Muqlah flew into a passion. "When did you give me the money?" he demanded. "I did not give it you in gold", replied Nasr, "but for the month of Ramaḍān I have freely eaten your bread and broken my fast at your table. Now that the Feast is here, it is my privilege that you no longer have a claim against me for gold."

Ibn Muqlah burst into laughter. "Take your quittance", said he, "and depart. I grant you the money as hire for your teeth and forgo it in your favour." And thus Nasr escaped being mulcted.

So you must be grateful to your guests and show them a pleasant face. But be sparing in your wine-drinking and never present yourself before your guests in a state of intoxication. Only when you have ascertained that the company has reached a state of semi-intoxication should you begin to put yourself into the same state. First drink a toast to your friends, then pleasantly and cheerfully drink and pass the wine. But do not indulge in foolish laughter over nothing. Foolish laughter is a form of lunacy, just as much as laughing too little is a form of excessive solemnity.

When a guest, having reached intoxication, wishes to depart, beg him on the first and second occasions [to remain], be polite to him and do not let him go; but at the third time do not detain him and in kindly fashion dismiss him. If your servants commit some fault, overlook it and do not show a sour visage in front of your invited company; also begin no quarrel with your servants by declaring one thing good and another bad. If something fails to please you, order them not to do it again, but tolerate it for that once. As for your guest, even if he says and does a thousand foolish things, never take him to task for it, but treat him with great regard.

I have been told that there was an occasion when [the Caliph] Mu'tasim ordered a criminal to be brought before him for execution. The man begged him, "Commander of the Faithful, for the sake of God and God's apostle, grant me the hospitality of a drink of water, then have anything you wish done to me. I am very thirsty." Being thus conjured, the Caliph ordered the man to be brought some water, which he drank, saying in Arab fashion, "God increase your goodness! Commander of the Faithful, I have become your guest by this draught of water. Now if nobility demands the slaying of a guest, order them to kill me; otherwise, pardon me that by virtue of your majesty I may repent."

Mu'tasim replied, "You speak the truth. Great is the privilege of a guest! I grant you pardon. Repent and beware not to sin again." So the man did penance and was released by the Caliph.

Now although hospitality is a duty, the hospitality which is worthy of recognition is not such as to require you to invite any undesirable person into your house and then to make a show of humility by saying, "This is my guest". You must be discriminating in your choice of the persons to whom you offer this generosity and friendliness.

If you go as a guest, let it not be to all and sundry—it would be derogatory to your prestige. When you go, do not be in a state of great hunger nor yet completely satiated; for if you eat nothing your host will be offended, and if you eat to excess it would be inelegant. When you go into your host's dwelling, sit where you are put and in what is your proper place. Even though it be the house of a familiar friend and you have business there, do not play the master at table or over the wine, and do not give orders to your host's servants, saying, "So-and-so, place that tray here and carry that dish there", giving it to be understood that you are a member of the household. Further, do not be over-officious as a guest, concerning yourself too familiarly with the bread and food of the company; and do not give your servant food from the table for him to carry away.

Never permit yourself to be completely overcome by wine, but rise in such condition that the signs of drunkenness will not be apparent in you. Drunkenness should not take possession of you to the extent that you lose the semblance of humanity, and practise all your drunkenness at home. Further, let us suppose you have drunk a single cup of wine; if your subordinates at the same time commit a hundred transgressions, do not punish a single one of them, however deserving of punishment they may be. If you do, no one will believe it to be a measure of discipline, but all will say it is merely drunken quarrelsomeness on your part. Whatever punishment you wish to inflict on them, do so before you have taken wine; then all men shall know it was your deliberate intention and not drunken quarrelsomeness. On such occasions everything is accounted drunken conduct, in accordance with the saying [of the Arabs], "Madness takes various forms, and drunkenness is one of the forms of madness".

Excessive talk (during intoxication) is a sign of drunkenness; so also are excessive hand-clapping, the stamping of feet and unnecessary displays of affection. Whether drunk or sober, hereafter guard against any of the things which I have designated drunken conduct. Never appear before any stranger in a state of intoxication nor indeed before anyone except your own family or servants.

Do not demand that all the music performed by the minstrels shall be in light modes, otherwise you will be charged with levity and frivolousness. Yet most young men demand the light or the sorrowful modes.

CHAPTER XIII

On Jesting and the Playing of Backgammon and Chess

UNDERSTAND, MY SON, that there is an Arabic saying that jesting is the forerunner of mischief. As far as lies in your power, refrain from jesting and particularly from tasteless jesting. If you indulge in jesting, let it not be while you are in your cups, because it is most often then that mischief is created. Be ashamed of unpleasant jests and of obscenity, whether you are drunk or sober, particularly when you are playing backgammon or chess, for when engaged in these two games a man becomes very impatient and has little tolerance of jesting.

Do not make a habit of constantly playing backgammon and chess. If you play, let it be only occasionally; and never for a stake, unless it be for a fowl or a dinner or the like. Beware against playing for silver or gold. Playing without money is training for the mind, but playing for gold or silver is gambling. However well you may play, do not play with a man notorious as a gambler, for you also will become known as one.

When playing with a person of higher rank than yourself at backgammon or chess, the etiquette is that you shall not put out your hand to move a piece unless he has first moved. Never play for a stake with persons who are drunkards, quarrelsome or morose, and thus avoid any bickering. Whenever possible avoid playing [with such persons] even without a stake. Never dispute with your opponent about the markings on the dice, nor swear an oath that he threw such or such a number. However right you may be, there will always be someone who will say you are lying.

Realise that the origin of all evil and quarrels lies in jesting. Yet jesting is neither dishonourable nor sinful, for the Apostle (upon whom be peace!) indulged in it. It is related in the Traditions that an old woman one day in the house of 'Ā'ishah[1] (God be gracious to her!) questioned the Apostle and said, "Apostle of God, is my countenance that of one destined for Paradise or of one destined for Hell?". By way of a jest the Apostle replied, "No old woman will enter Paradise". At this she was greatly distressed and wept; whereupon the Apostle said, "Do not weep! My words are not in dispute. I am speaking the truth; no old woman will enter Paradise. On the day of Resurrection all mankind will arise from the grave rejuvenated." And with that the old woman was consoled.

Although jesting may be allowable, no obscenity should be permitted. If you do speak or act obscenely, let it not be in the presence of anyone of a lower degree than your own, and so avoid exposing your self-respect to the indignity of his retort. If you *must* jest obscenely, let it be with men of your own standing, so that if they make a retort you

[1] Daughter of Abu Bakr (first of the Caliphs) and favourite wife of Muhammad the Prophet.

will not be accused of anything dishonourable or in bad taste. With your joking let there be some admixture of serious talk, and avoid obscenity, even though jesting is impossible without some levity and is the cause of the lowering of all values.

You will inevitably hear repeated all that you say, and you must expect to receive from other men the treatment you accord to them. Nevertheless, quarrel with nobody; quarrelling is not indulged in by men of dignity, but rather by women and little children. If a quarrel should on any occasion break out between you and another, do not utter all that you know and could say, but so conduct your quarrel as to leave a loophole for reconciliation. Do not be completely irreconcilable and stubborn, considering stubbornness and irreconcilability as the characteristics of persons of little worth. Realise that humility is the best of qualities, one of God's blessings which no one envies.

Do not with every word you address to others say, "O man"; this repetition of "O man" without reason detracts from a person's dignity as a man.

Whatever else may be said, wine-drinking and jesting are the occupations of young men. If you observe due limits, they can be enjoyed in the pleasantest way; but it is also possible to abstain, if you obey the dictates of wisdom.

The etiquette of wine-bibbing and jesting is now clear to you and, since I have made my comments on these topics, I will proceed to say something concerning the art of love, telling you a little of what I know, more especially in view of the difficulty of opposing one's heart.

CHAPTER XIV

On Romantic Passion

UNDERSTAND, MY SON, that no man can be passionate unless he is of a sensuous disposition, for passion arises from the sensuousness of a man's nature. What springs from a fineness of disposition is itself subtle, and, since love is subtle, it is characteristic of the subtle disposition. Do you not everywhere see how it is the young rather than the old who fall in love, for the reason that the disposition of the young is more concerned with the senses than that of the old? Moreover, no coarse-natured, heavy-witted person can be a lover; for passion is generally the special propensity of lively-spirited persons.

For your part, resist falling in love and guard against becoming a lover, for a lover's life is beset with unhappiness, particularly when he is without means. The penniless lover can never achieve his aim, more particularly if he is elderly; the goal cannot be reached except with the aid of money, and a lover not possessed of it will succeed only in tormenting his soul. On this theme I have said:

In poverty love swiftly turns to woe,
For lack of silver we must live apart.
Resembling me in my unhappy lot,
The pauper empty-handed leaves the mart.

Should it by chance happen at some time that you find happiness with someone, do not let your heart be completely captivated and do not accustom your heart to be for ever toying with love, nor be perpetually in pursuit of your desire. That is not the conduct of right-minded persons. Lovers are either united or apart, and a year together fails to compensate for the misery of a day's separation, seeing that the essence of the state of passion is misery, heartache and torment. The pain may be pleasurable, yet if you are apart from your lover you are in torment. When you are together, the object of your affection being aware of the state of your heart, her coyness, unreasonableness and cruelty, once apprehended, result in your being deprived of all pleasure in her society. Should a period of union be followed by one of separation, that union is worse than being apart.

Moreover, supposing the object of your affection to be the veriest angel, you would never be immune from the censure of mankind, because censoriousness has always been the nature of man. Abstain from such desire, therefore, in so far as you are able, because only philosophers have the ability completely to abstain. The argument for abstention is that it is impossible for a man to become enamoured at a glance. First the eye beholds, then the heart considers; and if the heart approves the object of love, one's physical nature conceives desire and demands further sight. If you submit your passion to the authority of your heart, whose dictates you will then follow, you will contrive to behold the object of your affection on other occasions. After further visual approval your physical inclination will be increased and the longing in your heart become even more urgent. You will then seek to behold your loved one again in order to have speech with her. Once you have spoken and heard the reply, the affair proceeds like a rope on a pulley—all your sagacity and good sense are in thrall to her, making you incapable of any independent action. Thereafter, even if you wish to put a restraint upon yourself, you will be unable to do so, because matters will have passed beyond your control and your passion will increase with every day. You will then perforce be compelled to follow your heart.

Nevertheless, if, when first you behold the beloved one you restrain yourself and, when your heart makes demands upon you, you set discretion in authority over it so that it will never again give a thought to her name, and if you occupy your mind with other things and drain away your feelings in other directions, closing your eyes to any sight of her, then your heartache will be past in a week. The memory of it will not recur and you will quickly be able to deliver yourself from torment. It is not, however, within the power of all men to act in this way. It requires an intelligent man with complete understanding to treat himself for this infirmity, for passion *is* an infirmity, as Muhammed ibn Zakarīyā of Rayy[1] has related in his *Classification of Diseases*. He there propounds the aetiology of the malady of passion and suggests remedies, such as continuous fasting, carrying heavy burdens, undertaking lengthy journeys and the like.

If you should find a friend in whose society and conduct you find happiness, I regard that as unobjectionable. Abū Sa'īd son of Abū'l-Khair[2] declared that a man finds four things essential to life; bread, a patched cloak, a land of

[1] Rhazes, who died in A.D. 923 or, according to some authorities, in A.D. 932.

[2] "The first master of theosophic verse" (Browne, *Lit. Hist.* II, p. 261), who died in A.D. 1049.

solitude and an intimate companion. To each man they are a necessity according to his circumstances and capacity, and in so far as they are lawful. Yet friendship is one thing and passion another.

In passion there is no happiness. A passion-struck man once composed this *bayt* on his own feelings:

Can passion's fire, my darling, comfort thee?
Who ever found relief in raging fire?

Be assured that through friendship a man's heart will ever be at peace, whereas through passion it will ever be in torment. Again, if during your youth you toy with passion, there will be some excuse for you; men will regard you with indulgence and say that you are young. But strive never to have such passion when you are old. No indulgence is granted to old men, although, if you were one of the ordinary run of men, the matter might be simpler. Being a prince, and old, by no means let your thoughts stray in that direction, nor let it be apparent that your affections are attached to any person. That a prince in old age should indulge in his passion is a matter of grave concern.

During the time of my grandfather, Shams al-Ma'ālī,[1] it was reported that a merchant at Bukhārā possessed a slave valued at two thousand dinars. Ahmad son of Sa'd brought the matter to the prince's attention, saying, "It would be fitting for us to send someone to buy that slave", and the prince replied that he, Ahmad, should go. On arrival at Bukhārā, he saw the slave-dealer and, the slave being produced, he made the purchase for the price of twelve hundred dinars. The slave was brought to Gurgān and inspected

[1] i.e. the great Qābūs ibn Washmgīr.

by the Amir, who appointed him to the office of towel-holder. [This meant that] when the Amir washed his hands, the slave held out the towel on which he dried them. Some time passed; then, one day, when the Amir had washed his hands and the youth was handing him the towel, as he was rubbing them his glance fell on him. The sight pleased him and he handed back the towel [without more ado]. However, some time later the Amir said to Abū'l-'Abbās 'Ālim, "I have given this slave his freedom and granted him such-and-such a village. I wish you to know this. Write title-deeds for him and ask the hand of a chieftain's daughter from the town for him in marriage. Instruct him, also, that he is to remain at home until his beard is grown and let him then present himself before me."

Abū'l-'Abbās 'Ālim was the vizier. He replied [to this]: "It is for my lord to command, but, if your discretion sanctions, will my lord inform his servant what his purpose is in this?" The Amir replied: "Today such-and-such an incident occurred. It would be a hideous offence if a prince over seventy years of age should become the victim of passion. I should at that age be fully occupied in the protection of God's servants and seeking the welfare of my people, my army and my possessions. Were I now to engage in dalliance, I should find forgiveness neither in the eyes of God nor of man."

Yet, when a man is young, excuses will be found for him whatever his conduct [in this respect]. Even so, there should never be any open display of passion. In spite of your youth, act with discretion, dignity and self-discipline, in order to give no man the pretext for meddling in your affairs. I once heard a man of high rank declare that Sultan Mas'ūd had ten slaves, Keepers of the Royal Robes, of whom one, named Nūshtagīn, was especially favoured by him. Several years passed without anyone's realising who the Sultan's favourite was, because the gifts he distributed were all alike. Then, after five years, in a fit of drunkenness he said: "Register in Nūshtagīn's name everything that my father granted Ayāz".[1] Thus it became known that the object of his affection was Nūshtagīn.

Even now, my son, although I have told you this story [as a warning], I know that if the occasion arose you would not apply my words. I have myself said in circumstances such as these

A man in lively health and sound of mind,
Must act like Wāmiq,[2] *who for 'Adhrā*[2] *pined.*
He but dissembles that behaves not so;
Who cannot love, for manhood's ill-designed.

Even though I composed the verse, you need not act in accordance with the quatrain, but strive rather not to be overwhelmed by passion.

If [nevertheless] there is someone of whom you are passionately fond, let it be a person worthy of love; although the object of one's affection cannot always be a Ptolemy or a Plato, he should have some endowment of good sense. Although I know, too, that not everyone can be Joseph[3] son of Jacob, yet there must be in him some

[1] Ayāz was the favourite slave of Sultan Mahmūd of Ghazna (*d.* A.D. 1030), the first real Muhammadan conqueror of India and the subject of many legends.

[2] Wāmiq the hero, and 'Adhrā the heroine, of a number of romances in Persian. The best-known is by 'Unsurī (poet laureate of Sultan Mahmūd), who died in 441/1049–50.

[3] The Muhammadan ideal of manly beauty.

pleasing quality which shall prevent men from cavilling and allow indulgence to be readily accorded you, since mankind is never immune from the commission of faults or from seeking them out. A certain man, being once asked if he had any faults, replied "No". Thereupon he was asked if there was anyone who found fault with him, and to this he replied, "There are many". "Then", came the retort, "it must be obvious to you that you are even fuller of faults than other men".

If you visit a house as a guest, do not let your favourite accompany you. If you do, then do not be for ever occupied with her in the presence of other persons, nor let your mind be always concerned over her; no one can eat her. Further, do not imagine that she is regarded by other people with the same eyes as your own. The poet says:

Alas for me if other eyes should see
You as through my eyes you appear to me.

It may be that although in your eyes she is the handsomest of creatures, in those of others she is the ugliest. Do not constantly be giving her fruit and making enquiries of her, nor be for ever calling to her or whispering in her ear.

Now that I have recounted the arguments for and against, it is your duty to make endeavours that men shall have no occasion to find fault with you.

CHAPTER XV

On Taking One's Pleasure

LET IT BE CLEAR to you, my son, that if you fall in love with a person, you should not indiscriminately and whether drunk or sober indulge in sexual congress. It is well-known that the seed which issues from you is the germ of a soul and of a person, so that when you have congress it should not be while you are in a state of intoxication, for in that condition it has detrimental effects. More properly and preferably it should come in the condition after intoxication. Yet do not indulge each time the thought occurs to you; that is the behaviour of beasts, which know not the season for any action but act as they find occasion. A man, for his part, should select the proper season and thus preserve the distinction between him and the beasts.

As between women and youths, do not confine your inclinations to either sex; thus you may find enjoyment from both kinds without either of the two becoming inimical to you. Furthermore, if, as I have said, excessive copulation is harmful, [complete] abstention also has its dangers. When you do it, let it be in accordance with appetite and not as a matter of course, so that it may have as little ill effect as possible. But, whether indulged in with appetite or not, have a care during the height of the hot weather or the depth of the cold; at these two seasons sexual congress has the most malign effect, particularly upon elderly men. Of the seasons, the spring is the most suitable, the air being then temperate, springs of water most abundant and the world indued with a pleasing countenance. Then, when the greater world renews its youth, and the strength of our body, which is the world in little, similarly behaves and the humours which are in conflict with it become temperate, the blood in the veins increases together with the semen in the loins. Irrespective of his own volition the need for intercourse and relief becomes urgent in every man and it is then, when the natural desires are genuine, that least harm is done.

In this respect also you should refuse as far as possible to have blood let from your veins either during the height of the warm season or in the depth of the cold. If you experience an excess of blood, still it by means of cold draughts.

During the summer let your desires incline towards youths and during the winter towards women. But on this topic it is requisite that one's discourse should be brief, lest it engender appetite.

CHAPTER XVI

Procedure when Visiting the Warm Baths

UNDERSTAND, MY SON, that when you go to the warm baths it should not be at a time when you are sated with food, that being a dangerous course. Further, do not indulge in sexual congress at the baths, especially in the hot chamber. Muhammad son of Zakarīyā of Rayy [Rhazes] somewhere says: "I marvel when any man, having eaten his fill and then had sexual intercourse at the baths, does not immediately die".

The baths in themselves are an excellent institution and from the time when wise men began to erect buildings nothing better than baths has been built. In spite of their excellence, however, it is of no benefit to visit them every day; it may indeed be harmful. To do so softens the sinews and joints, destroying their toughness; and it habituates the constitution to the practice of daily visits to the baths to such an extent that if on any day you omit to go, you feel that you are unwell and your organs do not behave properly. The correct procedure, therefore, is to go every second day.

When first you enter, remain for a while in the cool chamber; then, when your body has derived full benefit from that, enter the middle chamber and stay for a time until you have had the utmost enjoyment from it; then go into the hot chamber, where you should continue until you have derived full advantage from that also. When the hot chamber has taken complete effect, enter the private room and there wash your head. Never stay too long in the baths and never pour over yourself water that is either very hot or very cold. Let it be of a moderate temperature. If the baths should be empty, regard it (as all wise men do) as a great boon.

When you emerge from the baths, follow the same order as that followed on your entering. First dry your hair well and then come out. That is the practice of men of wisdom and dignity. Indeed, to leave the baths with hair wet and go into the presence of important personages is bad manners. As for the drinking of water or beer in the baths, refrain from it; it is harmful, conducing to dropsy. If, however, you are grievously suffering from the effects of intoxication, it is permissible to drink a little in order to allay the wine-sickness and so reduce discomfort caused by it.

CHAPTER XVII

Sleep and Rest

IT IS THE regular custom of the Greek sages on emerging from the warm baths to lie down in the disrobing-room of the bath-house for a period before they go out of doors. No other people have that custom. Now philosophers call sleep "The Lesser Death", because neither sleepers nor the dead have any consciousness of the world, and the sole difference between them is that these latter are dead and bereft of breath while those others are dead but still breathing.

Over-indulgence in sleep is a habit not to be approved. It renders the body slothful and disturbs the natural constitution. Moreover, it alters the appearance of the face from one aspect to another. Now, the conditions that may affect a man and immediately bring about an alteration in his face are six in number: sudden joy, unforeseen sorrow, anger, sleep, drunkenness and old age (though when persons reach old age they normally change in outward appearance, and that therefore stands in a category by itself).

Now men when asleep are in the category neither of the living nor the dead and no writ runs against any man asleep or dead. The poet has said:

Although I bow beneath thy cruelty,
My heart will never want for love of thee;
Thy dreaming saves thee, against those who dream
A charge becomes a nolle prosequi.

Just as sleeping to excess is harmful, so also is remaining without sleep. If a man is deliberately prevented for seventy-two hours from sleeping and is kept awake by force, there is danger of his suddenly dying. There are limits to everything that may be done. Philosophers say that a day-and-night consists of twenty-four hours, during two parts of which you are awake and during one part asleep. For eight hours you should be occupied in carrying out God's will, for eight hours engaged in pleasure, merriment and refreshment of your spirit, and for eight hours reposing so that the parts of the body, which have been active for sixteen hours, are rested. Foolish people are asleep for one-half of the twenty-four hours and are awake for the other half; but wise men sleep for one-third of the time and are awake for two-thirds.

By the division which I have indicated each period of eight hours should possess a different character. Understand that God created the night for the repose of his servants, as he says in his own words: "We made the night for a cloak and the day for livelihood" (Kor. 78, vv. 10 f.). Further, consider the reality that the vital principle is contained entirely in the soul, the body being the habitation in which the soul resides.

Now the soul has three qualities, namely life, lightness and movement, while the body also has three qualities, namely death, repose and inertia. As long as soul and body are together in the same place, the soul preserves the body by its own particular qualities, sometimes moving the body to action and sometimes restraining it from action and drawing it to inertia. [On the other hand] when the body displays its qualities, death, heaviness and repose sink down together, as though it were the collapse of a house.

When a house collapses it engulfs everyone within it. Similarly, the body, lapsing into sleep, engulfs all man's senses, with the result that hearing no longer hears, vision ceases to behold, taste distinguishes no savours, feeling perceives neither heaviness nor lightness, smooth nor rough, and speech makes no utterance. All, therefore, which lies asleep in its own place [internally], is engulfed. Memory and mind, however, being external, cannot be engulfed.

Are you not aware how, with the body asleep, the mind beholds visions of all kinds which the memory retains, so that on waking the person concerned can say that he has had such and such dreams? If these two also were in the places of the others [*i.e.*, internal], they would be engulfed, making the mind incapable of beholding and the memory of retaining. If speech also were in its place, the body could not fall asleep; if it did so, and speech gave utterance, there would be no sleep and hence no repose, because the repose of all living creatures comes during sleep. Thus God created nothing without wisdom.

As for sleep during the day, shun it as a matter of habit and, if you cannot avoid it, sleep only a little. To turn day into night is unwisdom. The practice of men of distinction and of the wealthy is that during the summer they rest for the siesta at midday. But for real enjoyment their method is to rest (as is their custom) for an hour, and then to seclude themselves with someone that gives them pleasure until the sun sinks and the heat is broken, at which time they emerge.

To sum up, your endeavour should be to spend the greater part of your life in a waking state, for the tendency is to sleep to excess. Whenever it is that you retire to sleep, whether by day or by night, refrain from going alone, but go with someone who refreshes your spirit; the reason being that the slumberer and the dead are one by analogy. Neither is conscious of the world, but the former sleeps while possessed of life and the latter without it. The distinction to be made between the two kinds is that the dead must of necessity sleep alone, being completely impotent; whereas the living are under no such compulsion. Why then go to sleep like one that is impotent of necessity? For the living person, a bed-mate who refreshes the spirit is therefore needful, but none is required for the dead man's bed. Thus is the slumber of the living distinguished from that of the dead.

It behoves you to make a habit of rising with the dawn, so that by the time the sun has come up you shall have performed your duty of worshipping God. He that rises only with the sun shall have scant prosperity, because the time for worship will have passed him by and the resultant misfortune will overtake him. Rise with the dawn, therefore, and fulfil your duty towards God. Then begin upon your own tasks.

If you have no task to be done in the early morning and you wish to go out for recreation, it is permissible to occupy oneself with hunting or some other pastime.

CHAPTER XVIII

On Hunting

BE WELL AWARE, my son, that riding and hunting are the occupation for gentlemen, particularly in youth. Yet there must be bounds and measure to every occupation, and one cannot hunt every day. In the week of seven days, hunt for two days, devote yourself to the fulfilment of God's commands for three days and to your own domestic affairs for the [remaining] two.

When you set out to ride, never mount a horse that is too small; however handsome a man may be, he appears insignificant on a little horse, whereas although a man may be insignificant in stature he appears to great advantage on a big horse. Also, except when on a journey, do not ride an ambling horse, because while riding an ambling horse a man holds himself in a bad posture. In the town, therefore, and in your own precincts, ride a spirited and high-stepping horse, so that because of the horse's mettle you are prevented from being careless of your own person. Always hold yourself erect if you desire not to display an ugly posture in the saddle.

When hunting do not urge your horse recklessly forward; to gallop rashly ahead is to act like a child or an immature youth. Do not go in chase of ferocious beasts; there is no benefit to be obtained and nothing is got from it except risk to one's life. It was thus, while hunting wild beasts, that two great princes of our line were killed, one being my father's grandfather the Amīr Washmgīr and the second my cousin Amīr Sharaf al-Ma'ālī. Let your attendants charge ahead—except when there are great princes present, and then it may be permissible with a view to acquiring a reputation and bringing oneself to their notice.

If you are fond of hunting, engage in it with falcon, white hawk, royal falcon, leopard [cheetah] or hound, in order not merely to have your hunting without hazard but to ensure that what you take may be of service. That is quite different from hunting wild beasts whose flesh cannot be eaten and whose pelts are useless for clothing. If you should choose hawking, princes use two methods. Those of Khurasan never fly the hawk from their own hand, while the practice of those of Iraq is to do so. Both are permissible and, if you are not a prince, you do as you please. If you are a prince, it is permissible for you to fly the hawk yourself, but do not fly the same bird more than once, that being a practice beneath the dignity of princes. Set the bird on once only and then observe; if the hawk secures its prey, all is well; otherwise take another and fly that.

The prince's aim and object in hunting must be the sport and not the meat. If he hunts with hounds, it is unfitting for him to hold them; his servants should unleash them in his presence, while he looks on. Do not gallop after the quarry!

If you hunt with the leopard, do not place it behind yourself on the horse; it is an undignified practice for a prince to act as leopard-attendant, as well as imprudent to keep a wild beast at one's back, particularly if one is a king.

That is the whole etiquette of hunting.

CHAPTER XIX

The Game of Polo

MY SON, IF your recreation is playing polo, do not be constantly indulging in it, for misfortune has overtaken many a man through so doing. The story goes that

'Amr son of Layth[1] was blind in one eye. One day, after he had become Amir of Khurasan, he went on to the field to practice with the ball. Now he had an army commander to whose every word he paid heed. This man came on to the field and seizing the Amir's rein said, "I will not leave you to practise with the ball, or play polo". 'Amr replied, "How is it that although you yourself play polo, you do not think it proper for me to play?" He answered, "Because I have two eyes. If one of them should happen to be struck by the ball, I should be blinded in one eye but one would still remain to me with which I should be able to behold the world. You have only the one eye, and if by accident the ball should hit it, you would be compelled to bid farewell to the amirate of Khurasan." To this 'Amr replied, "In spite of the annoyance of it all, you speak the truth. I agree never to practise with the ball as long as I live."

Yet, if once or twice a year you find pleasure in polo, I regard it as permissible. But you should not indulge in a great deal of riding, because in that there is danger. The men riding should number not more than eight in all; you should be stationed at one end of the field and another man at the opposite end, with six men on the field actually playing the ball. When the ball comes in your direction, return it and bring your horse up; but take no part in the scrimmage, thereby avoiding collision. You can achieve your purpose merely by looking on.

That is how men of distinction play polo.

[1] A famous warrior, founder of the "Coppersmith" dynasty (A.D. 868–903), and one of the earliest chieftains to claim independence in Persia from the Caliph of Baghdad.

CHAPTER XX

On Giving Battle to an Enemy

ONCE YOU ENGAGE in battle it is inexcusable to display any sloth or hesitation; you must breakfast on the enemy before he dines on you. When you have arrived in the midst of the fray, be remiss in nothing but take no precautions for your own life; he that is destined to sleep in the grave will never again sleep at home. This I have expressed in the following quatrain:

Though I should have a lion for foe I'd dare,
Were he unseen or seen, my sword to bare,
Who's destined friendless in the tomb to lie,
Can never sleep at home in friendship's care.

In the course of the battle, as long as you are able to advance a foot, never take a step backward. Even when you are hemmed in amongst the enemy, never cease the struggle; you may with your bare fist knock the enemy out of the fight. And as long as they see activity, proving you to be in good fettle, they will stand in awe of you. At a time like this reconcile your heart with death. Under no conditions be afraid, but be bold; for a short blade becomes elongated [grows longer] in the hands of the brave. Be remiss in nothing whilst you are in the battle, for if any mark of fear or cowardice is revealed in you, even if you had a thousand lives you would be unable to save a single one, and the humblest person could overwhelm you.

Cowardice results either in your being slain or in the besmirching of your name. Once you become notorious amongst men for poltroonery and for a display of sloth and feebleness in such circumstances as these, and for failing your comrades, you will be disgraced amongst your friends and associates. Neither repute nor comfort will be left to you; amongst your contemporaries and companions you will be stricken with shame. Death is preferable to such a life, and it is far better to die in good odour than to spend one's life in disrepute.

Do not be over-hasty in shedding innocent blood, and regard no killing of Muslims to be lawful, unless they are brigands, thieves and grave-robbers or such whose execution is demanded by the law. Torment in both worlds is inflicted for the shedding of innocent blood; you will find retribution for it on the Day of Resurrection, but also in this world your name will be besmirched. None of your subjects will trust you, those who serve you will despair of reward from you, your people will conceive hatred for you and will in their hearts become your enemies. Retribution for the shedding of innocent blood will assuredly not be confined to the next world, for I have read in books and ascertained by experience that the punishment for evil may also be inflicted on men even in this world. When they are gone, even if their own stars chance to be favourable, misfortune will befall their children. Therefore spare yourself and your offspring by shedding no innocent blood.

Yet do not neglect your duty where blood must rightfully be shed, for the general welfare demands it and out of remissness evil is born. It is told of my grandfather Shams al-Ma'ālī that he was a bloodthirsty man, never able to forgive an offence. He was a cruel man, and because of his cruelty his troops determined upon seeking vengeance. They accordingly entered into a conspiracy with my uncle, Falak al-Ma'ālī, who came and seized his father, Shams al-Ma'ālī, being compelled to that action by the army, which threatened to transfer the kingdom to a stranger if he did not agree to their terms. Realising that the sovereignty would thereby be lost to his family, he was thus driven by force to take the course he did.

Now comes the point of my story. The king, being seized and fettered, was placed in a palanquin and sent to the fort of Chanāshak [in Astarābād]. Amongst the men charged with his custody was one called 'Abd Allāh the Dromedary-guard. As they were proceeding on the way Shams al-Ma'ālī asked this man, "Have you any knowledge of the person who directed this affair and how it was planned; for here is a matter about which, though of great importance, I could gather no information?" "Such-and-such persons did it", 'Abd Allāh replied, mentioning five generals, "and they misled the army. I myself was at the centre of the affair; I made them all swear an oath [of loyalty], and it was I who brought the matter to this stage. But do not hold me answerable for it. Blame yourself, because all this has come about through your many killings and not because the army has changed its character."

Shams al-Ma'ālī's answer was that the other was mistaken. "This business has come upon me", he said, "through my failure to kill. If the possibility of such an affair had ever occurred to my mind, I should undoubtedly have slain you, together with the other five men. Had I done so, my affairs would have prospered and I should now have been in a place of security."

I relate this story to prevent you from being in any

degree careless over the duties of justice and governmental control and from treating over-lightly anything essential to these matters.

(Do not practise castration to procure eunuchs; it is the equivalent of shedding blood, because, for the sake of your own lusts, you lessen the number of Muslim offspring in the world, and there can be no greater wrong than that. If you need a eunuch, acquire someone who has castrated himself; the benefit of his action will be yours, the sin will be another's and you will be relieved of the consequences of it.)

Howbeit, in the matter of your conduct in battle, behave as I have advised; do not spare yourself, for unless you expose your body to be meat for dogs how shall you acquire yourself a lion's name? Strive therefore to get fame and bread, and, having got them, endeavour to acquire wealth. When you have that, guard it and expend it only by measure.

CHAPTER XXI

On the Acquisition of Wealth

MY SON, DO not be indifferent to the acquisition of wealth, yet do not cast yourself into danger for the sake of it. Assure yourself that everything you acquire shall be of the best quality and likely to give you pleasure. Once you have acquired it, preserve it, not letting it go for anything trivial; indeed, preserving is more difficult than acquiring. Should the time arrive when you are compelled to spend money, make every endeavour to replace it quickly, for if you remove without ever putting back, were it the treasure of Qārūn[1] it would come to an end. Yet do not have your mind constantly dwelling upon it nor regard it as something everlasting; then, if it should be consumed, you will not suffer regrets over it.

Should your wealth amount to a great matter, set it to good use and yet with proper control; a little used with circumspection is better than a great quantity extravagantly consumed. Also I should prefer you to leave behind a large sum rather than become impoverished; there is a saying that it is better to leave property to enemies than to stand in need of charity from friends. Thus, striving to keep is better than striving to find. However little the sum may be, realise that it is your duty to safeguard it, for he that can hold tight to a little can hold tight to much. Remember, also, that it is better to work for oneself than for others.

Furthermore, hold slothfulness in contempt as the disciple of misfortune, and be patient of toil, by which you accumulate wealth; just as greatly as wealth is increased by labour so it is diminished by slothfulness. Philosophers say, "Be unremitting in effort if you wish to prosper, be content if you wish to be rich and modest if you wish to be well beloved". To lose through sloth and neglect what you have won by toil and effort would not be agreeable with the conduct of wise men; to permit it would merely lead to regrets on your part in the day of need and would avail you nothing. On the other hand, when you have endured heavy toil, strive to enjoy what you have earned.

[1] Probably the Korah of the Old Testament and, according to the Koran, possessed of enormous treasure. Apparently there is some recollection of Croesus.

Then, however precious money may be to you, do not grudge it to the deserving; come what may, no man carries his wealth with him to the grave. Yet, if you have no liking for penury, your spending will accord with the extent of your income, because it is not always and only upon the houses of the impecunious that distress falls—it may descend upon any household. For instance, if your income is one dirham and you spend a dirham and a grain, you will always be poverty-stricken. When, therefore, your income is a dirham, you need only spend a grain less than a dirham for there never to be want in the house. And you must be content with what you possess (contentment being a second means of independence), remembering that your fortune will be what is destined for you.

Do not lavish your money on a matter which can be settled by fair words and cajolery; thus you will conserve your possessions against being wasted to no purpose, [knowing that] men lacking means enjoy no consideration.

You must realise that the common run of men have an affection for the rich, without regard to their own personal concern, and that they dislike poor men, even when their own interests are not at stake. The reason is that poverty is man's worst evil and any quality which is to the credit of the wealthy is itself a derogation of the poor.

Regard the virtue of men as lying in their generosity and judge their worth in accordance with their excellence in that virtue. Yet look upon extravagance as the enemy of God; anything which is hateful to God is a misfortune to his servants, as he has said in his noble Book: "Do not spend to excess; verily he loves not them that spend to excess". What God regards with dislike, do you also dislike. There is a cause for every misfortune; understand that extravagance is the cause of poverty.

Now extravagance does not lie merely in expenditure on disbursements. There must be no excess in eating, speaking, working or any other activity, for it wastes the body, harms the spirit and deadens the living mind. You observe that the life of a lamp is generated by oil; if you pour oil into the lamp without measure and limit, so that it overflows the spout of the container and passes beyond the tip of the wick, it immediately extinguishes the lamp. Oil itself then becomes the cause of the lamp's extinction, although, had it been present in moderate quantity, it would have been the means of keeping it alight; once there was an excess of it, it became the means of the lamp's extinction. Thus is demonstrated the fact that oil, which is the means of keeping a lamp alight, is also, if used without moderation and to an extravagant extent, the means of its extinction.

For such reasons as these excess is displeasing to God and disapproved by the wise in all matters, seeing that the consequences of excess are ever detrimental. Even so, you need not spend your life in misery nor close the door against your daily sustenance. Treat yourself generously and forgo nothing that is essential to you; he that neglects to satisfy his own needs can never enjoy happiness and will be disappointed in his ambitions. Therefore spend on yourself what you possess and disburse it on what is essential to you; for, when all is said, although possessions are precious, they are not more so than life.

In brief, endeavour to apply what comes into your hands to good purpose and do not entrust your possessions except to those who will be sparing of them. Place no reliance upon the gambler or the wine-bibber; and if you regard all men as thieves your possessions will be secure from theft. In your pursuit of the accumulation of wealth neglect nothing; bodily ease in the beginning means pain in the end and pain at first means comfort in the end, just as comfort today means toil tomorrow and toil today comfort tomorrow.

However acquired, whether with toil or without, out of your dirham spend two-sixths on your household and family; even though there are other essential requirements of which you stand in need, do not expend more. Having exhausted these two sixths, lay aside two-sixths in your treasury to meet [future] needs; keep it for your support and do not let your mind recur to it on any and every occasion when something is lacking. Transmit it to your heirs; so you will have something to succour you in the days of your feebleness and in your old age. Use the two remaining sixths for your own adornment, acquiring ornaments that will not perish or become antiquated, such as gems and objects made of gold, silver, bronze, copper, brass and the like.

Any money that is left over, bury in the ground; you will recover anything that you bury and your capital will always remain undiminished. Once you have bought your equipment, do not sell your household goods for any chance requirement or casual need that may come to you, and do not say, "Now that I have the need I will sell, and I shall buy again at another time". It is not a prudent course to sell your household goods expecting to replace them by purchase in the future, because it may not be possible to do so and then, having lost your possessions, your house will remain empty. Thus you will reduce yourself to the utmost poverty.

Furthermore, do not turn to borrowing for every need that may arise nor give your property in pledge, and in no circumstances either give or take gold for profit. Realize that borrowing is great infamy and, as long as you can contrive it, refrain from lending anyone even a silver dirham; particularly to friends, because, when the time comes for demanding back what is due, the greatest difficulty is encountered from your friends. Once you have lent money, cease to regard it as part of your possessions, and say to yourself, "I have given this money to my friend as a gift". However long the time before the borrower restores it, do not ask for it, because through such demands friendships are brought to an end. A friend can swiftly be turned into an enemy, but it is difficult to change an enemy into a friend; the one is child's play but the other requires the negotiation of elders.

Whatever your possessions may be, let them that deserve it have a share. Covet no other man's goods and thus you will become the best of men. Consider what is yours to be yours and what is other men's theirs; thus you will become recognised for trustworthiness and men will place their confidence in you. By thus conducting your life, you will ever be rich.

CHAPTER XXII

On the Placing of Trusts for Safekeeping

IF YOU SHOULD be offered a valuable object for safeguarding as a trust, in no circumstance accept it; but, having accepted, keep it safe. To accept an object on trust is to accept misfortune, because there are three things[1] which cannot fail to be the consequences before you have surrendered it to its owner (as God in his own well-founded revelation commands, "Restore objects entrusted to you to their owners" (Kor. 4, v. 61)). The manly, humane and generous path is not to accept trusts, but, once having accepted them, to safeguard them and restore them intact to their owners.

I have been told the story of a man who left his house early one morning while it was still dark to go to the warm baths. On the way he saw a friend, to whom he suggested that they should go there in company. The friend replied that he would go with him as far as the door of the baths, but that he would not enter because he had other business. Accordingly he went to within a short distance of the baths to a place where there was a parting of the ways, and there, without any warning, turned off and continued by the road leading away from the baths.

Now it chanced that a pickpocket, going to the baths for his own nefarious purposes, was behind the first man, who happened to look round but thought in the dark that it was his friend whom he saw. In his sleeve he had a hundred dinars tied in a kerchief. He took this out of his sleeve and handed it to the pickpocket, saying, "Brother, take charge of this until I come out of the baths; then give it back to me". The pickpocket received the gold and settled down where he was. By the time the other was ready to emerge from the baths, it was light. He put on his clothes and was about to depart when the pickpocket called to him and said, "Young man, take your gold and go. Because of this thing which you deposited with me I have had no success with my own business today."

[1] Explained subsequently.

The man asked, "What thing have I deposited with you and what kind of man are you?". The pickpocket answered that he was a pickpocket by profession but that the other had entrusted him with the gold to keep until he came out of the baths. The man asked in reply, "If you are a pickpocket, why did you not make off with it and leave me?" "Had I been engaged in my own business", said the other, "I should have made off with it, even if there had been a thousand dinars there, and not left you a barleycorn. But you handed me the money for safeguarding and as a trust; it would not have been honourable for me to be dishonest with you when you came to me on a matter of confidence."

I tell you this story to make you realize that when even a cutpurse respects the confidence reposed in him, the acceptance of a trust is a grave matter attended with hazard. Suppose the thing deposited with you should be destroyed while in your hands, though without any intention on your part; if you bought another in replacement and gave it him, then well and good; but suppose that an evil spirit led you astray to covet it, that would mean disgrace both in this world and the next. Even when you restore it to its rightful owner, having endured such troubles in the safeguarding of the trust, the owner bears you no gratitude. He merely says that the article was his and it has been given back to him. He remains entirely ungrateful towards you for all your trouble and your sole reward from him is the possibility that he would besmirch your garments.

If any harm befalls the article, without any conceivable dishonesty on your part, no one will accept that excuse as true. In the thoughts of all you will be a rogue; the regard in which you are held by your peers and associates will vanish and none will ever place reliance upon you again.

Were, in fact, a single particle of that valuable object to remain with you, it would be a contravention of the law, and great misfortune would cling to you. In this world you would not prosper and in the next you would earn God's punishment.

On the other hand, when you, for your part, entrust something to another for safe keeping, never do it covertly but take two equitable witnesses and ask for a document [of receipt] from the depositary, thus relieving yourself of any litigation. Then, should the matter come to litigation, do not be over-exigent; to be so is the mark of the oppressor. As long as you can avoid it swear no oath, whether true or false, and never gain a reputation as a swearer of oaths, so that, should the occasion arise when you are compelled to swear, men will believe by that oath that you are telling the truth. However rich and powerful you may be, if your reputation is not good and you do not speak the truth, you will be one of the poor, seeing that the man of ill repute and the liar must inevitably decline at last into poverty. Put into practice your reputation for trustworthiness—it has been called the Philosopher's Stone for making gold—and thus live rich and powerful. That means that you must be trustworthy and truthful, because the wealth of the whole world is the possession of them that are trustworthy and truthful. Strive never to mislead, but also be on your guard against being misled, especially in dealings in which the appetites are concerned.

CHAPTER XXIII

On the Purchase of Slaves

WHEN YOU SET out to buy slaves, be cautious. The buying of men is a difficult art because many a slave may appear to be good, who, regarded with knowledge, turns out to be the opposite. Most people imagine that buying slaves is like any other form of trading, not understanding that the buying of slaves, or the art of doing so, is a branch of philosophy. Anyone who buys goods of which he has no competent understanding can be defrauded over them, and the most difficult form of knowledge is that which deals with human beings. There are so many blemishes and good points in the human kind, and a single blemish may conceal a myriad good points while a single good point may conceal a myriad faults.

Human beings cannot be known except by the science of physiognomy and by experience, and the science of physiognomy in its entirety is a branch of prophecy that is not acquired to perfection except by the divinely directed apostle. The reason is that by physiognomy the inward goodness or wickedness of men can be ascertained.

Now let me describe to the best of my ability what is essential in the purchasing of slaves, both white and black, and what their good and bad points are, so that they may be known to you. Understand then that there are three essentials in the buying of slaves; first is the recognition of their good and bad qualities whether external or internal, by means of physiognomy; second is the awareness of diseases, whether latent or apparent, by their symptoms; third is the knowledge of the various classes and the defects and merits of each.

With regard to the first requirement, that of physiognomy, it consists of close observation when buying slaves. (The buyers of slaves are of all categories: there are those who inspect the face, disregarding body and extremities; others look to the corpulence or otherwise of the slave.) Whoever it may be that inspects the slave must first look at the face, which is always open to view, whereas the body can only be seen as occasion offers. Then look at eyes and eyebrows, followed by nose, lips and teeth, and lastly at the hair. The reason for this is that God placed the beauty of human beings in eyes and eyebrows, delicacy in the nose, sweetness in the lips and teeth and freshness in the skin. To all these the hair of the head has been made to lend adornment, since [God] created the hair for adornment.

You must, consequently, inspect everything. When you see beauty in the eyes and eyebrows, delicacy in the nose, sweetness in the lips and teeth and freshness in the skin, then buy the slave possessing them without concerning yourself over the extremities of the body. If all of these qualities are not present, then the slave must possess delicacy; because, in my opinion, one that is delicate without having beauty is preferable to one that is beautiful but not possessed of delicacy.

The learned say that one must know the indications and signs by which to buy the slaves suited for particular duties. The slave that you buy for your private service and conviviality should be of middle proportions, neither tall nor short, fat nor lean, pale nor florid, thickset nor slender, curly-haired nor with hair over-straight. When you see a slave soft-fleshed, fine-skinned, with regular bones and wine-coloured hair, black eye-lashes, dark eyes, black eyebrows, open-eyed, long-nosed, slender-waisted, round-chinned, red-lipped, with white regular teeth, and all his members such as I have described, such a slave will be decorative and companionable, loyal, of delicate character and dignified.

The mark of the slave who is clever and may be expected to improve is this: he must be of erect stature, medium in hair and in flesh, broad of hand and with the middle of the fingers lengthy, in complexion dark though ruddy, dark-eyed, open-faced and unsmiling. A slave of this kind would be competent to acquire learning, to act as treasurer or for any other [such] employment.

The slave suited to play musical instruments is marked out by being soft-fleshed (though his flesh must not be over-abundant, especially on the back), with his fingers slender, neither lean nor fat. (A slave whose face is over-fleshy, incidentally, is one incapable of learning.) His hands must be soft, with the middles of the fingers lengthy. He must be bright-visaged, having the skin tight; his hair must not be too long, too short or too black. It is better, also, for the soles of the feet to be regular. A slave of this kind will swiftly acquire a delicate art of whatever kind, particularly that of the instrumentalist.

The mark of the slave suited for arms-bearing is that his hair is thick, his body tall and erect, his build powerful, his flesh hard, his bones thick, his skin coarse and his limbs straight, the joints being firm. The tendons should be tight and the sinews and blood-vessels prominent and visible on the body. Shoulders must be broad, the chest deep, the neck thick and the head round; also for preference he should be bald. The belly should be concave, the buttocks drawn in and the legs in walking well extended. And the eyes should be black. Any slave who possesses these qualities will be a champion in single combat, brave and successful.

The mark of the slave suited for employment in the women's apartments is that he should be dark-skinned and sour-visaged and have withered limbs, scanty hair, a shrill voice, little [slender] feet, thick lips, a flat nose, stubby fingers, a bowed figure and a thin neck. A slave with these qualities will be suitable for service in the women's quarters. He must not have a white skin nor a fair complexion; and beware of a ruddy-complexioned man, particularly if his hair is limp. His eyes, further, should not be languorous or moist; a man having such qualities is either over-fond of women or prone to act as a go-between.

The mark of the slave who is callous [insensitive] and suited to be a herdsman or groom is that he should be open-browed and wide-eyed, and his eyelids should be flecked with red. He should, further, be long in lips and teeth and his mouth should be wide. A slave with these qualities is extremely callous, fearless and uncivilised.

The mark of the slave suited for domestic service and cookery is that he should be clean in face and body, round-faced, with hands and feet slender, his eyes dark inclining to blue, sound in body, silent, the hair of his head wine-coloured and falling forward limply. A slave with these qualities is suitable for the occupations mentioned.

Each then, should have the essential characteristics which I have recounted. But I will also mention the defects and virtues which should be known in respect of each separate race. You must understand that Turks are not all of one race and each has its own nature and essential character.

Amongst them the most ill-tempered are the Ghuzz[1] and the Qipchāqs[2]; the best-tempered and most willing are the Khutanese, the Khallukhīs[3] and the Tibetans; the boldest and most courageous are the Turghay (?)[4] the most inured to toil and hardship and the most active are the Tatars[5] and the Yaghmā[6], whereas the laziest of all are the Chigil[7].

It is a fact well-known to all that beauty or ugliness in the Turks is the opposite of that in the Indians. If you observe the Turk feature by feature [he has] a large head, a broad face, narrow eyes, a flat nose and unpleasing lips and teeth. Regarded individually the features are not handsome, yet the whole is handsome. The Indian's face is the opposite of this; each individual feature regarded by itself appears handsome, yet looked at as a whole the face does not create the same impression as that of the Turk. To begin with, the Turk has a personal freshness and clearness of complexion not possessed by the Indian; indeed the Turks win for freshness against all other races.

Without any doubt, what is fine in the Turks is present in a superlative degree, but so also is what is ugly in them. Their faults in general are that they are blunt-witted, ignorant, boastful, turbulent, discontented and without a sense of justice. Without any excuse they will create trouble and utter foul language, and at night they are poor-hearted. Their merit is that they are brave, free from pretence, open in enmity and zealous in any task allotted to them. For the [domestic] establishment there is no better race.

[1] *Cf. Hudūd al-'Ālam*, tr. Minorsky, Gibb Series (New, XI), London, 1937. p. 311.
[2] *id.* p. 315.
[3] *id.* p. 286.
[4] *id.* p. 308 n. 2.
[5] *id.* p. 94 [*Toghuzghuz.*]
[6] *id.* p. 277.
[7] *id.* pp. 98, 297.

Slavs,[1] Russians[2] and Alans[3] are near in their temperament to the Turks but are more patient. The Alans are more courageous than the Turks at night and more friendly disposed towards their masters. Although in their craftsmanship they are nearer to the Byzantines, being artistic, yet there are faults in them of various kinds; for example they are prone to theft, disobedience, betrayal of secrets, impatience, stupidity, indolence, hostility to their masters and escaping. Their virtues are that they are soft-natured, agreeable and quick of understanding. Further they are deliberate in action, direct in speech, brave, good road-guides and possessed of good memory.

The defect of the Byzantines is that they are foul-tongued, evil-hearted, cowardly, indolent, quick-tempered, covetous and greedy for worldly things. Their merits are that they are cautious, affectionate, happy, economically-minded, successful in their undertakings and careful to prevent loss.

The defect of the Armenians is that they are mischievous, foul-mouthed, thieving, impudent, prone to flight, disobedient, babblers, liars, friendly to misbelief and hostile to their masters. From head to foot, indeed, they incline rather towards defects than to merits. Yet they are quick of understanding and learn their tasks well.

The defect of the Hindu is that he is evil-tongued and in the house no slave-girl is safe from him. But the various classes of the Hindus are unlike those that prevail amongst other peoples, because in other peoples the classes mingle with each other, whereas the Hindus, ever since the time of Adam (Upon whom be peace!), have practised the following

[1] *Hudūd al-'Ālam* pp. 158, 427.
[2] *id.* pp. 159, 432.
[3] *id.* pp. 42, 160, 444. (Their territory lay to the north of Byzantium.)

custom: namely no trade will form an alliance with any outside it. Thus, grocers will give their daughters only to grocers, butchers to butchers, bakers to bakers and soldiers to soldiers.

Each of these groups therefore has its own special character, which I cannot describe one by one because that would entail a book in itself.

However, the best of them, people benevolent, brave or skilled in commerce, are [respectively] the Brahman, the Rāwat and the Kirār[1]. The Brahman is clever, the Rāwat brave and the Kirār skilled in commerce, each class being superior to the one after. The Nubian and the Abyssinian are freer of faults, and the Abyssinian is better than the Nubian because many things were said by the Prophet in praise of the former.

These then are the facts concerning each race and the merits and defects of each.

Now the third essential is being completely alive to defects both external and internal through knowledge of symptoms, and this means that at the time of buying you may not be careless. Do not be content with a single look; many a good slave may appear vile at first sight and many an extremely vile one appear to be good. Further there is

[1] "Under Muhammadan rule the Rajput disappeared [in the Panjab] and for the Hindu population the Brahman took his place. In the Hills, the stronghold at once of Rajput power and of Hinduism in its most primitive form, we have the *Brahman* . . . we have the Rajput, a name strictly confined to the royal families and their immediate connections . . . we have the great cultivating class including the Thakars and Rāthīs of acknowledged and immediate Rajput descent . . . and the *Rāwats*, Kanets and Ghiraths of somewhat lower status; we have the *Kirār* or Mahājan, including not only traders, but all the Kāyaths and the clerkly class, and even the Brahmans who take to these pursuits" etc. Sir D. Ibbetson, *Panjab Castes*, Lahore 1916, p.16.

the fact that a human being's visage does not continually bear the same complexion. Sometimes it is more inclined to be handsome, at other times to be ugly. You must carefully inspect all the limbs and organs to ensure that nothing remains hidden from you. There are many latent diseases which are on the point of coming but have not yet appeared and will do so within a few days; such diseases have their symptoms.

Thus, if there is a yellowness in the complexion, the lips being changed [from the normal] in colour, and dry, that is the symptom of haemorrhoids. If the eyelids are continuously swollen, it is a symptom of dropsy. Redness in the eyes and a fullness of the veins in the forehead are the mark of epilepsy. Tearing out the hair, flickering of the eyelashes and chewing of the lips are the signs of melancholia. Crookedness in the bone of the nose or irregularity in it are the symptoms of fistula; hair that is extremely black, but more so in one place than another, shows that the hair has been dyed. If here and there upon the body you perceive the marks of branding where no branding should be, examine closely to ensure that there is no leprosy under it. Yellowness in the eyes and a change [from the ordinary] in the colour of the face are the symptoms of jaundice.

When you buy a slave, you must take and lay him down, press him on both sides and watch closely that he has no pain or swelling. If he has, it will be in the liver or spleen. Having looked for such hidden defects, seek further for the open ones, such as smells from the mouth and nose, hardness of hearing, hesitation in utterance, irregularity of speech, walking off the [straight] road, coarseness of the joints and hardness at the base of the teeth, to prevent any trickery being practised on you.

CHAPTER XXIV

The Purchase of Houses and Estates

UNDERSTAND, MY SON, that whenever you make a purchase, whether it be lands, houses or anything else you wish, you must observe the provisions of the law. Further, you must buy when the market is slack and sell when it is brisk. Look for profit and do not account it a fault; the wise have said, "You must take devious paths if you wish to buy". And do not be careless over the bargaining, for bargaining is the half of commerce. Whatever you buy must be bought with profit-and-loss in mind, and if you have no wish to be reduced to pennilessness you will not spend money out of profits as yet unrealized. Furthermore, if you wish to safeguard your capital against harm, have a care about such profits as may ultimately result in losses; and if you wish to have wealth in plenty and not be poor, do not be avaricious. Further, endure any form of toil, for persistence means added cleverness; and never, in anything that you do, lose sight of your own interest—to do so is superfluous folly.

Whenever your course becomes obscure and you are faced by a door which is closed against action on your part, make haste to discover the right track. But exercise the utmost patience until the signs of what you are seeking make themselves apparent; no affair can succeed that is transacted in haste. When you come to buying and selling, if you wish to buy a house, buy one in a street where prosperous people reside and not one on the outskirts. And do not buy one which lies under the city wall, or one which is cheap because it is in a state of dilapidation. Also, look first of all to your neighbour; the Arabic proverb says: "The neighbour, then the house". Buzurjmihr[1] too declared that there are four things which are great misfortunes: a bad neighbour, a large family, a quarrelsome wife and poverty.

Do not purchase a house in the neighbourhood of 'Alawids[2] or of philosophers (because it is difficult to maintain the duty of revering them), nor in the neighbourhood of your own retinue. Endeavour to buy your house in a street where there is no one richer than yourself, but choose honourable neighbours. Once you have bought your house, respect the rights and the honour due to your neighbours; there is an [Arabic] saying. "The neighbour has first right". Live on good terms with the inhabitants of your street and quarter; go and make enquiries after the sick, condole with them that are in sorrow, and attend funerals; but also take your share in any other of your neighbour's activities. Thus, when there are rejoicings, rejoice with him and send such gifts as are within your means. By so acting you will become the person most honoured in the quarter.

Engage the children of the quarter in conversation and be pleasant to them, and ask the older people about their health, treating them with respect. Maintain the congregation in harmony at the mosque of your quarter, never neglecting to send candles and lamps in the month of

[1] The vizier of the Sasanian king Khusraw (Chosroes) the First (A.D. 531–578) and a character of legendary wisdom.

[2] The descendants of the Caliph 'Alī and hence of the Prophet, through his daughter Fatima.

Ramaḍan. Men do themselves receive the treatment they have accorded to others; remember that what inevitably befalls them, whether it be good or evil, they experience as the result of their own doings. Therefore, neither do what it is improper to do nor say what it is improper to say; he that does what he should not, suffers what he need not.

Provided you are able to do so, make your home in large towns; live in the town most agreeable to you and buy a house whose roof is higher than that of others and so prevent people from staring into your house. At the same time you must avoid giving annoyance by your own prying.

When you are buying an estate, never buy one where there are no near neighbours and no permanent quarters; and, whatever it is that you buy, make your purchase in a year of plenty, not closing the bargain until the land has been valued and is free of doubtful qualities. An estate, you must understand, represents wealth without risk. Yet once you have purchased your land you must constantly consider how you may improve it. Each day you must cultivate some fresh part and so be always finding some new source of income. In no circumstances may you rest from cultivating your estates and fields, because estates become valuable through their product. If you are indifferent whether they produce or not, then any desert can be your estate. A land-owner is valued by his villages and [cultivated] estates, and estates by their produce, which, in turn, is not to be procured except by cultivation.

CHAPTER XXV

Buying Horses

WHEN YOU BUY horses, be on your guard against making any mistakes. In essence horses and human beings are alike in that you may value a good horse or a good human being at as high a price as you like, in the same way that you may depreciate a bad horse or man to any extent possible. There is a saying that the world persists through mankind and mankind through animals; and the horse is the best of all animals because its maintenance is required both by husbandry and knightly duty. It is proverbial that you must keep horses and garments in good condition if you wish them to maintain *you* in good condition.

It is more difficult to judge horses than men, because something of the true significance of men can be obtained from what they claim, whereas all the horse's pretensions lie in his external appearance. In order to discover what its claims are, first consider its external aspect, because in general a good horse has a good appearance and a bad one the reverse. The teeth must be without gaps, thin and white, the lower lip longer than the upper, the nose high, wide and straight, the forehead broad, the lower part of the ears smooth, the ears long with the upper part pointed and raised, the middle of the ear being straight, the neck well extended, the barrel [*lit.* "place of the girth"], the base of the neck and of the ear fine, the cannon heavy, with the upper bone shorter than the lower, the hair scanty, the hoof long and black, the sole round, the back arched [*lit.* "high"], the part between flank and belly short, the chest broad, the space between fore and hind leg well open, the tail bushy and long, the root of the tail fine and short, the scrotum black, eyes and lashes black also.[1] On the road it should move with caution.

Further, its shin should be smooth, the quarters well-suspended, the crupper wide, the inner side of the thigh fleshy and well-knit. As the man riding it moves, it should be aware of his movement.

These good points which I have detailed should be present without fail in every horse. There are others which may be present in one horse but not in another. Amongst colours, bay is reputed best, but date-colour is good too. The horse should be able to tolerate both heat and cold, and be a willing worker. It is a good quality if the scrotum, the middle of the thighs, stifle, tail, fore and hind legs, breast and forehead are black. A dun-coloured horse is good too, especially if the colour is deep, the face flecked with black, and it is black in the breast, forehead, tail, scrotum, stifle, the middle of the thighs, the eyes and the lips.

A cream horse should be similarly variegated, but a light bay should be all of one colour, without any contrasting flecks. The black horse must be shining black. Horses must not have red eyes; generally a red-eyed horse is unmanageable and vicious. The ash-grey with black legs and possessing the qualities I have described for the dun is good, but the piebald is of small worth and not well regarded, being generally bad-tempered.

[1] *Cf*. Shakespeare, *Venus and Adonis*:
Round-hoof'd, short-jointed, fetlocks shag and long,
Broad-breast full eye, small head and nostril wide,
High crest, short ears, straight legs and passing strong;
Thin mane, thick tail, broad buttock, tender hide.

Now that you know the good points of the horse, you must also learn the bad ones. There is a particular fault which is damaging to a horse's capacity for work and has an ugly appearance but only means that the animal is on heat; but there are also faults due to defects and ugly qualities of which some can be tolerated and others not. Each blemish and defect has a name by which it is identified, as I shall set out.

Of the defects in a horse, one is dumbness; the dumb horse has very little value. The sign of it is that when it sees a mare, although it may erect the penis, it fails to neigh. Then there is the half-blind horse, which is night-blind. The sign of it is that it has no fear at night of those things which horses usually fear and will not shy, and it will venture on to any ground however bad on to which you ride. A deaf horse also is bad. The sign of it is that it does not hear the neighing of other horses and never answers although it always has its ears forward and open. A "left-legged" horse is bad also, constantly stumbling. The mark of it is that when you lead it into a passageway it puts forward first its left fore-leg. Furthermore it cannot swim. The pur-blind horse is bad because it cannot see in the daytime. The mark of it is that the pupil of the eye is black verging on green, it keeps its eye always open so that the lids never touch. This may occur in one eye or both. Although this defect may appear to be a bad one, both Arabs and non-Arabs are agreed that it is well-omened, and I have heard that Duldul[1] had strabismus, that is, was squint-eyed. The "stockinged" horse has a white fore or hind-leg; if the left fore and hind-legs are white it is ill-omened.

[1] The Caliph 'Ali's mule, a fabulous runner.

If the horse is blue in both eyes, that may pass; but if it is so in one only, then it is defective, particularly if it is the left eye. The wall-eyed horse is bad, that is, the horse that has a white eye; and the blue roan is bad too, so is the long-necked horse, that is, the one which has its neck stretched out straight. No regard should be paid to a horse of that description. The (?) "crab" horse is bad because both its hind legs are crooked; in Persian it is called "bow-legged". It frequently falls down. The hairy-backed horse is bad, having hair on top of its back and round its hind legs. The hair-ringed horse similarly is bad because it has hair round its legs and under its hoofs. It is worst if the hair grows on both sides, but it is bad if the hair is about the legs above the hoof on the inner side. If it is on the outer side, it is tolerable.

The horse with distorted hoofs is bad also, that is, one which has the hoofs turned inwards. (It is also called *ahnaf*.) Bad also is the horse which has an overlong fore or hind-leg, whether in descent or ascent. (It is called *afraq*, i.e., "That which has one haunch higher than the other".). The crooked-tailed horse (called *a'zal* or *akshaf*) is bad; it is one that has the genital organs open to view. So also is the dog-tailed horse and that whose [hind-] legs are set wide apart in such fashion that they cannot follow in the traces of the fore-legs. The limper is bad too, always falling lame because of a malady in the joints of the fore-legs. It is called *afran*, if the infirmity is in the hind-legs; and that is equally bad. Bad also are the horses which refuse harness, bore, bite, neigh frequently, break wind, kick, are slow to eject their droppings, or maintain the penis erect.

The "crow-eyed" horse is blind at night. I was once told the story of how the herdsman of Ahmad son of

Farīghūn[1] one New Year's Day presented himself before him without the [customary] New Year's gift but said, "Long live my lord! I have brought no New Year's gift, because I have news which is better than any gift". Ahmad son of Farīghūn bade him tell it and he replied, "Last night the herd dropped a thousand crow-eyed foals". At this Ahmad gave the order that he was to be beaten a hundred blows of the stick, saying, "What sort of good tidings is this which you have brought me—that a thousand night-blind foals have been born?"

Now that I have said all this and you know the failings of horses, you must know that each has a name: [*Here follows a list.*] If I were to explain all these infirmities which I have mentioned, it would become a lengthy matter. All are defects. The worst defect of all is old age; one may contrive with any of the other disabilities to have some work done, but with old age it is impossible.

Buy large horses, because even though a man may be fat and of goodly figure he has an insignificant appearance on a contemptibly small mount. Another thing to know is that there may be a bone more in the left side than in the right; count them, and if the bones on either side balance in number, then buy the horse for more even than it is worth, for no horse could be better. Whatever you buy, whether it be animals or lands, let it be such that you will enjoy the benefits of it during your lifetime and your friends and heirs will do so after you.

Next, you will, of course, have a wife and children; it is proverbial that anyone who is [veritably] a man will have a wife for his mate.

[1] He was the first of a line of three rulers of Juzjān and Balkh, incorporated into the Ghaznawid empire in 401/1010.

CHAPTER XXVI

Marrying a Wife

IF YOU MARRY a wife, my son, treat her with the utmost consideration. Even though material goods may be valuable to you, they are not more so than wife and children, to whom you should not begrudge them, at least if they are a good wife and obedient children, and that is a matter within your own control. I have said something to this effect in a line of verse:

> *Why nurture sons or keep a wife, if neither brings you joy in life?*

When you seek a wife do not demand her possessions also; and look well to her character, refusing to be enslaved by beauty of face—for prettiness, men take a mistress. A wife, to be good, should be chaste and of sound faith, capable in household-management and fond of her husband, modest and God-fearing, brief-tongued, sparing and economical of materials. Men say that a good wife is one who looks to the consequences of every action. Yet even if a woman is affectionate, handsome and well-beloved, do not submit yourself entirely to her control nor be subservient to her command. Someone asked Alexander why he did not marry Darius's daughter, who was very beautiful. He replied, "It would be an ugly matter if we, who have become master of all men in the world, should have a woman as master over us".

Howbeit, do not marry a wife of nobler birth than yourself. And you must marry a virgin, so that there shall be no room in her heart for love of anyone but you, and, further, in order that she shall think all men alike, thus preventing her from conceiving a desire for any other man. Flee from the power of a woman with a loose [*lit.* 'long'] tongue; men say that the master of the house swiftly runs away when the wife is not to be trusted with confidences. It is improper for her to assume control of your possessions or to prevent your having the disposal of them; if that occurs, you are the woman and she the man.

Marry a woman of honourable family, because men marry in order to have a lady for the house and not to indulge in sexual pleasure; to satisfy your desires you can buy slave-girls in the bazaar, which involves neither so much expense nor so much trouble. Your wife must be of sound health, of mature age and intelligent and a person who in her parents' house has seen how the mistress of the house conducts her affairs. If you find a woman of those qualities, do not fail to ask for her in marriage; do your utmost to marry her and endeavour at all costs never to display jealousy in front of her. If you are of a jealous disposition, it is better for you not to marry, because a display of jealousy does nothing but suggest impropriety. Also, it is as well to know that women frequently destroy men because of jealousy, but will sacrifice their persons only for very few; moreover, they have no fear of jealousy and rage.

On the other hand, if you never display jealousy and are generous in your conduct, not begrudging the things with which God has endowed you, your wife can be more gracious to you than your father and mother; therefore, do not hold your own self more dear than you do her. If you ever give vent to your jealousy, she will be more hostile to you than a thousand enemies—and while you may be able to protect yourself against an enemy who is a stranger, you cannot protect yourself against her.

Once you have married a wife, being greatly in love with her, even though you may be infatuated with her, do not spend every night in her society. Let it be only from time to time, thus leading her to think that such is the universal custom, so that if on occasion you have reason for excusing yourself or wish to go on a journey, your wife will be forbearing towards you. But if you customarily visit her every night, she will acquire a propensity for it and it will be difficult for her to exercise forbearance. You must realize that a woman cannot steadfastly resist a man, however old or ugly he may be; so admit no male slave into the women's apartments, even though he is black, old and ugly.

Observe what is due to a sense of honour and account no one who is deprived of it as being a man; because he that has no sense of honour has no true faith.

Now when you possess a wife of the character I have described, if God grants you children, take thought to their upbringing.

CHAPTER XXVII

On Rearing Children

MY SON, IF a son is born to you, you must endow him with a good name, because one of the claims which children have upon their fathers is to be endowed by them with a good name. Another duty is to entrust your children to intelligent and affectionate nurses. Then, when the time comes for circumcision, have it performed; and hold it essential to celebrate it with as resplendent and joyful a feast as lies within your power. Afterwards teach your son the Koran so that he shall be known as having it by heart.

When he grows up, let your son be instructed in the arts of wielding arms and of horsemanship. Also teach him how to maintain his weapons and what methods are applicable to them, so that he shall understand the proper manipulation of each separate arm. When he is freed of concern from weapons, teach him to swim, just as I was taught. At the age of ten I had a chamberlain called Munzir, who had great skill in horse-breaking and riding. I also had an Abyssinian slave called Raihān who was clever in various arts. My father handed me over to them to be taught riding, javelin-throwing, archery and wielding of the spear. They further taught me how to play polo and bowls and how to throw a lasso, as well as acquainting me with all forms of skill and athletic prowess.

In time, the chamberlain Munzir and Raihān presented themselves before the Amir and said, "My Lord, our master's son has now learned all that we know. If you grant permission, we will take him to the hunting-field tomorrow, so that he can display his skill." My father replied that that would suit his pleasure. On the next day I went out and made a display before him of all that I knew. My father bestowed robes of honour upon them and said, "All that my son here has learnt is good, but there is one art better than any of these which he has not acquired". When they inquired what it was, he answered, "All these arts that he has acquired in the way of skill and prowess are of a kind that can be exercised by others on his behalf, if he is himself incapable of exercising them. But the art which he is compelled to exercise for himself and which no one else will, or can, exercise for him is the one which you have not taught him; and that is how to swim. No one can swim for him.''

He then gave orders that two clever sailors should be summoned. To them he handed me over for instruction in swimming and by compulsion, since I did not learn of my own inclination. But I learnt to swim well. Now it chanced, in the year that I set out on pilgrimage to Mecca by way of Syria, that I was waylaid by highwaymen at the gates of Mosul so that the caravan was overwhelmed; for the Arabs were there in force and we had not the strength to cope with them. In brief, I entered Mosul naked, and having no other recourse I boarded a ship on the Tigris and went to Baghdad. There my fortunes improved to the extent that I was able through God's grace to perform the pilgrimage successfully.

Now comes the point of my story. Before one reaches Baghdad, there is a dangerous place with a strong whirlpool, through which it requires a very experienced sailor to make the passage. If there is no one [on board] with the necessary experience of what to do, the ship is wrecked. There were several people on board, but the sailor in charge was inexperienced, and when we arrived at the spot he was ignorant of the direction to take. Mistakenly he drove the ship into the middle of the whirlpool, and the ship was about to sink when I and several Basrans and a servant of mine called Zīrak cast ourselves out of it and into the water, saving ourselves by swimming, while the rest were drowned.

Ever afterwards my affection for my father grew and I gave alms for him and sent out many gifts of mercy. I realised that the old man had foreseen just such a day and had therefore taught me to swim.

You must, consequently, teach your children all that needs learning in various arts and accomplishments, in fulfilment of your duty as a father and the exercise of your lovingkindness as a parent. One can never be secure against the accidents of fate nor foresee what can occur to men, whether of good or ill. Every art and accomplishment is of service some day, therefore permit no neglect in your own acquisition of accomplishments, nor in the training of your children, nor in their instruction in the arts.

Whatever the art, teach it with eagerness, and if your children's instructors should beat them in the course of their lessons, do not be over-compassionate, but allow them to be beaten; children acquire the arts, as well as skill and learning, not by the light of nature but by use of the rod. Yet if a child should be unmannerly, rousing you to anger against him, do not strike him with your own hand but threaten him with the instructors. Bid them inflict the correction and so prevent any rancour against you from lodging in his heart.

Do you for your part always behave with dignity towards him, so that he shall not regard you with disrespect but stand ever in awe of you. Do not grudge him such silver and gold as he needs, if you wish to avoid his praying for your death merely because of money. In teaching him the arts neglect no aspect of them. If he is ineffectual and unsuccessful—from which God spare us!—you will have done your duty as a father and the responsibility will not lie about your neck. If he is successful and prosperous, he must take the instruction to heart and find experience, reaching perfection through his own wit and the trials of fortune. There is an [Arabic] saying that a man who is not chastened by his father is chastened by [the passage of] day and night, or, in a different form, "A man unchastened by his parents is chastened by time".

You for your part must strictly observe the obligations laid upon a father, while your son must live as destiny has planned for him; for at the time when a man emerges into being out of non-existence, his disposition and habits are present with him. As he burgeons and grows each day, his disposition and habits are trained up with his physical growth until they reach completion, when the likelihood of his advancement or decline is revealed. Do not withhold your own portion from him; the sons of men of quality can have no better heritage than accomplishments and skill in the arts, while for the sons of the common people there is nothing better than craftsmanship and learning.

Yet craftsmanship is also the concern of the nobleman's son; accomplishments are one thing and crafts are another, yet in my view, and if truth be told, a craft is the best of all accomplishments. Even though the sons of men of quality and high birth acquired a hundred crafts (provided they did not employ them for gain) it would be no fault; nay, rather, it would be a virtue. Every form of art and skilled workmanship at some time bears fruit; it is not wasted.

When Gushtasp fell from his throne—it is a long story, but the point is as follows—he went to Greece, to the city of Constantinople, which he entered completely without worldly goods. It irked him to beg and ask for food, accounting it a dishonour; but as a child, in his father's palace, he had seen smiths at work making knives, swords and spear-heads. Thanks to his good star his attention had been attracted to the craft and every day he walked about looking on, and so learned something of it.

On the day that he entered Constantinople, having no other recourse, he went to a blacksmith's shop and said that he knew something about the work. He was hired for a wage and was given the money he earned by his skill, spending what he received on necessities. He was thus saved from holding out his hand to beg from anyone. At last he returned to his own country and when he had again assumed the kingship, he made proclamation that no man was to restrain his son from learning a craft and that this was no longer to be regarded as dishonourable; for, he declared, the occasions were many when ancestry and gallantry were of no use to a man, but every form of skill that a man possessed would some day be of benefit to him.

From then onwards that became the custom in Persia, and there was never a nobleman who did not know a trade; even though he had no need of it, he practised it. Learn, therefore, anything that you can, for the advantages of doing so will accrue to you.

Now when your son reaches puberty, scrutinize him. If he is a proper youth, capable of having charge of a household, and you know that he can carry out a task and earn something by doing so, and, further, if you are assured of his success, then set about the task of seeking a wife for him. Having provided him with a wife you will have discharged that duty also. But make no alliance with your own kinsfolk, seeking a woman rather from amongst strangers. If you form a union with your own relatives, they are like your own flesh. Therefore seek a woman from a different tribe, thus converting strangers into kinsfolk, doubling your strength and acquiring helpers from two sides.

But if you realize that your son is unworthy, without capacity to be the head of a household and lacking the power to succeed, do not cast a Muslim maiden into unhappiness; for each will suffer misery at the hands of the other. Let matters rest until he is of full age, when he may do as he wishes.

If you have a daughter, entrust her to kindly nurses and give her good nurture. When she grows up, entrust her to a preceptor so that she shall learn the provisions of the sacred law and the essential religious duties. But do not teach her to read and write; that is a great calamity. Once she is grown up, do your utmost to give her in marriage; it were best for a girl not to come into existence, but, being born, she had better be married or be buried. The Prophet said, "The burial of daughters is an act attended with honour", but as long as she is in your house, treat your daughter with compassion.

Daughters are the captives of their parents; sons, even if they have no parents, from the mere fact of being sons are able to keep themselves and find employment, whatever it be. A girl, on the other hand, is helpless and incapable of finding employment. Make such provision for her as you are able and contrive matters properly for her; fasten her about someone's neck so as to escape from anxiety for her. If the girl is a virgin, seek for a son-in-law who shall be a virgin also; in that way the husband will have an attachment for his wife as great as the wife's for her husband, and he will desire no one else because he will have known no other person.

I have been told the story of the daughter of a Persian

king who was brought as a captive from Persia to Arabia, and whom [the Caliph] 'Umar son of al-Khattāb ordered to be sold. When she was taken to the market-place, the Commander of the Faithful, 'Alī, (Whose visage God ennoble!) came and said, "The Prophet declared that the children of kings are not liable to sale". When he recited this Tradition of the Prophet, the selling was annulled and she was lodged with Salmān the man of Pārs[1] until a husband should be found for her. When the question of a husband was proposed to her the princess said, "I will take no husband before I have seen him with my own eyes. Place me in a spot from which there is a view and let the Arab chieftains pass by me. He upon whom I fix my choice shall be my husband." Accordingly they seated her in a place in the house of Salmān from which she could see, while he, being seated before her, presented the people to her and gave her each man's name. She spoke to each in turn but approved of none until the Commander of the Faithful and Foremost of Loyal Believers, 'Alī son of Abu Tālib, passed by her. On her enquiring who he was, she was told that he was the Commander of the Faithful, 'Alī, the cousin of Allah's Chosen [the Prophet]. At that the princess said, "He is truly noble and suited to me; yet in the next world I shall be shamed by Fātima[2] the Glorious. For that reason I cannot marry him."

Hasan, 'Ali's son, then came by, and being informed of his birth and story, she again said, "He too is a fitting match for me, but I have heard that he has made many marriages". Lastly Husain, 'Ali's son, came by. When she had inquired

[1] Salmān of Pārs—an intimate companion of the Prophet Muhammad.

[2] Daughter of Muhammad the Prophet who became one of 'Ali's wives.

his history, she said, "He must be my husband, for he has never taken a wife just as I have had no husband; we are suited to each other". Thus then, to abbreviate the story, they married her to Husain ibn 'Ali.

As for your son-in-law, he must be of handsome appearance; a beautiful girl will never give her heart to an ugly husband. If she does, the possibility of scandal is created, for the girl may take herself a lover who is handsome, and thus evil report may arise. Your son-in-law, therefore, must be of clean appearance and sound faith, of pure and honourable lineage and a member of a family of notables. Yet he must hold lower rank than yourself, so that his boast may be concerning you, not yours of him, and your daughter will live at ease and in splendour. If your son-in-law is such as I have described, demand nothing further from him.

Never sell your daughter; that is conduct which your own sense of honour should not permit. Yet lavish all you possess in the endeavour to prevent your daughter from remaining in your house; quickly hand her to a husband and, as speedily as you can, rid yourself of trouble. Give all your friends this same counsel, for much profit lies in it.

CHAPTER XXVIII

On Friendship and the Acquisition of Friends

UNDERSTAND, MY SON, that as long as men are alive, friends are indispensable to them; they were better, indeed, bereft of brothers than of friends.

When a certain sage was asked whether it was better to have a friend or a brother, he replied, "It is best for the brother to be also a friend". Take thought therefore to the matter of your friends, keeping evergreen the custom of giving presents and showing kindnesses.

He that never spares a thought for friends never has them. Form the habit, therefore, of making friends with all manner of persons; many of a man's faults are hidden from his friends, although his virtues are revealed to them.

When you find new friends, never turn your back on old ones and so you will always possess a host of them; and there is a saying that a good friend is a rich treasure. Give a thought also to the people who are advancing towards friendship with you but are only quasi-friends, to whom you should make yourself well-disposed and affable, agreeing with them in all matters good or bad and showing yourself to be favourably inclined towards them. In that manner, experiencing nothing but civility from you, they become whole-heartedly your friends. When Alexander was asked by virtue of what it was that he had been able to acquire so great an empire in so short a space of time, he replied, "By winning over enemies by kindliness and gathering friends about me by solicitude for them".

Regard as your friends also your friend's friends, but fear any who are friendly with your enemies—their friendship with that enemy of yours may outweigh their friendship for you, and they may therefore not hesitate to do you an injury in order to help your enemy. Also, beware of a person who without any excuse or argument becomes estranged from you. Place no reliance upon his friendship. Regard no one in the world as faultless, yet hold fast to the friendship of an honourable friend, for honourable men have fewest faults.

Take no unprincipled person for your friend; no good comes from an unprincipled friend.

As for your companions of the cup, regard them only as drinking-associates and not as true friends; they are well-disposed merely towards your cups, not to you. But make friends with persons both good and bad and be affable with both classes of men, having sincere friendship with the good and making a show of friendship with your tongue towards the bad; thus you will gain the friendship of both classes. One's need is not always for good people; occasionally help in need comes from the bad ones, because what one can do cannot always be done by the other. Even though your connection with the wicked may displease the good, and, conversely, your connection with the good displease the wicked, do you so order your life with both groups that the feelings of neither are injured by your actions. Yet do not attach yourself so closely to either group that the other becomes hostile to you; tread the path of wisdom and understanding and watch either side, thereby securing your safety.

Never seek the friendship of fools; a foolish friend in his unwisdom can do [such harm] to you as a clever enemy could not. Rather cultivate the friendship of men who have talent, are faithful to their trust and are good-natured; you will thus become known and praised for the same virtues as those for which your friends are known and praised. Further, bear in mind that solitude is preferable to evil associates. The poet has said:

O heart, like creature wild thou'rt fled to deserts rude;
Upon my sorrow, or thine own, thou hadst no mind to brood.
An evil mate wast thou; thy fleeing then was best.
Than life with ill companions better far is solitude.

Never permit the claims which your friends have upon you, nor the regard due to them, to be lost to view, [if you wish] to prevent exposing yourself to obloquy. It is said that there are two kinds of men deserving of harsh words, namely those who lose sight of the claims of their friends and those who are ungrateful for kindnesses received. There are two things by which you may know whether men are deserving of your friendship or not. The first is that when hardship befalls a friend they do not grudge him a share of their own possessions to the extent of their powers nor forsake him in adversity. The second is that if a friend departs this life, they seek out his children, enquire about their welfare and indulge them with kindnesses. Moreover, from time to time they visit his grave, albeit that it is not the grave of the friend but of the friend's body.

I have been told that when Socrates was being borne away to be executed and was being tortured to induce him to become an idol-worshipper, his constant reply was, "God forbid that I should worship the Creator's creature". Some of his disciples, who in tears escorted him, addressed him and said, "Sage, now that you have reconciled your heart to death, express your last wish and tell us where we are to bury you". He smiled and said, "If it is possible that you will find me again. . . Bury me where you like," as much as to say, "It will not be I, but my body".

In your friendship with others, keep the middle way, never attaching yourself to men on account of any hopes you cherish or thinking to yourself that you have many friends. Be your own especial friend and look before and behind yourself; nor, in your reliance upon friends, be at all heedless for yourself. Even though you possess a thousand friends, there will be none more friendly disposed towards you than yourself. Test your friends at times of adversity, because in times of prosperity all men will be friendly to you; and be the same to your friends whether in sorrow or happiness. In brief, hold that man in affection who holds you so.

Yet do not confide to your friend any secrets of which a knowledge would enable him to do you mischief in the event of a quarrel breaking out between you that leads to hostility; regrets would then be of little profit.

If you are poor, do not demand rich friends; nobody, and particularly so the rich man, requires a friend who is poor. Choose friends of your own degree, therefore; yet if you are rich and have a friend who is poor, that is well enough. In your friendships with men let your heart be constant and remain steadfast in them; in that manner your life will be firmly established. If a friend, through no fault on your part, destroys his affection for you and harms you, do not preoccupy yourself over winning him back, for he is not worth the trouble. And never set your affections upon the man who makes a practice of such conduct. Also, keep at a distance from a covetous friend; he cultivates your friendship for selfish ends. Never have a rancorous man as your friend; he is not fitted for friendship, because rancour is never far from the heart of such a man, and since he is everlastingly malicious and vengeful there will never be [true] friendliness in his heart for you.

Now that you understand the conditions and rules of friendship, you must in turn consider the character and the activities of an enemy. Hearken well and remember [my counsel]; act in accordance with it if you wish to prosper.

CHAPTER XXIX

On Taking Thought Concerning the Enemy

USE YOUR BEST endeavours, my son, not to make enemies. If you should have an enemy, be neither afraid nor anxious; for the man who has no enemies is an easy prey to enemies. Yet never remain uninformed of your enemy's doings whether they are secret or open; never feel secure against his mischievous activity against you, and be constantly planning how to outwit and injure him. At no time can you be sure against his stratagems and contrivings. Make continual inquiry about the state of his affairs and the opinions he expresses, keeping both ear and mind alert for them; thus you may keep the door of calamity and misfortune closed for yourself.

Until your affairs are in a complete state of preparedness, do not reveal your hostility to the enemy; then show him a bold front and, even if you fall, exercise your courage and ardour, refusing to admit yourself among the defeated. Place no reliance at all on the enemy's good words or on his beneficence; cherish no expectations from him and do not descend into the well on his rope. If you receive sugar from the enemy, account it colocynth[1]. Always be apprehensive concerning a powerful enemy; there is a saying that there are two persons whom one must fear; a powerful foe and a treacherous friend.

Never openly despise an insignificant enemy, saying

[1] *Cf.* Shakespeare (*Othello*, i, 3, 355), "As bitter as coloquintida."

"Who is this fellow?", but deal with a weak foeman as you would with a mighty one. I have been told that there once lived in Khurasan a bold, witty and well-regarded brigand named Muhadhdhab. Going along the road one day his foot slipped on a piece of melon-rind and he fell. Whereupon he drew his knife and stabbed the melon-rind. His attendants remarked, "Master, you are a man of dignity and wit, are you not ashamed to strike at a melon-rind?" He replied, "The melon-rind overthrew me; it is my enemy. An enemy must not be despised even though he or it may be worthless." Any man that despises his enemy himself swiftly becomes a person regarded with contempt.

Always, therefore, be planning how to destroy your enemy before he begins to take action over destroying you. If you come to be another's foeman, do not decry him or point out his feebleness when you have overcome him, otherwise you will diminish the glory of it. Do you not observe how, when a monarch gains a victory, even though the enemy may not have been very powerful, the scribes who write the proclamation of triumph begin by entitling him "The Mighty"? They then proceed to liken him to a lion and a dragon, lavishing praises on his troops both horse and foot, and belauding the enemy's battle-array and the commanders of the centre and the wings to the full extent of their powers. Finally they say, "It was forces of this strength that our Lord So-and-So, on his arrival, by one single onslaught put to flight and destroyed". In that way they proclaim the qualities of their patron and the power of his troops.

I have been told that at one time there lived in the city of Rayy a certain old woman, a chaste and pious princess, my mother's cousin and the wife of Fakhr al-Dawlah[1]. When he died he had left a young son, entitled Majd al-Dawlah, who was declared king, although his mother in verity directed the affairs of state. When he grew older he proved no true heir to his father and showed himself unfitted for kingship, his sole occupation being to sit at home in the company of his slave-girls. For thirty-nine years it was his mother who governed.

Now comes the point of my story. Your ancestor, Sultan Mahmūd, sent an envoy to her with the command that she was to acknowledge his sovereignty by inclusion of his name in the *Khutba* [Bidding-Prayer] in the Mosque and on the coinage of the land. If she disobeyed, he would come and seize Rayy and destroy her. When the envoy arrived and delivered his message, the Princess replied, "Say to Sultan Mahmūd, 'Throughout my husband's lifetime, I ever had the apprehension that the thought of attacking Rayy would occur to you. When he died, and affairs passed into my hands, that apprehension was lifted from my heart. I said to myself that Sultan Mahmūd was a wise monarch and that a prince like him would know that he could never go to war with a woman. There are females among lions as well as males; if you should come, God most High knows that I will not flee but will stand firm in battle. For there are but two alternatives possible: either that victory should come to me or that I should be defeated. If the victory is mine and I defeat you, I shall write to the whole world that I have overthrown Sultan Mahmūd, and great glory will be mine.

[1] A member of the family of warrior-princes known as the Buyids or Buwaihids, who for a time held Baghdad and controlled the destinies of the Caliphate. Fakhr al-Dawlah became governor of Rayy (ancient Rhages), near the modern Tehran, in A.D. 976–7.

" 'Now, you are a monarch who has overthrown a hundred kings and more; should I overthrow you, it will spread over the whole world that a woman has overthrown and defeated Sultan Mahmūd. Your fame will be brought to nothing, and for you no shame or dishonour could be worse than that people should say that Sultan Mahmūd had been defeated by a woman. Should the victory, on the other hand, be yours, and I be defeated by you, no glory or fame will accrue to you; nor will anyone compose an epic to celebrate the victory, for no fame or glory is acquired by defeating women.' "

From the time when these words and this message were delivered to Sultan Mahmūd, and for as long as he lived, he refrained from making any onslaught on Rayy, his intention being halted simply by that speech.

And so, do not disparage your enemy overmuch and in no circumstances trust him. Most of all, be on your guard against the enemy who is within your own household; no stranger has such opportunities of informing himself concerning your affairs and of spying upon them as fall to the member of your own household. When he becomes detached from you, his heart is never empty of malevolence towards you; he will continually be inquiring about your activities and will know what an outside enemy could never know. Therefore do not entrust a [possible] enemy with your complete friendship.

Yet always show him the semblance of friendship; it is possible for the fiction to become a reality and out of enmity friendship may spring just as enmity out of friendship. Strive to make the number of your friends twice that of your enemies; be, indeed a man of many friends and few enemies. Yet in your reliance upon a thousand friends, never be off your guard concerning a single enemy. A thousand friends may be neglectful of their solicitude for you, but that one enemy of yours will never forget his hatred.

Never begin hostilities with an enemy who is more powerful than yourself, and never rest from pressing home your hostile activities against one who is weaker. Yet, if your opponent throws himself on your mercy, however great his hostility has been and however far from friendly his actions towards you, grant him an armistice and reckon it a great advantage. The saying goes, "What difference between enemies dead, fled, or come in to throw themselves upon your mercy?" Yet even if you find him meekly submissive, do not refrain from all action against him.

If an enemy meets his doom at your hands, it is permissible for you to exult; but if he dies a natural death, do not rejoice over much, and then only when you are assured that you yourself will not die. The sages say that a man who lives a single breath longer than his enemy must acknowledge it a blessing; yet since we know that we must all die, one must not be over-exultant—as I have said in a quatrain:

Why, when your foeman is throttled by fate,
Express exultation so swift and so great?
When other men die, how can you rejoice?
Since death must destroy you too, early or late.

I have been told how [Alexander] the "Two-Horned", having travelled about the world and subdued it to his power, set out on his homeward journey. On his arrival at Dāmghān[1] he made a will, desiring that when he died he was

[1] Capital of the ancient province of Kumis, at the foot of the Elburz range.

to be placed in a coffin pierced with [two] holes, through which his hands were to be extended with the palms open. It was to be borne along in such fashion that men should see that although he had seized the whole world, he was departing from it with empty hands. He made the further request that his mother should be told that if she desired to please his soul, she should seek consolation for him from someone who had never lost a dear one by death.

Now, my son, if you overthrow a man by [the might of] your hands, draw him to his feet again; for, if you twist a rope up to a particular limit and extent, the strands combine together; if you twist to excess, they are torn apart. Therefore observe a proper measure in your conduct, whether in friendship or enmity, for moderation forms a part of universal understanding. Be forbearing towards simple persons but show yourself haughty towards the haughty; and in all your actions be careful to play a man's part. When circumstances point to anger, impose it upon yourself as a duty to swallow your rage and remember your dignity. Yet regard it as a disgrace to tolerate all kinds of treatment, good and bad [*lit.* hot and cold]; the man that does not recognise his own worth is lacking in his quality as a man.

Whether with friend or foe be deliberate in speech and courteous in language; courtesy is a form of enchantment. Further, whatever you say, whether good or bad, have an eye to the answer; and what you would dislike to hear, do not force upon another's hearing. What you cannot say to men's faces, do not repeat behind their backs; do not threaten men emptily; neither boast of what you have not done nor proclaim what you are going to do. I have said (in a quatrain):

From mine heart, Idol, have I thrust the love I bore thee;
Level with the plain is woe's mountain thou heapedst upon me.
Not today shall I reveal to thee my doings;
Tomorrow, when I speak, the results of my deeds shalt thou see.

Remember that deeds are more than words; and as for your tongue, do not lengthen it against the man who, if he desired, could loosen his own against you. Do not be two-faced in your conduct and keep at a distance from two-faced persons; fear slanderers more than raging dragons—the wound caused by them in a moment cannot be repaired in a year. The philosopher counsels you to practise ten qualities if you would escape a multitude of ills: though you are noble and great, engage in no contention with one more powerful than yourself; do not dispute with a man of sharp temper; do not associate with miserly men; do not argue with fools; do not drink wine with men given to jealousy or quarrelsomeness; do not consort too frequently with women; tell your secret to no one, so that you may not destroy the lustre of your greatness and honour; if anyone finds fault with you, banish the cause of it from yourself; never bear yourself with such lofty ceremony that anything else is an undignified descent; belaud no person to such a height that you will be unable to say anything in dispraise of him if the need should at some time arise, but also, never disparage a man to such extent that you will never be able to praise him if the occasion should arise; never over-awe a man with your anger and displeasure if he has achieved some task without your aid, for he who is independent of you has no fear of your anger and displeasure and, if you threaten someone who has no fear of you, you bring ridicule on yourself; on the other hand, do not regard as entirely spiritless the man who achieves nothing without your aid and do not behave in overbearing fashion towards him; do not be offensive towards him that is envious of you nor direct the anger of others against him; if one commits a fault, overlook it.

Against men subordinated to you bring no [false] allegations; thus remain their master, from whom they will not flee. Let your subjects thrive; they are your estates. If you maintain your estates in good condition, your affairs will prosper; if your estates are ruinous, you will be bereft of goods and resources.

A servant who will do your bidding, even though it be faultily, is better than one who will do it correctly but is unwilling to obey. If you order a task to be done, do not appoint to it two persons together, if you wish to avoid failure. There is a saying that a pot with two in attendance never comes to the boil, just as a house with two mistresses is never swept. The poet Farrukhī says:

If in the house two mistresses be,
The dust will lie as high as your knee.

And if you yourself are engaged on any task, do not desire any assistant or partner, if you wish it to be executed without imperfection and also to maintain your place in your master's good opinion.

Whether towards friend or foe be generous; let no man's faults anger you to excess, nor twist a man's least word about your finger [to take offence], nor exact retaliation for any trifle, be it true or false. Keep to the path of generosity, so that you may ever enjoy the praises of your fellow men.

CHAPTER XXX

Pardon and Punishment

MY SON, DO not feel that men must inexorably be punished for every misdeed. If a man commits a fault, ask forgiveness of yourself for him in your heart, for he too is the offspring of Adam, who first brought sin into existence—and who was our father.

Rubā'ī:

> *Should I once break allegiance to Thee.*
> *Contrition hundred-fold were forced on me.*
> *Turn not thy face from me for one sole sin;*
> *'Twas Adam first transgressed—our father he!*

Inflict no punishment for a triviality, for fear that you may yourself be made liable to penalties even when innocent; and let nothing rouse you to anger. Where there is cause for wrath, make it a habit to swallow down your vexation, and when you are petitioned for forgiveness of a transgression, forgive; and deem forgiveness your duty, even though the fault committed be a grievous one. For if the servant never transgressed, the master's pardon would never come into being; and, further, once you have exacted retaliation for an offence, what place is there for the exercise of your clemency? Knowing the necessity of forgiveness, you will never lack nobility and dignity.

Once you have forgiven a man, do not be for ever rebuking him and reminding him of his crime; that means no forgiveness. For your own part, endeavour not to commit a fault which will put you under the necessity of begging forgiveness. However, if you should commit a fault, have no shame in asking pardon for it and so end any bitterness.

If anyone commits a crime which demands punishment, inquire into the penalty for the offence and inflict the punishment appropriate to it; that is the injunction of those concerned with equity. In my opinion, however, if a man commits a crime for which he must be punished, you should not inflict the full penalty but should pardon him, thus treading the path of clemency and mercy. Yet, if you must punish and see no necessity for pardon, then contrive in requital for a dirham's worth of crime to inflict only half a dirham's worth of punishment; thus you will be numbered amongst men capable both of generosity and of exercising discipline. It would be improper for men of generosity to conduct themselves like those who are ungenerous.

I have been told that in the reign of Mu'āwiyah[1] a group of men committed a crime which rendered them liable to the death-penalty, and he commanded that they should be executed in his presence. As they were bringing one of the men forward for execution, he said, "We deserve all that you charge against us; we confess our crime. Yet, for the sake of God most High, listen to two words from me and vouchsafe an answer."

Mu'āwiyah bade him say on.

"The whole world", then said the criminal, "is aware of your clemency and nobility. Now, had we committed this crime against a monarch who was not, like you, noble and clement, what would he have done to us?"

[1] First of the Umayyad Caliphs; reigned at Damascus, A.D. 661–680.

"The same", said Mu'āwiyah, "as I am doing".

"In that case", retorted the man, "of what benefit are your clemency and generosity to us, since you merely act in the same way as that merciless tyrant?"

"If only the first of you had said this to me", said Mu'āwiyah, "I should have pardoned you all. I now grant pardon to those remaining."

If a criminal, therefore, should beg for pardon, you are under an obligation to grant it; and never believe that it is possible to commit an offence too grievous for pardon. Further, if a petitioner has fallen into need and asks your help, do not leave him in anxiety and desperation (provided that it is possible without offence to your religion or injury to your status in the world), merely out of consideration for your worldly possessions. Do not turn such a man away without satisfying his need, nor destroy his good opinion of you; for if he had not thought well of you, he would not have made his request to you. Once he makes his petition to you, he is your captive; indeed, the saying goes that a man in need is nothing but another captive—and it is a duty to treat captives with compassion; it is not praiseworthy to slay them, doing so being highly execrable.

In this matter, then, permit yourself no remissness; thus will you gain honour in both worlds. If necessity should arise for you yourself to seek help from another man, observe well whether he is generous or mean. Should he be generous, make your request; yet wait for the right moment. Make no demand of him when he is vexed, or before dinner when he is hungry, if you wish to have any hope of a propitious answer. Moreover, do not ask for impossible things, and when making your request give good consideration to your words. Having laid the foundations properly, utter your chosen words and depart. Display great delicacy in what you say, because delicacy in the making of a request is a second petitioner. Once you understand how to make your request, you will never be disappointed over its fulfilment; as I have said in my quatrain:

O Heart, if your ambition is to your delight to win,
With gladness to that Moon, that Queen of Night, to win,
Then rule your life as she desires, my Heart, because,
With knowledge dight, your prize you'll bring in sight to win.

Yet, whoever it is of whom you stand in need, you [promptly] become his bondsman and servant; we worship God because we have need of him, for if there were no need of him, no one would turn in obedience to him.

Once you have received a favourable reply to your request, do not fail to express your thanks. Allah says, "If you are grateful, I will give you increase" (Kor. 14, v. 7). Not only does God love them that are grateful, but thankfulness for a first favour gives hope of an affirmative answer to a second request. If your need is not satisfied, blame your own fortunes and not the person of whom you asked the favour; if he had any fear of your complainings, he would have granted your request.

If a man is close-fisted and mean, never ask anything of him while he is sober, for he will not give it. Ask him when he is intoxicated; mean and close-fisted men are generous when they are in a state of intoxication, even though they regret their generosity the following day. If you are condemned to make a request of a mean-spirited man, you are truly worthy of commiseration; there is a saying that three kinds of men deserve pity: the wise man in the power of a fool, the strong man subject to a feeble one and the generous man compelled to ask favours of a mean one.

Now that I have completed all that I desired to say as a preliminary, I will set down to the best of my ability a section on a variety of topics, in my desire to give my ideas their full scope. I will provide some account, therefore, of various occupations for you to read and learn about, in case the need should ever occur for you to make use of it. If I knew the wisdom of [all] the ancients and the moderns, I would teach and reveal it to you, that at my death I could leave this world without a pang. But what am I to do? In knowledge I am a veritable pedestrian; and even if there were anything I knew, of what advantage is my utterance, though you were to listen to me as I did to my father? In any event, you have no room for reproach if I do what is my duty. Whether you listen or not, I will say a word or two under each head, both in order not to be niggardly over words and to recount what I have experienced in the course of my life.

CHAPTER XXXI

Religious Science and Allied Topics

YOU WILL REMEMBER, my son, that earlier in my discourse I said that I would give some account of various occupations. By occupation I do not mean merely tradesmanship, but every form of work which men undertake and is regarded as a profession. Whatever the trade, it is necessary to be well acquainted with its practice in order to derive advantage from it. In my view there is no trade or employment followed by human beings which is without its traditional system and methods; for all require to have their regulations.

The number of professions is very large and to expatiate on each separately impossible, since otherwise my book would become excessively long and be diverted from its original plan. Now whatever the quality of a profession, it must fall into one of three categories, namely, a science linked with a craft, a craft linked with a science or a craft existing independently. Of the science linked with a craft, examples are: geometry, medicine, surveying, versification and the like; of the craft linked with a science, examples are: musicianship, the veterinary art, architecture, the construction of underground channels[1] and the like. Each has its own subject-matter, and if you are ignorant of its rules and subject-matter, even though you may be a master in other respects, in that respect you are no better than a poor captive.

The professions which are specifically so called are so well known as to need no exposition by me, but I will set out the substance of each as far as is practicable. And my reason for this is that one or other of two alternatives is inevitable; either that you may some day stand in need of a knowledge of the secrets of any one of the professions (through the accidents of fate or the vicissitudes of fortune), or that you will never have need of the knowledge and will remain a prince. In the latter case you will be in possession

[1] Over a large part of Persia, water for agricultural and domestic purposes has from time immemorial been conveyed from the mountains by means of underground channels excavated and maintained by men specially skilled, who appear to inherit their aptitude for the work.

of that knowledge of the various professions which is indispensable to princes.

You must realise, my son, that you may only enjoy the fruits of a [pure] science in the form of a reward in the next world. If you wish to enjoy mundane benefits from a science, you can only do so by means of some profession which you combine with it; the law, for example, or the judge's art, or the proportional division of the estates of deceased persons[1], or homiletics, or preaching. Not everyone can attain to this, but those who do so reap great profit.

From astrology, calendar-making and the interpretation of omens, so long as they go unprovided with embellishment, whether solemn or farcical, no mundane profit comes to the astrologer. Similarly with medicine, as long as there is no manipulation, quackery, or indiscriminate bolus-mongering, the physician is unable to earn a livelihood. The loftiest branch of learning, therefore, is that of religion, the principles of which lie everlastingly in the declaration of the unity of God. The practical applications of that declaration constitute the provisions of the religious law, and its profession brings blessings both in this world and the next.

For that reason, my son, to the extent of your powers, concern yourself with the faith, in order to secure for yourself the rewards of this world and the next. If you would receive divine assistance in this matter, acquire first an accurate knowledge of jurisprudence and then of the practical applications, for without a knowledge of jurisprudence

[1] By Muhammadan law a testator has power to assign only one-third of his property, the rest of his estate falling to be divided according to prescribed fractions. The calculation of shares is often complicated, with results that lead to prolonged litigation.

the practical side consists merely of a perfunctory execution of religious duties. When therefore you have decided to take up, out of the various professions which I have described, that of a student of the [divine] laws, you must become chaste, contented, the friend of learning and the foe of worldliness, patient, light of spirit, accustomed to retiring late to rest and rising early, avid of writing and study, unassuming, unwearying in labour, retentive, constant in repetition of the principles of theology, eager in the investigation of [sacred] biographies and delving into mysteries, a friend of scholars, grave and reverend. In learning you must be eager and without shame and cognisant of the debt you owe your master.

It behoves you always to have at hand an abundance of books and pens, pen-sharpeners, pen-holders, ink-holders, knives, compasses, line-pens, rulers and similar articles. Your mind should dwell on nothing else. Retain in memory all that you hear, but speak little and think deep, never being content with blind formality. The seeker after knowledge who is endowed with these qualities will swiftly become the unrivalled paragon of his age.

If you become a jurisconsult, practice your religion, be assiduous in study and in committing the Koran to memory, and perform the duties of worship, prayer and fasting, none of which you must neglect. Be pure in your faith, clean of raiment and ready of answer. Yet pronounce no decision on any matter until you have considered it well. Do not consent to take action where proof is inadequate or merely on your own precedent, nor blindly follow the example of others. Set a high standard for your own judgment and never be content with ambiguity and equivocation. Take no action except on the word of persons who are to be trusted and do not consider every document and every paragraph [in a document] as deserving respect.

When you hear a tradition [of the Prophet] scrutinize the persons transmitting it, but reject any doubtful tradition even from a recognized traditionist. Have no confidence in statements [concerning the Prophet] transmitted by single individuals, unless they are reliable traditionists; and do not evade a well-established tradition.

Exert your faculties in the elucidation of points of law, but exercise no partiality and make no prejudiced utterance. When you engage in discussion, have regard to your opponent; if you have the ability to cope with him and know that you can defeat him in argument, then enter upon what questions you wish. Otherwise refrain from action. Do not be content with a solitary precedent, nor reject and rebut a case by reason of a single argument. Have a care in the early part of your utterances in order not to destroy the effect of what you say later. If the discussion turns on a point of applied law, give the text of the Koran precedence over Tradition, and Tradition precedence over inference and probability. If the discussion turns on jurisprudence, there can be no objection if positive, negative and conditional arguments are granted equal importance. Do your utmost to make your meaning clear, setting forth your words in due order, neither curtailing them nor expanding, and saying nothing which is without value.

Should you become a preacher, you must have the Koran by heart and commit many other things as well to memory. In the pulpit engage in no wrangling or argument, even though you know that your adversary is weak. But you may make any statement you wish from there, and if anyone should ask questions, it makes no matter. Make your tongue eloquent and remember that the people in your audience are stupid brutes, to whom you may speak as you wish—only avoid being at a loss for words. But you yourself must be immaculate in person and raiment.

Get together disciples who shall always sit amongst your audience and, at every point you make, shall applaud loudly and keep the assembly warm. If some [of your hearers] weep, do you also shed a tear from time to time. Should you ever be at a loss for what to say, let it not trouble you; engage in prayer and recital of the creed. Never be sour-visaged, otherwise your congregation may become as heavy of spirit and sour-visaged as yourself, in accordance with the Arabic proverb that "What issues from the ponderous is itself ponderous".

During your discourse be animated, and do not suddenly in the midst of a lively speech fall into listlessness. Study your audience constantly; if it demands wit, speak wittily; if stories, tell stories; in short let your discourse be anything for which there is common demand. Once you have won success, fear nothing; offer the worst discourse as though it were the best of all things, for when you are successful with the audience they will eagerly accept it. Yet even when you are successful exercise some caution, for the preacher's adversaries appear when he is most successful.

Do not persist in a place where you fail to find success. When questions are launched at you in the pulpit, reply to those to which you know the answer; but where you do not know the answer, retort, "Such questions are not suited for the pulpit; come to my house, so that I can answer you". No one will ever come to the house. If men act with intent to bring about your downfall and write you frequent questions, tear up the papers and say, "This is the kind of question put by misbelievers and heretics; the questioner is a heretic''. Everyone will call out, ''Curses upon the heretic and misbeliever!'' and thereafter no one will have the audacity to ask you questions.

Bear in mind what utterances you make before an audience, so as not to repeat them. Your appearance should ever be new and unfamiliar; therefore do not dwell over-long in any one city; the livelihood of preachers and fortune-tellers depends upon their legs, and their success upon the unfamiliarity of their faces. Cherish the preacher's good name and ever keep your person and raiment unspotted. Let your performance of the requirements of the religious law be good; pray frequently and undertake voluntary fasts. In speech be polite.

Do not be found too often in the bazaars, through which the mass of the public passes; you will thus contrive to remain a spectacle unfamiliar to the common gaze. Avoid unworthy associates and maintain the etiquette of the pulpit; that is a rule which I mention elsewhere. Keep yourself clear of bombast, lying and bribery, and bid men do only those things which you do yourself; thereby you will show yourself a man of integrity as well as of religious knowledge. Make yourself very familiar with your branch of learning and expound your doctrine as clearly as possible if you wish not to be shamed through words which lack significance.

In your discourses and sermons let all your utterances inspire either fear or expectation; but never allow men to despair completely of God's mercy, nor yet unfailingly admit them to Paradise without regard to their goodness. In general, speak on those matters in which you are properly versed and of which you have a good knowledge, for the result of unsubstantiated pretence is disgrace.

Should you reach high distinction in your learning and become a qadi, once you have acquired the qadiship be forbearing and gentle; but also be quick-witted, discerning, of good judgment, perspicacious, understanding of human nature, profound in religious knowledge, familiar with the ways of every [social] group and their artifices and with the organisation of every people and sect. You must be acquainted with the expedients open to judges, so that if an aggrieved person should appear for justice, having no witnesses and in danger of being victimised or of being deprived of what is lawfully due to him, you may come to his aid and by some contrivance or subterfuge convey to every possessor of a just claim what is duly his.

To illustrate: there was in Tabaristan[1] a certain chief qadi called Abu'l-'Abbās Rūyānī, a person of distinction, endowed with learning and dignity, far-sighted and of great good-sense. One day a man appeared in his court with a claim against another person for a hundred dinars. The qadi questioned the defendant, who denied the debt; whereupon the qadi asked the claimant if he had any witness. When he had replied that he had not, the qadi proposed to administer an oath to the defendant. At this the claimant burst into tears and appealed to the judge not to let the man swear an oath, because he would not scruple to swear falsely. "I cannot", said the qadi, "go outside the provisions of the law. You are under an obligation to produce a witness, otherwise I must administer an oath to him."

The claimant grovelled in the dust before the qadi. "I claim your protection", he cried, "I have no witness. He will swear a lying oath and I shall be deprived of justice. Devise some way of furthering my cause!"

[1] Modern Māzandarān, a province to the south of the Caspian Sea.

It became clear to the qadi, seeing the man's distress, that he was telling the truth. "Master", said he, "relate to me in exact terms the circumstances in which you gave the loan, so that I may understand what is at the root of the matter".

He replied, "O Qadi! This man was for several years my friend. It chanced that he fell in love with a slave-girl, whose price was a hundred and fifty dinars. But he had no money, and, like other people distracted with love, he went about day and night weeping and moaning. One day, he and I had gone walking together for recreation into the open country. We sat down for a while and this man talked of the girl, weeping bitterly. My heart was so touched—he had been my friend for twenty years—that I said, 'My dear friend, you have no money; I am not in possession of the whole sum and you know of nobody who will come to your aid in a matter of this kind. However, I have, as the whole of my savings, the sum of a hundred dinars, which for years I have been gathering. I will give you these hundred dinars and you must by some method or other contrive to acquire the rest. With that sum buy the girl, keep her for a month and enjoy your pleasure with her; then when the month is past, sell her and return me my money.'

"He rolled in the dust before me and swore an oath that he would keep her for one month and then sell her, whether she sold at a profit or a loss, and return me my money. Thereupon I unloosed the money from my girdle and gave it to him. The only ones present were he and I and God Almighty. And now four months have passed and I have not seen my money, nor will he sell the girl."

"Where were you sitting," asked the qadi, "at the moment when you gave him the money?"

''Under a tree'', was the answer.

''Well'', said the qadi, ''since you were sitting under a tree, why did you tell me that you had no witness?'' Turning to the defendant he asked him to be seated before him, while to the claimant he said, ''Do not be anxious. Go to that tree; under it bow down twice in worship and call down blessings on the Prophet a hundred times, then tell the tree that the qadi wishes it to come and give evidence.''

The defendant smiled at this. The qadi observed his doing so but pretended not to have seen and kept the matter to himself. Meantime the claimant said, ''O Qadi, I fear the tree may not come at my bidding''. To this the qadi answered, ''Take this seal of mine; tell the tree that it is the qadi's and that he desires that it [the tree] will come before him and give testimony as in duty bound''.

Thereupon the claimant took the qadi's seal and departed, the defendant at the same time seating himself in front of the qadi, who now busied himself with his other cases, although from time to time throwing a glance at the man. Suddenly and unexpectedly, in the middle of a case he was deciding, he turned to him and asked ''Can So-and-so have arrived there?'' ''Not yet'', said the man, whereupon the qadi continued with the case.

The claimant meantime had displayed the qadi's seal to the tree and told it that the qadi required its presence. When he had waited a little while and began to realize that he would receive no answer from the tree, he sorrowfully returned into the presence of the qadi, to whom he reported that he had presented the seal but that the tree had not come.

''You are in error'', retorted the qadi. ''The tree came and gave testimony.'' Turning to the defendant he said, ''Give the man his money''.

"No tree has come since I have been sitting here", said the man, "nor has any given evidence".

The qadi retorted, "If you did not receive this money from him under that tree, why did you reply, when I asked you whether he had reached it, 'Not yet; it is some distance from here to there'? Why did you not say, 'Which tree? I know of no tree under which I received money from him and I do not know where he has gone'?"

In that fashion he proved the man's guilt, and, having exacted the money from him, he restored it to its owner.

Not all decisions, therefore, should be made from books. Inferences should be drawn and devices invented on one's own initiative.

To touch on another matter; although you should be very unassuming at home, yet in a court of law the more awe-inspiring, stern-faced and unsmiling you are, the better, in order to preserve the distinction and eminence of your position. Further, be dignified and of few words, but never weary of listening to argument or of making decisions. And never display impatience, but be forbearing; if a problem occurs, do not be content to rely upon your own judgment, but seek advice of the jurisconsults also. Keep your judgment unclouded and never rest from studying problems and beliefs, after the manner which I have suggested. Bear actual cases in mind, for in the practical execution of the law the qadi's ideas are on an equality with the views expressed in the codes. Frequently a cause comes for judgment which, if it depended on the codes, would be difficult to decide but which the qadi grasps easily. And, provided the qadi is able to elucidate the law for himself, such a course is permissible.

The qadi, then, must be a person self-controlled, God-fearing, pious and capable of elucidating the law. There are certain times at which he should refrain from sitting in judgment. They are when he is hungry or thirsty, on emerging from the warm baths, at times of personal distress or when some anxiety over everyday affairs distracts him. He should have competent assessors[1], whom he must not permit, at the time when he is delivering judgment, to interject comments or relate experiences or to make personal explanations. It is his duty to pass judgment, not to make investigation (and many an inquiry were better not made). He should be brief in his discourse and turn quickly to the witnesses and the administering of oaths.

In cases where he knows that large sums are at stake and the parties unscrupulous, he may bring to bear any form of test or investigation familiar to him. He must neglect nothing and assume nothing to be simple, and should always have competent assessors with him. It behoves him always to keep his authority effective and firm. He should refuse to write deeds and decrees in his own hand, except where it is essential; for he should regard his script as something rare and valued. Let him have his decisions registered. [And, lastly,] the highest virtues of a qadi are learning and scrupulousness.

Should you [after all] not make this your career nor yet follow the profession of arms, then take the path of commerce, from which you may perhaps derive profit. What accrues from trade is always lawful and it finds approval with the majority of men.

[1] Who speak to the credibility of witnesses.

CHAPTER XXXII

Being a Merchant

MY SON, ALTHOUGH commerce is not an occupation which can with complete accuracy be called a skilled craft, yet properly regarded it has its laws just as the professions have. Clever men say that the root of commerce is established in venturesomeness and its branches in deliberateness, or, as the Arabs express it, "Were it not for venturesome men, mankind would perish". What is meant by these words is that merchants, in their eagerness for gain, bring goods from the east to the west, exposing their lives to peril on mountains and seas, careless of robbers and highwaymen and without fear either of living the life of brutal people or of the insecurity of the roads. To benefit the inhabitants of the west they import the wealth of the east and for those of the east the wealth of the west, and by so doing become the instrument of the world's civilization. None of this could be brought about except by commerce, and such hazardous tasks would not be undertaken except by men the eyes of whose prudence are stitched up.

Commerce is of two kinds, each of which has its own risks; one is buying and selling [locally] and the other travelling. The one is undertaken by people settled in one place, who buy merchandise when it is not in demand in the hope of increase. This means a risking of money, and it needs a venturesome, long-sighted man to have the courage to buy goods in little demand on the expectation of increase. What travel involves I have already said. On either aspect it is essential for the merchant to be bold and fearless with respect to his person and property. But he must also be honest and not seek other people's loss for his own gain, nor desire to bring other men into misfortune for his own benefit.

The merchant should trade with those whose position is inferior to his own; if he does so with those in a superior position, let them be men possessed of honesty, religious integrity and honour. He must be on his guard against tricksters and do no business with men who have no understanding of commodities, if only to protect himself against a constant knocking at his door. He should have no dealings with persons of scanty capital nor yet with simpletons, and he should never do business with close friends. If he does, he must abandon any desire for profit if he wishes to prevent the friendship from being destroyed, for many a friendship has been terminated by reason of some trifle of profit or loss. And let him never deal on credit in the hope of increment; many is the increment which has borne loss as its fruit.

Further, let him not cut the time for inspection too short: too brief a time for viewing may mean extensive loss, as I say in my quatrain:

Methought if from her arms I found release,
Perchance the pain within my heart might cease;
Since parting, though, I neither sleep nor eat;
Out of her sight my anguish doth increase.

The roots of bankruptcy for a merchant lie in extravagance. Unless money is actually in hand as profit it should not be spent out of capital, for the greatest loss that a merchant can incur is the result of spending out of capital.

The most profitable merchandise, let it be clear to you, is that which is bought in wholesale quantity and sold retail by the dram—the worst being the opposite. Avoid buying grain in the expectation of profit; the grain-dealer is always branded as disreputable and evil-intentioned.

The truest form of integrity is [for the merchant] never to lie about goods [he has] for sale; unbelievers and Muslims alike hold in detestation any lying about goods that are for sale. I have said something to this effect in my quatrain:

See, in my heart, the flame of love arise!
Love, like a yoke, upon my shoulders lies;
Dearly, with heart and soul, my love was bought;
No man should lie about the things he buys.

No merchant should permit goods to leave his hands before completion of a sale and there should be no shame about bargaining; wise men declare that moderation reduces a man's fortune. One should not make a practice of restraint in demanding more; nevertheless there should be no unconscionable dealing in the course of trade, for those who engage in this occupation declare that although the basis of trading is gain, lofty principle in the matter of gain is a guarantee of wealth and a safeguard to one's dignity.

On this point there is a story which I have heard, about a merchant who was one day bargaining in a tradesman's shop over an article costing a thousand dinars. When the chaffering had been concluded, a dispute broke out in the reckoning between merchant and tradesman over a single carat of gold, the tradesman saying "I owe you a gold dinar", whereas the merchant said, "It is a dinar and a carat".

Over this reckoning the dispute raged from dawn till afternoon, the merchant clamouring, storming and refusing to abate anything of his claim, until at last the trader in despair handed over a dinar and a carat. The merchant took the money and departed, with every one of those who had observed the incident declaring him to be in the wrong. As he left, the trader's apprentice ran after him to demand the usual apprentice's gift, and received both the dinar and the carat. On his return, his master remarked, "That man agitated himself from dawn to mid-day about a carat of gold shamelessly in the middle of a crowd of people. Did you expect him to give you anything?" Thereupon the boy displayed the gold, to the amazement of the trader, who thought to himself, "This boy is not good-looking and is very small. He cannot be suspected of any improper conduct. But why did a man who is of so grasping a nature act in this [generous] fashion?"

Some time later he met the merchant and remarked to him, "That was strange conduct I observed on your part, Sir, that day. You disputed hard with me from dawn until the afternoon prayer in the midst of a crowd of people over a single carat of gold, and then gave the whole sum away to my apprentice. Why did you give me such trouble and then follow it up with this open-handedness?"

The merchant answered, "There is no need to be astonished, Sir, at what I did. I am a merchant, and it is the rule of commerce during buying, selling and negotiation that if one should be beguiled out of a single dirham it is as though one were tricked out of half one's life. On the other hand, when the time comes for generosity, if one were to be guilty of ungenerous conduct, it were as much as to assert one's origin to be unclean. I had no taste either to be tricked out of half my life or to attribute any unclean origin to myself.''

A merchant whose capital is small should be cautious over taking a partner. Should he do so, the partner ought to be someone who is at the same time generous, wealthy and modest, so that when it comes to division [of profits] he will not treat him harshly. He must never buy with new capital any merchandise of a nature to deprive him of a percentage of profit or which involves him in heavy expenditure. Nor should he buy anything at all where the harvest goes to another, or anything that has died naturally, or anything broken. He should not test his luck with his capital unless he knows that, in the event of his losing, it will not be more than half.[1]

If the merchant is handed a letter with the request that it be delivered in such or such a place, let him read it before accepting it, for many misfortunes may be contained in a sealed letter and one never knows how conditions may be. But he need take no precautions over the messages of needy people. Whatever the town he enters, he should give no news of calamity, and when he returns from a journey he should not carry the report of a death. But he must not fail to report news of a pleasant nature.

No merchant should set out on a journey without a companion, and when travelling with a caravan he should alight [at the halting-place] in the midst of a group and place his goods where people are crowded together. He should not penetrate amongst the arms-bearers nor halt amongst them, for brigands first attack the men bearing arms. If he goes on foot, he should not accompany the mounted men. Never let

[1] A more cautious version reads ''unless he knows that if he does not win, his capital will not be diminished''.

him inquire the way of strangers, but only of someone whom he recognises as worthy of respect; it often occurs that unscrupulous men give false directions about the way, then follow behind and rob one of one's goods.

He should greet with an untroubled face any persons encountered on the way, without any hint of apprehension or distress. He must attempt no dishonesty with the road-guardians charged with exacting dues, but need not neglect to beguile them by putting a bold front on his utterances. He should never embark on the road without provisions and food, nor set out in summer without clothes for the winter, even though inhabited places are frequent on the way. The drivers of the animals should be kept contented.

When the merchant arrives in a town where he is unknown, or when lacking in confidence, let him choose out a trustworthy salesman. His acquaintanceship should lie with three classes of men; those that are generous and quick-witted, those that are rich and of an honourable character and those that are acquainted with the roads and familiar with the country.

Strive your utmost to inure yourself to cold and heat, to hunger and thirst; when you are in easy circumstances, do not be extravagant, so that if at any time you are compelled to suffer hardship, it will fall the more lightly upon you. Where there is a task which you are capable of doing, do it yourself and trust no one; the world is swift to deceive, even though the real capital of commerce is honesty. Be brisk in buying and selling, trustworthy and honest. Let your commerce be on a large scale. As far as may be possible, do no trading on credit. Should you do any, then let it never be with learned men, with 'Alawids [''Saiyids''], with men who have newly acquired wealth or who possess little, with confidential agents of the qadi, with children or with courtiers. He that deals with them never escapes headache and regrets.

Never entrust your goods to men whose own goods have not been seen by you, nor rely upon men untried by yourself. Then, once you have tested a man, do not be continually testing him further, nor exchange one you have tried for one untried; many a long day is needed before a man who is proved trustworthy comes to hand, and there is a proverb that the devil you have tried is better than human beings you have not tried. Judge men first by what others say of them and then test the men in their own persons; those who are of no use to themselves will not be of use to others. Prove men by their actions and not by their words—a sparrow cash down is better than a peacock at a date.

As long as you can by land-journeys obtain a profit of one-half on a capital of ten, never embark on the sea in your eagerness to obtain a profit of fifteen on the same capital. On sea-voyages there may be profit as high up as the heels, but there is peril up to the neck; do not cast great substance to the winds for the sake of a trifle. If on dry land an accident occurs through which your goods are lost, there is a chance that your life will be saved; whereas at sea there is peril to both. You may find a replacement for your goods but not for your life. And a career on the sea has been likened to that of a king, at a bound to fortune and at a bound destroyed. Yet it is allowable to embark on a ship once in order to satisfy your curiosity when you have reached affluence. The Prophet said: "Ride once upon the sea and behold the mighty works of God".

At the time of negotiation, do not forgo bargaining; but once the contract is made, bargain no further. Do not resign your business wholly into the hands of others; the saying goes, "With other men's hands grasp serpents, and with other people's feet trample down thistles". Keep a complete tally of all your profit and loss, and have all written down in your own hand to protect yourself from oversight and error. Furthermore, always keep a reckoning with your slaves and those about you; but undertake no obligation in your own handwriting, so that if ever you wish to denounce it, you may do so. Make constant inquiry into the state of your economy, looking at the profit and loss and the credit or debit brought about by your dealing; by keeping yourself informed, you will never suffer through ignorance of the state of your profit and your loss.

Avoid all dishonesty; he that deceives his fellow-men should realise that thereby he deceives himself. I have been told the story of a man who possessed large numbers of flocks and herds. He had a shepherd, a God-fearing and honest man, who every day collected all the sheep's milk and brought it in to the owner. He, whatever the quantity, mingled a like amount of water with the milk, which he then bade the shepherd go out and sell. The man constantly urged and counselled him to refrain from acting as he did and from defrauding his fellow-Muslims. "The ultimate destiny", said he, "of the man who defrauds his fellows, is humiliation."

However, the owner refused to listen to the shepherd's words and continued his malpractice. It chanced that one night the shepherd brought the sheep to lie down in a dry torrent-bed, while he himself went to sleep on a piece of higher ground. It was then the spring season and, by God's decree, heavy rain fell upon the mountains and the flood which arose launched itself down the torrent-bed, destroying the sheep. Next day the shepherd came in to the town and faced the owner without any milk.

"Why have you brought no milk?", he asked. "I told you, master," said the shepherd, "not to water the milk; for it was dishonest. But you would not do as I asked; and now, the water which you sold to men at the price of milk gathered itself together in a mass, rushed down and swept away your sheep."

To the full extent of your power, therefore, refrain from dishonesty; the man who has once been dishonest will never find anyone to trust him again. Make a habit of integrity; it is the finest adornment. Bargain hard, giving and taking to good effect; make promises to no one, but, having promised, do not go back upon your word. Do not say overmuch but let what you say be the truth, that God may bless your dealings. In your negotiation have a care over the demanding and the giving of documents; if you must give a receipt, do not let it leave your hand until you have received what is due to you.

Wherever you go, seek acquaintanceship, and if, being a merchant, you have not previously visited a particular town, go provided with a letter from some well-regarded person through whose personal introduction you may become known. Frequent the society of well-endowed persons and undertake no journey with anyone who is incompetent, ignorant, foolish, lazy, neglectful of worship or irreverent. The Arabs say, "First choose your fellow-traveller, then travel". On the other side, when people regard you as trustworthy, do not belie their opinion of you.

When you make purchases, buy nothing which has not been seen by you or been displayed to you; and, if you wish to sell goods, first inform yourself of the market-rate and sell according to proper conditions and contract, to avoid any litigation and dispute. Keep to the path of balanced domestic economy, which is the highest form of commerce; and never permit household purchases to be made without discretion. Buy household necessities once a year at the appropriate season; then buy all the articles which are of use to you and in the quantity you will require during the year. Keep yourself informed of the market price; when it rises, sell one-half of all you have bought and so live gratis during the year. There is no sin in this nor anything disgraceful, and no one will accuse you of avarice on its account, for it is an integral part of household economy.

Should defects appear in your economy, plan to increase your income so as to prevent the occurrence of deficiencies, and if you are unable to increase your income, reduce your expenditure and thereby secure what you otherwise would by means of an increase.

Now if it should happen that commerce does not appeal to you and you wish to become an honourable man of learning, there is no branch of learning more noble or more profitable than the science of medicine. The Prophet said: "Learning has two sides, namely the science of bodies and the science of beliefs".

CHAPTER XXXIII

The Science of Medicine

IF YOU BECOME a physician, my son, you must be familiar with the principles of the science of medicine, both in the theoretical and the practical aspects. Understand, then, that everything which is found in the human body is either natural or extra-natural. The natural is composed of three parts; first, that on which the stability and subsistence of the body depend; second, that which is composed of what is consequential on those things on which the stability and subsistence of the body depend; third, that which transports the body out of one condition into another. The extra-natural is that which causes disorder of [bodily] functions, either mediately or immediately, or is itself the disorder of the functions.

The part on which the stability and subsistence of the body depend is composed either of what is classed as matter or of what is classed as form. What is classed as matter is either very deep-seated [fundamental] like the elements (which are four in number—earth, air, fire and water), or less fundamental than the elements like the temperaments (which are nine in number—one equable and eight non-equable, four being simple and four compound), or less so than the temperaments, like the humours (which are four in number—yellow and black bile, phlegm and blood), or less so than the humours, like the organs (which, according to one opinion, are four in number or, according to another view, two).

To explain further what I have said: the organs are composed of humours, the humours of temperaments and the temperaments of elements, which are the ultimate form of matter.

What is classed as form consists of three parts: faculties, functions and spirits.

The faculties have three parts: spiritual, animal and physical. The spiritual consists of the five senses: sight, taste, hearing, smell and touch, and, in addition, the faculty of movement. Its parts correspond in number with the organs endowed with power of movement. The spiritual also includes the inward perceptive faculty, which consists of three parts: imagination, thought and memory.

The animal has two parts: active and passive.

The physical has three parts: generative, educative and nutritive.

The functions have the same number of parts as the faculties—spiritual, animal and physical; for the spirit is the servant of the faculty, the faculty the source of the function and the function the effect of the faculty. The functions therefore are exactly equal in number to the faculties.

As for what is consequential to those things on which the stability and persistence of the body depend, examples are: obesity, the result of coldness of temperament; leanness, the result of warmth of temperament; floridity of complexion, the result of a sanguine temperament; pallor, the result of yellow bile; blood-pulsation, the result of the active animal faculty; anger, the result of the passive animal faculty; valour, the result of equability of the animal faculty; chastity, the result of equability of the appetitive faculty; wisdom, the result of equability of the logical spirit; and all the accidents and qualifications which are the result of matter or form.

The things which carry the body out of one condition into another are called "Essential Causes" and consist of six parts: air, food, movement and rest, sleep and waking, cheerfulness or sadness of disposition and emotional disturbances such as anger, fear and the like. These are called "essential" because they are all indispensable for every human being, each of the number having its own influence on the human body. When each is in a proper state of equilibrium man's activities are more complete, exact and better balanced. When an alteration occurs in any one of the number, or if man abuses any one of them, sickness and decay become apparent by reason of excesses committed.

The extra-natural is in three parts: cause, disease and symptoms. Cause is in three [!] parts: namely the cause of malady in the paired "instrumental" organs, the cause of hot maladies (in three parts), the cause of cold maladies (in eight aspects), the cause of moist maladies or the cause of dry maladies. Each has four divisions.

As for the cause of disease in the "instrumental" organs, it may be such as affects structure, size, position or number. In disease of structure the cause may be a defect of shape, soft tissue or marrow (divided into seven classes), or hardness (divided into two classes) or softness (divided into two classes).

The cause of diseases affecting size is of three kinds, while each of those affecting position and number is of two kinds. The cause of break in continuity (called "associated disease") occurs in the paired organs and in the "instrumental" ones. Diseases of the paired organs fall into eight classes, four simple—warm, cold, moist and dry, and four compound—warm and moist, warm and dry, cold and moist and cold and dry.

Diseases of the "instrumental" organs are of four kinds: those affecting structure, size, position or number. Diseases affecting structure fall into four classes: those affecting shape, those affecting soft tissue, those causing hardness and those causing softness. Diseases affecting size are of two varieties, those bringing enlargement and those bringing diminution. Those affecting position too are of two varieties, being either those whereby the organ is moved from its normal place or those whereby harm is caused to the organs by the adhesion of one to another. Diseases affecting number are also of two varieties, in respect either of increase or diminution. Discontinuity affects either the paired organs, or the "instrumental" ones or both.

Symptoms fall into three classes: those associated with function, those which appear during particular bodily states and those which appear during evacuations. Those associated with function are in three classes, those associated with particular states are in four and those associated with evacuations in three.

You must clearly realize that there are the two sides to medicine, namely the theoretical and the practical. The theoretical is what I have just expounded to you; and now I will tell you where you are to seek for information on the various branches of the science, so as to acquire a wide and thorough knowledge of each. All the various branches of the science which I have touched upon have been dealt with extensively and thoroughly by Galen in his Sixteen Books and occasionally in some outside the Sixteen.

On the elements, you will find as much as suits your purpose as a physician in the "Book of the Elements", one of the Sixteen. Material on temperaments must be studied in the ''Book of Temperaments'', one of the Sixteen, and on humours in the second discourse of the ''Book of Natural Faculties'', likewise one of the Sixteen. For information on the symmetrical organs look in the ''Shorter Anatomy'', one of the Sixteen, and for information on the instrumental organs in the ''Greater Anatomy'', which is outside the Sixteen. Study natural faculties in the ''Book of the Natural Faculties'', one of the Sixteen, and animal faculties in the ''Book of the Pulse'', also one of the Sixteen; but spiritual faculties in the ''Dogmas of Hippocrates and Plato'', a work of Galen's outside the Sixteen.

If you wish to become more profound and to advance beyond the student stage, you must study the science of the elements and temperaments in the ''Book of Existence and Corruption'' and in the ''Book of the Heavens and the Universe'', the science of faculties and functions in the ''Book of the Spirit'' and the ''Book of Perception and the Perceived'' and the science of the organs in the ''Book of Animals''. The classes of diseases are to be studied in the first discourse of the ''Book of Maladies and Diseases'', one of the Sixteen, the causes of symptoms in the second discourse of the book I have mentioned, the classes of symptoms in the third discourse of the same book and the causes of diseases in the fourth, fifth and sixth discourses of the book.

Now that I have dealt with the theoretical side it is my task to deal with the practical side even though it means speaking at some length, because theory and practice are associated like body and soul. A body without a soul or a soul without a body is incomplete.

When you embark on treatment, take into consideration

the diet of old persons and infants; the treatment of patients being of two kinds. The physician dealing with a patient must on no account embark on a course of treatment before he has informed himself about the patient's strength, the class of malady, the cause of the malady, the patient's temperament, age and occupation, his statements and character, the character of the place and the condition of his temperament.

The physician must know about the state of the urine and the pulse, the species of malady, the external symptoms, good and bad signs, kinds of sediment, the signs of maladies which occur internally and tokens of crises which may arise. He must familiarize himself with the various kinds of fevers and know how to deal with acute diseases. Further, he should be skilled in the compounding of medicines, through studying both the methods of the men who pursue analogies and the Canons of Treatment. If I were to expatiate on each of these, the story would become a long one, but I will say in which books information about each may be sought, so that it may become familiar to you and you may have recourse to it in an emergency.

On the subject of the preservation of health, study the "Regimen of the Healthy", one of the Sixteen; on the treatment of the sick and the canons of treatment consult the "Art of Healing"[1], one of the Sixteen. For symptoms, good and bad, consult the "Preface to Knowledge" and the "Aphorisms of Hippocrates", for pulse-lore consult the lesser and greater works on the "Science of the Pulse"; for the urine consult the first discourse of the "Book of Crises" (one of the Sixteen) and Galen's "Book of the Urine" (which is external to the Sixteen); for the

[1] *i.e., De methodo medendi.*

symptoms of internal diseases, study the "Instrumental Organs of the Body", for crises the "Book of Crises" (one of the Sixteen) and for fevers the "Book of Fevers" (one of the Sixteen likewise). The regimen of acute diseases should be studied in the "Book of Barley-Water" (one of the works of Hippocrates) and in the "Book of Medicaments" composed by Galen.

The physician who undertakes therapeutics should make frequent experiments, though he should not experiment on men well known or of high repute. He must have seen much service in hospitals, examined many patients and undertaken many treatments, so that rare diseases shall present him with no difficulty and diseases of the internal organs be no mystery to him. What he has read about in books he must actually see with his own eyes and never be at a loss for a treatment. He should have read the "Testaments" of Hippocrates, so that in his treatment of the sick he shall act in accordance with the rules of honour and integrity. His person and dress must ever be clean and he should be agreeably perfumed. When visiting a patient, he should go with a pleasant face and untroubled mind and have pleasant words with which to encourage the sick. The physician's heartening words to the patient increase the power of the natural heat of the temperament.

If a patient whom you think to be asleep on your visiting him replies to you, although without recognising you, when you call him, and opens his eyes and then goes back to sleep, the prognosis is bad. Further, if you see an unconscious person who throws his arms and legs about in all directions and keeps himself in violent agitation, the prognosis there also is bad. If he is unconscious but utters constant loud cries and clutches his hands and fingers, wringing them, the prognosis is bad. If the whites of the patient's eyes are whiter than is normal with him and the black blacker, and if he passes his tongue constantly around his mouth, drawing his breath from deep down, that too is a bad sign. If a person falls into sickness through jealousy or heavy grief, or struggles for breath, it is bad; and if the patient vomits matter variously coloured—red, yellow, black and white, or if the vomiting is incessant, it is dangerous. Further, if the patient suffers from serious wasting and cough, the physician should take some of his spittle on a piece of rag, which he should dry. He should then wash the rag and, if any mark is left, that also is a bad sign.

Give no medicine to any patient in the circumstances which I have described, for, as long as they have these symptoms, treatment is useless. But then, my son, if, when you visit a patient, none of these symptoms is present, it is right to be the more hopeful.

Next [after observing symptoms] place your hand on the patient's pulse; if it leaps and runs under your finger, understand that the blood predominates. If it is feeble and soft and the beat is rather slow, you must understand that moisture predominates. If it pulsates slowly but thickly and feebly, black bile predominates. On the other hand, if it is the reverse of these, make your diagnosis according to the signs indicated to you.

Then, when you have ascertained the state of the pulse, inspect the urine-bottle. If you see the water is white and clouded, the patient has sickened through grief; but if it is white and clear the disease is due to raw air and unhealthy moisture. If it is clear as water, the patient is ill through some aversion; if it is citron-coloured with particles floating in it, the disease is due to some flux of the belly. If the water appears oily to you and a line shows at the bottom of the bottle, the disease is of short duration. If you see that the urine is saffron-coloured, infer that the patient is suffering from yellow-bile fever; there may also be blood associated with the yellow bile. If upon the surface of the liquid there is yellowness, with the bottom of a dark hue, the cause is black bile and it is useless to prescribe medicine. Similarly if there is blackness on the surface of the liquid.

If the bottom of the bottle inclines to yellowness or greenness, the patient will speedily recover. If he is delirious in speech and his water is red and very dark, [it means] there is black bile mingled with blood and the particles in it have risen to the surface; pay good heed to that patient. If the water is black with something like blood deposited upon it, then bid him farewell. If it is black and there be a bran-like substance in it, or if there be something like blood deposited upon the surface, visit that patient no more. If the water is yellow and appears to have the sun shining through it, or if the yellowness inclines to dark red, the disease is in the blood and the patient must be bled for speedy recovery. If the water is yellow with white streaks in it, the illness will be rather lengthy; if it is green in colour, the disease is in the spleen. If it has in it some green and some black, the disease is the result of heat; if it has in it something resembling rectal worms, the disease is haemorrhoids and coitus will be impossible for him.

When you have inspected the urine and tested the pulse, seek to discover the class of the disease, for the classes of diseases are not all alike. Then, when you have discovered the class, do not concern yourself with medicine or poultice so long as diet suffices; and so long as powders or unguents suffice, have no recourse to pills or concoctions. Do not be too venturesome with medicaments; if the desired result can be achieved by sedative and gentle methods do not give emetics to excess, but where matters threaten to pass beyond control, busy yourself with good remedies and waste no time over sedatives.

Never accuse your patient [of disobeying orders] nor exact promises from him; if he is a glutton, lay no commands upon him [to diet himself], for he will not consent to them, although you must exert yourself to fend off the ill consequences of what he has eaten.

The finest quality in a physician is to be familiar with medicaments and have ability in diagnosis. I have said a great deal on this head because I have a liking for medical science. It is a highly regarded science and I have expatiated on it for the reason that a man talks at length about the things which he likes.

Now if it happens that *this* science does not fall to you as a profession, the science of astrology is a noble one. When you study it, exert yourself to the utmost, because it is a very great science, being one of the miraculous possessions of apostleship and therefore indubitably a science linked with prophethood, although, at the present time, by command of the law of Allah's Apostle Muhammad, it has been abrogated as such.

CHAPTER XXXIV*

On the Science of Astrology

IF YOU BECOME an astrologer, constrain yourself to take great pains over mathematics. The science of judicial astrology is a many-sided one, and perfect justice, without the commission of any error, cannot be done to it, there being nobody so accurate that he never commits an error. Be that as it may, the fruit of astrology is prognostication,

* It is not entirely inappropriate to give here a translation of the comment on this chapter made by Heinrich Friedrich von Diez, Member of the Royal Prussian Privy Council and quondam Envoy Extraordinary and Minister Plenipotentiary to the Palace at Constantinople, in his translation of the *Buch des Kabus*, "A Work for all Times", published at Berlin in 1811. He says:

"This chapter has proved one of the most difficult for the translator, and for our age also the most worthless, particularly since it has suffered greatly at the hands of copyists and translators [from the original Persian into Turkish and Arabic]. Yet all this could not induce me to omit it tho' it needed a great many explanatory notes because only a general view is given of astrology, the technicalities of the art being assumed as commonly familiar.

"Although the chapter purports to deal with astronomy, it is actually devoted to astrology, the latter being in Asia the true bread-winning art to which the former serves only as an introduction. This was so formerly in Europe too. The history of the science teaches us that astronomy ceased to be a general object of study to the learned when astrology was separated from it and repudiated. . . . All sciences have their fanciful conceptions and it would have fulfilled an extremely useful purpose to leave them in possession of them as satisfying a human need. . . . How many good inventions and contrivances would have been lost to the world if there had been no pursuit by chemists of the Philosopher's Stone, by mechanical scientists of perpetual motion, by geometricians of the square of the circle, by politicians of the balance of power and by moralists of altruism."

and when you have constructed an almanack the advantage of it lies in its prognostications. Since, therefore, prognostications are essential, endeavour to become well acquainted with their principles and be competent in the art of almanack-making. It is only when the star-almanack is exact and the ascendant star rightly identified that prognostication is accurate.

Look to it that you place no reliance on an ascendant estimated by guesswork, but only on one which is based upon calculation and upon indications strictly and thoroughly ascertained. When calculation and indications are verified, the prognostication which you make from them will be right. Whatever the decision you make, whether on a nativity or a hidden future destiny, do nothing until you are familiar with the states of the stars, the ascendant, the degree of the ascendant, the moon and its mansions, the lord of the mansion of the moon, the quality of temperament of the stars which are in each mansion, the lord of "The House of Need", the stars from which the moon turns away and the star with which the moon will be in conjunction, the star which is master in the degree of the ascendant, the house of the star which is master in the degree of the course of the stars, the fixed stars which in their course have reached it [*i.e.* that degree], the degree of the illuminant and the felicitous, the degree of the obscurant, the degree of the traces, the degree of the combust which is in the sun's body, nor of any star rising or setting.

Nor must the astrologer neglect the lots of the twelfths of the Signs[1] the decanate[2], the lords of the triplicities[3], the

[1] Every Sign of the Zodiac could be divided into twelve, each with its "lord". *Cf.* Al-Biruni: *The Book of Instruction in the Elements of Astrology* (written in Ghaznah 1029 A.D. Translated by R. Ramsay Wright. London 1934), p. 267, para. 456. [Notes [2] and [3] on next page]

term[1], the exaltation, fall [dejection] and house of detriment[2], joy, misfortune, apogee and perigee. When you have ascertained these, turn to the states of the moon and the stars—good and evil, aspect, "companionship"[3], application and separation[4], that whose light is distant, that whose application is distant, that which is void of course[5], that which is feral in its course[6], the conferring of counsel [by planets][7], evasion[8], reception[9], orientality and occidentality[10] both conjunctional and when in a position confronting

[2] The third of a Sign. *Al-Biruni*, p. 263, para. 451.

[3] The Twelve Signs were divided into four Triplicities, each with common characteristics. *Cf.* E. J. W. Gibb, *History of Ottoman Poetry*, Vol. I, p. 328, note 3.

[1] Terms are unequal divisions of the Signs with each of which a planet is associated. *Cf.* Al-Biruni, para. 453.

[2] Each of the Signs was said to be the "house" of one or other of the Seven Planets. The sun and the moon had only one "house" each, the rest of the planets had two apiece. When in its own "house", a planet was supposed to have more than usual influence; the sign opposite its "house" was its "detriment". When in its "exaltation" it was in the position of greatest power and it was weakest when in "dejection" in a Sign not its own. *Cf.* Gibb, *op. cit.* Vol. I., p. 329, note, and Al-Biruni, paras. 442 f.

[3] The two days before the "new" moon, during which it is in close association with the sun. *Al-Biruni*, p. 65, para. 154.

[4] *Id.* p. 303, para. 489. Formation of "aspects" between the planets and withdrawal from such positions.

[5] *Id.* p. 310, para. 504. A planet which does not enter into conjunction with another while within a Sign.

[6] *Id.* p. 310, para. 505. A planet in a Sign with no other in aspect with it.

[7] *Id.* p. 311, para. 506.

[8] *Ibid.* Occurs when an inferior planet is about to conjoin with a superior one.

[9] *Id.* p. 312, para. 507. When an inferior planet arrives in one of the dignities proper to a superior one, there is an exchange of compliments.

[10] *Id.* p. 63, para. 152. A planet's becoming visible in the east and its becoming invisible in the west.

the sun[1]. Then acquire knowledge of the hyleg[2] and the lord of the House[3], of providing gifts, of the diminution and increase of life and the fivefold calculation of the distance between the hyleg and the nearest fortunate or unfortunate indication.[4]

When you have satisfied yourself with regard to these, utter your words in such fashion that your decree will be true, basing it upon a reliable almanack, the elucidation of which shall be carried out by means of astronomical tables made in a legible script. It behoves you, moreover, to have observed carefully the middle signs, and the various parts in combination and singly, and considered the equality of degree of the stars.

Even with all this, guard yourself carefully against any oversight or error, so that no mishap may befall. Once having taken these precautions you must have the assurance to say, "Every decree I have elaborated will come about as I have said". If you have no confidence in your words, you will have no success. When a question is asked you, you may give any explanation you please of the inward meaning of your words and so make it more probable that your decree will come true.

On the matter of nativities, I heard it from my own master that in verity the nativity is not the moment when the child is severed from its mother. The original nativity is the horoscope of the insemination, the moment of the incidence of the semen, when the sperm from the male

[1] *Id.* p. 65, para. 154.

[2] In a nativity, an element in the indication of the length of the child's life. *Chahār Maqāla*, tr. E. G. Browne (1921), pp. 132, 167.

[3] The planet which rules the Sign in which the hyleg is found at birth. *Ibid.*

[4] *Mafātiḥ al-'ulūm* ed. Van Vloten, p. 230.

passes into the womb of the female and conception takes place. That is the original nativity and, good or ill, everything is linked to that. The horoscope of the moment of severance from the mother is called "The Great Anniversary", the occurrence of the return of the year is called "The Middle Anniversary" and the return of the months[1] is called "The Lesser Anniversary".

Man's career is determined by the horoscope at the moment of conception, and proof of the fact is contained in the tradition of the Prophet, who said, "The fortunate man is he that became fortunate in his mother's womb, and the unfortunate one is he that became unfortunate there". The idea contained in the Prophet's words is identical with that which I have propounded. For you, however, the question of a horoscope of the conception is best left undiscussed; it is material not woven according to your measure.

When you discuss the matter of the Great Anniversary, observe the practice of the bygone masters and, when you make an astrological decree, let it be in accordance with the instructions I have already given you. If you are ever consulted, first observe the ascendant of the time, then the moon, the Sign of its lord, the star with which the moon is about to be in conjunction and that from which it has turned away, then the star which you find in the ascendant or at a "pivot".[2] If you find more than one star at a "pivot", observe which is dominant and has the greater weight of testimony, then give your opinion by it to ensure your being right.

[1] Since the Muslim year is a lunar one, the months recur at different points of the solar year.

[2] Those houses, of the twelve contained in the Zodiac, which are situated on the east and west horizons and on the meridian above and below the earth, are called the four angles or *cardines* (cardo) or pivots. (Al-Biruni, p. 149, paras. 246 f.)

The rules for astrological decrees are such as I have laid down. Now, if you wish to be a geometer or an expert in mensuration, you must be competent in reckoning and be careful not for an hour to omit conning over the rules of arithmetic, which is an intractable science. To begin with, when you are measuring a piece of ground, first acquaint yourself with the angles, being careful not to treat polygons of irregular sides as unworthy of attention or to say that you will do one piece by mensuration and the rest by guesswork, because the calculation of an area may make a great difference [to the result]. Use your best endeavour to ascertain the angles; my professor used to warn me never to neglect them in calculation, for the reason that there are many polygons which contain a curved angle of this shape or that, while there are also many acute angles which look like obtuse ones. Those are the cases in which considerable differences occur. If there is a difficult shape, do not assume its area by guesswork, but divide it all up into triangles or squares; there is no shape which will not come out by this method and you can measure each part separately to secure an exact answer.

Even though I were to say a good deal on this head, there is much more that could be said, though this book [of mine] would then change its character. What I have said, however, was indispensable because, having spoken about the stars, I wished to say a few words on this topic too, so that you might be endowed with some portion of each science.

CHAPTER XXXV

How to be a Poet

IF YOU ARE A poet, see to it that your verses are, within limits, easy of comprehension,[1] and guard against making your utterances too profound. There may be subjects familiar to you but not to other people, who will need a commentary; these subjects are to be avoided, because poetry is composed for the benefit of the general public and not for oneself alone. Never be content merely with metre and rhyme; compose no verse which is lacking in craftsmanship and artifice; verse unadorned is displeasing, therefore let your poetry have art and movement.

Whether in poetry, instrumental-music or singing there should always be present a tremolo to give true pleasure, or else some artifice of the kind permitted by the rules of verse. Examples of these are [the figures and metres] known as, paraonomasia [punning], parallelism, antithesis, balance, simile, metaphor, duplication, refrain, pairing, coupling, equipoise, quotation, allusion, concatenation, rhymed prose, equalisation, acrostic, composition of words in which the Arabic letters are all joined by ligatures, or in which some remain unjoined, (?) unshackling, the ornate poem, the "ingenious" two-rhymed poem, the *rajaz*, *mutaqārib* and anagram[2].

[1] A Persian commentator remarks: In the technical vocabulary of the art of poetry, this phrase means that people reading verse may find that it flows along easily, but realize the difficulty of it when they try to compose something similar.

[2] For explanations and examples of most of the figures mentioned, *cf.* E. G. Browne, *Literary History of the Persians*, Vol. II, pp. 41–78.

If you wish your verse to be endowed with distinction and possessed of permanence, let it have plenty of metaphor in it drawn from what is possible [in nature], using it even in your panegyrics. If you compose odes and lyrics, let them be light and delicate, with rhymes that are familiar, and avoid tasteless unfamiliar Arabisms. Your love-songs should be apposite, your verses witty and your similes pleasant, in order that they shall appeal to men of all kinds. Make no verses that are no more than clumsy exercises in prosody; only men of an inferior talent, men incapable of sweet words and witty ideas, will cling slavishly to prosody and heavy metres. Yet if there is a demand for the other kind of verse compose it; excuses will be found for you.

Make yourself familiar with the science of prosody and learn the art of versification, the forms of address [to patrons] and the criteria for judging verse, so that if ever a dispute arises or someone displays his rivalry with you or you are put to the test, you shall not fall short. Further, you must know the seventeen metres which occur in the Persian system of prosody[1] and also the metres of the Arabs.[2] Make yourself fully acquainted with them all.

Whatever the form of your verse-composition, whether it be a religious poem, a panegyric, an ode, a satire or an elegy, let it be in the best style of which you are capable. Never utter anything of an inferior style. Should the theme be one best suited for prose do not put it into verse; prose may be likened to subjects and verse to a king—what is fitted for the king is not so for his subjects. Let your odes

[1] The text gives their names:—"Hazaj, Rajaz, Ramal, Hazaj-i makfūf, Hazaj-i akhrab, Rajaz-i matwi, Ramal-i makhbūn, Munsarih, Khafif, Mudāri', Muqtadib, Sarī', Mujtathth, Mutaqārib, Qarib-i akhrab, Tawil."

[2] The text gives their names: "Basīt, Madīd, Kāmil, Wāfir and the like."

and lyrics be in brilliant style. As for your panegyrics they should be strong, bold and of lofty spirit; you yourself must know each man's worth, so that when you are composing a laudatory ode it shall be suited to the person to whom it is addressed. Do not say of the man who has never so much as girt on a dagger, "Your sword brings low the lion, with your lance you move the mount of Bihistun, with your arrow you can split a hair", and when a man has never even bestridden a donkey, do not compare his horse to Duldul,[1] Burāq,[2] Rakhsh[3] or Shabdiz[4]. Have a clear understanding of what may fittingly be said of any person; nevertheless, it is the poet's duty to judge the character of his patron and know what will please him, for until you say what he desires, he will not give you what you need.

Yet do not be abject-spirited, nor call yourself 'slave' or 'servant', except in a panegyric upon someone who is worthy of it. Moreover, do not make a practice of composing satires; the pitcher does not always return from the river unbroken.

If you have some talent for pious poems and those which proclaim the oneness of God, then do not neglect it; it will stand you in good stead both in this world and the next. In your verse do not carry invention beyond proper limits,[5] even though hyperbole is a virtue in poetry and elegies on friends and honoured persons demand it. If you wish to compose a satire, say the exact opposite of what you

[1] The mule of the Caliph 'Ali, fabled for its speed.

[2] The fabulous steed on which Muhammad mounted into Heaven.

[3] Rustam's famous horse which saved him from a lion.

[4] The equally renowned horse of Khusraw, the king who was the lover of Shīrīn.

[5] There is an Arabic proverb to the effect that the poet is a liar, *i.e.* a creator of fictions.

would say in a panegyric, for the satire is the reverse of an encomium, and similarly for the love-lyric and the threnody.

Whatever the composition, let the material come out of your own quiver. Do not cling to other men's words; thus you will permit your talent to develop, the field of poetry will expand before you and you will not linger at the stage at which you first entered on to the composition of verse. Even when you have mastered the art of poetry and your talent has developed with your increase of skill, if you hear of some unusual turn of phrase which pleases you, you should not precipitately adopt it for a similar theme nor use the selfsame words. If you find it in a panegyric, adapt it for use in a satire, and if it was contained in a satire use it in a panegyric. Similarly, if you hear it in a love-lyric, adapt it to a threnody, and if you hear it in a threnody, use it in a love-lyric; in that fashion no one will know whence it came.

Lastly, when you are looking for a patron, do not go about the bazaar with a gloomy countenance and soiled garments, but rather be ever of an agreeable and smiling appearance. Learn anecdotes, rare quips and amusing tales in abundance, and repeat them to your patron. It is an exercise indispensable to the poet.

CHAPTER XXXVI

On Being a Musician

IF YOU BECOME a musician, my son, be sweet-tempered and light of spirit. Furthermore, keep your garments clean, fragrant and perfumed. Be polite of speech, and when you enter a house to play as a minstrel do not be sour-faced and reserved. Do not let all your musical modes be heavy ones nor yet all light ones; it is unsuitable always to play in one style, for not all men have the same character. They are as varied in nature as they are in their bodily composition, and for that reason the musical experts have given the art an especial pattern.

They invented the "Royal Melody" to be played in an assembly where kings were present. Then they set down certain styles of playing in a solemn measure to which songs can be sung—styles which they also called modes—the measure being such as was appropriate to the disposition of old men and others of serious character. These heavy [solemn] modes were invented for such persons.

But, seeing that not everyone was old or of a serious disposition, they said, "We have invented a mode for the sake of old people; now let us invent one also for them that are young". Consequently they sought about and invented poems which were in a lighter measure and suited to light modes. These they called "Nimble"; and matters were so arranged that after every "heavy" mode something was played in the light mode. In that way, at a musical session there was something both for the older people and also for the younger ones.

Then, in order that women, children and men of more effeminate taste should not be left unprovided for, they composed the *tarāna*[1] for their benefit in order that they might derive pleasure. And in verity there is no measure so delicate as that of the *tarāna*.

Do not therefore either play or sing regularly in one mode, but practise your minstrelsy as I have described, so that all may derive some pleasure from hearing you. When you are seated with a company, look about you. If the audience is composed of men of ruddy and sanguine complexion, let your music be largely on the bass strings; if the audience is pale and bilious, let the music be chiefly on the short strings; if your hearers are pale-faced, obese and large, play mostly on the bass; if they are dark-complexioned, lean and melancholic, play on the lute for them. These modes have been invented to suit the four different human temperaments; I wished to familiarize you with this fact in order that you might bear it in mind, even though it forms no part of the principles and art of minstrelsy.

Next, exert yourself to become a *raconteur*; by telling a number of stories, witticisms and jests you can rest yourself and so diminish the strain of minstrelsy. If, in addition to your musicianship, you are skilled in poetry, do not be enamoured of your own verse nor let all your recitations be confined to your own compositions. Others may not be as pleased with your poetry as you are yourself, because minstrels are rhapsodists for poets in general and not mere reciters of their own verse.

Next, if, when you have been engaged as a minstrel, you

[1] A style of composition of undefined character.

find two people playing at backgammon, even if you are yourself a player of the game, do not waste your minstrelsy. Do not sit down to teach backgammon nor take a hand yourself at backgammon or chess; you have been called upon for minstrelsy, not to gamble.

Further, when you are learning a song, keep discreet measure, never singing (or learning) a lyric or quatrain out of time; it is disagreeable when your song is in one place and the musical accompaniment in another. Should you happen to fall in love with someone, do not every day be singing of what suits your mood; it may please you to do so, but it will not please others. Let each of your songs be on a different theme; memorize large numbers of poems and lyrics, on [lovers'] parting and meeting, coyness, reproaches, upbraidings, refusal and consent, loyalty and cruelty, kindness and yielding, and all those things which are appropriate to times and seasons, like the songs of spring and autumn, winter and summer. You must be acquainted with what may fittingly be recited at each period, not singing an autumn-song in the spring nor a spring-song in the autumn, nor a song of winter in the summer nor a summer-song in the winter. In fact, you must know the appropriate time for every song.

Even though you are an unrivalled master, be attentive to the craftsmanship of your fellow-musicians.

If your audience consists of men especially qualified, elderly and wise, who are acquainted with the profession of music, be lavish in your minstrelsy and play your tunes well; and let most of your songs then be about old age and scorn of the world. If your audience consists of young men and boys, play chiefly in the lighter modes; sing melodies picturing women or in praise of wine and wine-bibbers.

If you see that the audience is military or given to living by freebooting, sing them quatrains of Turkestan [*lit.* 'of beyond the Oxus'], songs about battle and bloodshed and in praise of an adventurous life. Do not be sad, nor play all your melodies in the 'Royal' mode, claiming it is the rule of minstrelsy.

First play something in the true key, then, in due order, in all the keys such as those of "Iraq", "The Lovers", "The Overthrowing", "Ispahan", "The Hostage", "The Barred", "The Husaini" and "Bā Kharzī". Thus you will discharge the duty expected of you as a minstrel. Then return to the ordinary run of melodies, so that while you are executing the programme of minstrelsy your colleagues will have reached the stage of intoxication and taken their departure.

Devote yourself to discovering what mode each [member of your audience] desires. When the cup in circulating reaches him, sing what he desires so that you may receive from him whatever it is that *you* desire. The greatest skill in a minstrel is the capacity to penetrate into the character of his audience.

Should you be in a company, do not show excessive haste to take wine nor call for too large a measure of it. Drink wine sparingly until you have received your fee; then, when you have reached your objective (having obtained your money), devote yourself to the wine. In your capacity as minstrel, do not dispute with intoxicated men over any song they may call for, however ridiculous. Pay no regard to that, but permit them to say what they wish. When you have drunk wine and all are intoxicated, do not enter into dispute and argument with your fellow-minstrels; you gain no money and you only cause annoyance.

Take good heed never to engage in drunken brawling with another minstrel; thereby your fee as a minstrel is lost and you return home with head and face damaged, your clothes torn and your instrument broken. You must understand that musicians are hired by topers, who refuse to pay quarrelsome musicians. If there is anyone in the company who applauds you, show yourself very much at his service, sing whatever he demands of you and thus attract the applause of the rest.

At first, while the audience is still sober, you will gain applause but no money, but as the members become intoxicated, money follows the applause. If those who are intoxicated there insist strongly upon a particular mode or tune, as is the habit of drunken men, you must never become wearied until you have attained your object from them. The highest form of skill in a minstrel is the ability to exercise patience with intoxicated men; those who cannot be patient with them always remain disappointed.

Furthermore, it has been said that a minstrel should be deaf, blind and dumb. That is to say, he should not turn his ears in any direction that is not meant for him, nor look in any direction in which he should not look, nor report anything which he has seen or heard in a particular company. The minstrel with those qualities will never lack a host.

CHAPTER XXXVII

The Service of Kings

IF IT SHOULD befall you to become one of the king's retinue and to attach yourself to his service, however close to himself he may establish you, do not be puffed up; prefer rather to refuse office. Yet never evade your duty; from familiarity with the king estrangement may emerge, but close intimacy comes from doing one's duty. Should he at any time pretend to you that you are completely secure with him, begin from that moment to feel insecure; if you are being fattened by someone, you may expect very quickly to be slaughtered by him. However greatly you may be held in honour, never cease to be aware of your position nor speak any word that is not to the king's taste. Do not persist when in argument with him; there is a proverb that he who argues with a king dies before his allotted time, and it is folly to thrust one's hand against an awl.

Never direct your master upon any road but that of righteousness; if you teach him wickedness, he will practise wickedness upon you. In the reign of Faḍlūn son of Māmān,[1] who was king of Ganjah and Arrān, a certain Dailamite nobleman acted as his adviser. Now it was Fadlūn's practice to seize any nobleman who in any way made himself liable to fetters or imprisonment and to cast him into a dungeon. But his Dailamite adviser's counsel to him was that he must

[1] Otherwise "Mamalān" *i.e.* Muhammad, Abu'l-Aswār. Fadlūn reigned 466/1073–468/1075 over Arrān in the Caucasus. *Cf.* E. Zambaur, *Généalogie de l'Islam* (Hanover, 1927), p. 184, No. 171. In 1075 the country was absorbed into the Seljuq empire.

never inflict an injury upon a nobleman, yet that once having committed the injustice he should put the victim to death. In consequence of this advice a number of men of noble birth had been slain.

It happened that the Dailamite himself became guilty of a misdeed and was at the king's command seized and thrown into prison. Thereupon he sent a messenger saying that he would give such-and-such a sum of money if the king would refrain from slaying him. To this Fadlūn son of Māmān replied, "It was from you that I learnt not to do a nobleman an injury, but, having done the injury, to slay the victim." That Dailamite had inculcated an evil doctrine in the course of his duty.

I hold it preferable for you to be rebuked by a good man than praised by an evil one. Remember that once beyond the fulfilment of a desire, there results harm. Be not puffed up by power, seeking dignity rather than wealth from service of the monarch; wealth comes running after dignity, and the honour of the sultan's service is a form of riches. But when you become obese from office under the king, display a lean front to the world if you wish to guarantee your safety. Do you not observe that the sheep is secure from slaughter as long as it remains lean, with no one trying to slaughter it, but that as soon as it is fattened there is aroused in everybody the desire to slaughter it.

Do not be the man to sell your master for money; money gained from office under the sultan resembles roses and jasmine, which in a single day make themselves beautiful, sweet-scented and highly reputed. But also it is as ephemeral as the flowers, and like them the profits derived from office cannot be hidden away. Money acquired in the service of the sultan is more easily dissipated than the dust on the surface of the world, and although the honour of service of royal masters is the best form of capital, the money which accrues from it is no better than usury. Do not let the capital go merely for the sake of the interest. As long as the capital remains secure, there is always the hope of interest, whereas if the capital is lost no profit can ever be gained. He that holds money in higher regard than his life will fall from a position of honour into one of ignominy, for remember that avarice in the acquisition of wealth means the destruction of honour and the dismissal of men who are held in honour—unless you acquire your wealth with due moderation and give others a share in order to keep their tongues still.

When you become important in the royal service and have achieved high rank, never behave treacherously towards your master; if you do, it will have been prescribed for you by the pen of ill-fate. When a great man raises a humbler person to a position of greatness and he requites his benefactor with treachery, it is a sign that God (Be he exalted!) will revoke that greatness; for had it not been that an evil destiny had overtaken that man, he would not requite his benefactor with evil for good. Thus, to provide an example, when the Amir Fadlūn Abu'l-Aswār sent his chamberlain Abu'l-Bashīr to Barda'[1] to take charge of the troops there, Abu'l-Bashīr replied that he would not set out until the winter, because the climate of Barda' was unhealthy, particularly in the summer. There followed a long argument on this subject, and at last the Amir Fadlūn remarked:

"Why should one hold opinions of that kind? Surely no man ever dies before his fated time?"

[1] Probably Barda'ah, capital of Arrān, in the Caucasus.

Abu'l-Bashīr replied, "It is as your Majesty says; no man dies before his fated time. But also no one goes to Barda' unless his time has arrived".

Never omit to inform yourself of the doings of others, whether friends or enemies, and thereby ensure that your rewards and punishments reach your friends and enemies. Greatness becomes sweet when you can requite your friend with benefactions and your enemy with injuries; no man of rank should be a tree without fruit. Greatness demands power, and the man from whom there comes neither good nor ill is like the Jew who owns a hundred thousand dinars; since mankind neither benefits nor is harmed by him, he lives disregarded.

Next, understand that your own advantage lies in liberal beneficence; do not withhold largesse from your fellow-men, for the Prophet has said, "The best of men is he who benefits his fellows".

Seek no employ under a prince whose fortunes have reached their zenith, for they are then approaching their decline; nor attach yourself to a dynasty that has grown old, for although there may be life left in an old man, the world regards him as nearer death than younger men. Furthermore, there is rarely an old man with whom fate deals trustworthily. If you wish to retain your position in the service of kings, be such a man as the Prophet's uncle 'Abbās described to his son 'Abd Allah when he said, "My son, you must understand that this man—namely the Commander of Believers, 'Umar—has stationed you in his presence to perform a given task and relies upon you more than upon the remainder of mankind". Now, if you do not desire your rivals to overthrow you, observe five rules of conduct in order to safeguard yourself. First, never permit anyone to hear you lie; second, in his presence never calumniate another man; third, never practise treachery towards him; fourth, never fail to obey his commands; fifth, never reveal his secrets. By these five things you may achieve success in the service of masters of flesh and blood.

Next, when in the service of a patron, leave no command unfulfilled. Should a failure of this kind occur, do not admit your remissness to him, thus preventing him from realizing that your failure to act was intentional and leading him to believe that your neglect of duty was due to ignorance rather than to lack of courtesy or to disobedience. Ignorance on your part would not be regarded as a misdemeanour, but lack of courtesy or disobedience would be so.

Constantly busy yourself with your duties, anticipating commands issued to you. If there is a task which others wish to do, make haste yourself to do it, so that whenever his glance falls upon you he beholds you engaged upon some task of his. Be assiduous in your attendance in the palace, so that whenever he should call for someone he finds *you*; for it is part of the lofty character of kings that they are constantly testing their subordinates. If, each time that he calls, whether it be once, twice or ten times, he discovers you engaged in your duties and assiduous in your attendance at court he will give you his confidence in important tasks. As Qamarī Gurgānī[1] says:

To utter words in your presence meant hazard for me.
But only by suffering hazard are pearls brought up from the sea.

Until you have borne the drudgery of subordinate

[1] A panegyrist at the court of Tabaristan in the fourth/tenth century, who had written poems in adulation of Qābūs ibn Washmgīr, the author's grandfather.

positions you will never attain to the comforts of high rank. Do you not observe how indigo is only obtained after the leaves of the indigo-plant have been rotted? And God created the king to be such that all men in the world are obliged to hold themselves in servitude and submission to him. Never appear before him imbued with envy, for if thereafter you have occasion to report the words of someone whom you have envied, he will not listen to you, reckoning your words as due to envy even though they are in fact true.

Stand ever in awe of the king's wrath, for there are two things which may never be held in contempt—first the king's wrath and second the counsel of the wise. He that holds these two things in contempt, will himself come to be held in contempt.

These are the conditions of service of the king. Should it happen that you pass beyond that stage and reach the higher rank of intimate association with the king, it becomes necessary for you to become acquainted with the duties of the king's boon companion; and these I now proceed to recount.

CHAPTER XXXVIII

The Function of Boon Companionship

SHOULD THE KING confer upon you the office of boon companion, do not accept the position if you have no aptitude for it. He that fills the office should possess certain qualities; for example, if his master's assembly gains no adornment from him, he should at least not disfigure it. Therefore, to begin with, he must be possessed of all five senses and he must present an appearance from which men's eyes are not averted in disgust, so that his own patron will not weary of it. Further, he must have the ability to act as secretary both in Arabic and Persian; for, if while in his private quarters, there arises for the king the necessity to have something read or written, and, there being no secretary present, he calls upon you to read or write a letter, you must not lack the capacity to do it.

Next, although the boon companion need not be a poet, he should know what is bad and good in poetry and the art of versification be no mystery to him. Also, he should commit to memory poems both Persian and Arabic, so that if there is need for a verse, whatever the occasion, it shall not be needful to summon a poet; for he himself will be able either to compose a verse or to recite one of someone else's composing. Similarly with medicine and astrology, of which he should have some knowledge, so that if ever there is conversation involving these arts, or if there is need to apply them, he can say what he knows while awaiting the arrival of the physician or the astrologer. Such then are the qualities requisite for fulfilment of the duties of boon companionship and whereby the king is induced to repose confidence in you, with the result that he becomes eager for your service and company.

The boon companion should have some skill with musical instruments and be able to play, so that if the king has a private session in which a minstrel would be out of place, you may cause the time to pass agreeably for him by means of your skill. That will provide a further motive for his liking you and increasing his regard. In addition, you should be a *raconteur*, retaining in your memory a large number of anecdotes, jests and clever witticisms; a boon companion without stories and quips is imperfectly equipped. Then again he should know how to play backgammon and chess, though not to the extent of being a gambler, for where your instincts are those of a gambler you are unfitted to be the intimate companion of a king.

In addition to all that I have mentioned, you should have the Koran by heart and, in a measure, know how to comment upon it. Also you must know some of the Traditions of the Prophet, something of jurisprudence and something too of the practical application of the law. Of none of these categories of subjects should you be ignorant, so that if there is any discussion of them in the king's assembly, you may be able to answer queries on them and obviate the necessity of summoning a qadi or legist.

Moreover you must have read much concerning the lives of monarchs, to enable you to discourse to your master of the character of past kings and thus have an influence upon his heart with beneficial and favourable consequences for Allah's servants.

You must be endowed with both seriousness and humour, yet conscious of the appropriate time for each; utter no jests when the occasion demands seriousness nor discuss serious matters when there is jesting afoot. Whatever the talent with which you are equipped, if you are ignorant of when to apply it, it is a matter of indifference whether you possess it or not.

Combined with what I have said above, it behoves you to possess the qualities of chivalry and manliness, for the king is not perpetually engaged in pleasure. When the occasion arises for you to display the qualities of manliness, display them; indeed you must have the ability to contend with any one man, or even with two. Should it befall (which Heaven forfend!) that in the midst of a convivial gathering in the privacy of the palace someone conceives treachery against the king, or if some other unfortunate emergency arises, you must do your duty as a man of valour to enable your patron to find deliverance through your efforts. If you are slain, you will have performed the duty owed to your patron, you will have emerged with credit and provided your children with a claim upon the prince. If you escape with your life, you will have secured fame and goodly sustenance for as long as you live.

If the qualities I have described exist in you, then you are equipped for the function of boon companionship with the king. But if you regard the purpose of such companionship to be no more than eating, drinking and jesting, [you are wrong]; that is the conduct merely of worthless people. Train yourself in boon companionship with ordinary people to ensure that this form of service shall not be a burden to you.

Next, as long as you are in his presence, never be unaware of your master and never cast glances at his slaves. When the cup-bearer passes the goblet to you, do not gaze into his face but keep your head bent forward as you accept the wine. While you are drinking it and when you return the goblet to him you must not stare at him nor give your patron cause to conceive any suspicious fancies. Be vigilant in not permitting yourself any misdemeanour such as was committed by the qadi ‘Abd al-Malik ‘Abkarī.

I have been told that the Caliph Māmūn conferred the privilege of intimate boon companionship to himself upon the qadi ‘Abd al-Malik. (The qadi was a wine-bibber and had therefore been dismissed from his office.) One day at a drinking party, a slave handed the wine to the qadi, who, as he received it, gazed at the youth and made a signal to him with one eye. Māmūn was watching and saw what occurred, whereupon 'Abd al-Malik, realizing that Māmūn had observed the signal, kept his eye as it was, half-closed. A little while later Māmūn asked him meaningly what had happened to his eye. 'Abd al-Malik replied, "I do not know. It has just closed". Thereafter and for as long as he lived, whether travelling or in his ordinary place of residence, in private or in public, he never completely opened that eye, until finally suspicion had passed out of the mind of Māmūn.

To sum up, the person who would be the intimate of a king must be competent in the respects here described.

CHAPTER XXXIX

The Secretary and the Art of Secretaryship

IF YOU BECOME a secretary, you must have a command of words and a good knowledge of script. You should not make a habit of extravagance in your phraseology, but must constantly practise writing to acquire proficiency. I have heard an anecdote about the Sahib Ismā'īl ibn 'Abbād,[1] who one Saturday was writing at the Ministry when he turned to his secretaries and said, "I always see some blemishes in my writing on a Saturday. It is because I have

[1] See p. 42.

not attended at the Ministry and written something on the Friday''.

Occupy yourself constantly, therefore, with writing in an open clear hand, with the tall letters well up and the words close-knit. Your missives should be so written that a multitude of topics and ideas are expressed in a minimum of words. As the poet says:

A subtle thought that issues from the very mouth of time,
A missive full of meaning in the briefest form of speech.

Adorn your own letters with quotations, proverbs, Koranic verses and traditions of the Prophet; and if a letter is to be in Persian, do not write it in pure Persian, because that would be unacceptable, more especially in dialectal Persian, which is unfamiliar and should never in any circumstances be written. It is generally known how the formal turns of expression used in Arabic letters should be employed. In such letters, rhymed prose[1] is a sign of talent and is regarded with great favour as an agreeable feature, whereas it is disapproved in letters written in Persian, and much better omitted Let all the language you use be elevated, metaphorical, mellifluous and terse.

It behoves the secretary to be quick of perception, familiar with the mysteries of the secretarial art and capable

[1] Composition, generally of ornate or rhetorical character, in which certain words rhyme together or have the same final vowel, although metre is absent. The resultant effect is a kind of jingle. Much of the Koran is written in this style, as, for example [Surah 109]:

Qul, ya ayyuha 'l-kāfirūn, la a'budu ma ta'budūn, wala antum 'ābidūn ma a'budu. [*Say, ye that are misbelievers, I do not serve what you serve, nor are ye servers of what I serve.*]

This effect is due to the abundance of similar grammatical endings in Arabic.

of appreciating the significance of allusions. I have been told that your ancestor, Sultan Mahmūd (Allah compassionate him!), once wrote a letter to the Caliph of Baghdad, Al-Qādir-billāh, saying, "You will surrender Transoxiana to me and grant me written title which I can display to the province. The alternatives are either that I shall take the province by the sword or that its subjects shall pay obedience to me by reason of your command and written title." The Caliph replied that in the whole realm of Islam there was no people more obedient than those of Transoxiana. He continued, "Allah forbid that I should do what you demand. If you attack them against my will, I will rouse the world against you."

Enraged by these words Sultan Mahmūd said to the envoy, "Ask the Caliph what he is saying. Am I less than Abu Muslim?[1] This has become an issue between you and me. Behold me arriving with a thousand elephants to trample the seat of the Caliphate into desolation under their feet and to carry away the earth of it upon their backs to Ghazna"[2]. And to these words he added many other violent threats.

The envoy departed and when, in due season, he returned, Sultan Mahmūd seated himself upon his throne with the chamberlains and palace-slaves drawn up in their ranks, the elephants stationed at the palace gates and the army mustered and arrayed, to give him audience. When the envoy approached, he laid before the Sultan a letter consisting of nearly a whole sheet of Mansuri paper put together in sections, rolled up and sealed. "The Commander of the

[1] The famous intriguer and agent who helped the Abbasids to overthrow their predecessors (the Umayyads) in Persia and to mount the throne of the Caliphate.

[2] The capital (now in Afghanistan) of the Ghaznawid empire.

Faithful'', he said, ''says that he has read your letter and heard your extravagant demands and that the reply to your letter and pretensions is all written down in this letter''.

Master Abu Nasr son of Mushkān, who was head of the Chancery, put out his hand, took the letter and opened it in order to read it out. At the beginning of the letter there was written ''In the Name of Allah, the Compassionate, the Merciful[1]'', followed by a single line laid out thus:

ALM[2]

Then came the conclusion of the letter, ''Praise be to Allah, the Lord of all worlds, and blessings upon his Prophet Muhammad and his kin universally''. There was nothing more written.

Sultan Mahmūd together with his secretaries fell to cogitating what this enigmatical word could mean. They read every verse in the Koran containing ALM and interpreted them, but they contained no reply to Mahmūd. Now there was there present a certain Master Abu Bakr Qūhistānī, a young man who had not yet achieved the eminence of a seat but had a place amongst the courtiers who stood. Addressing the Sultan, he said, ''The Caliph has not written the letters *alif*, *lam*, *mim*. Rather the matter is this. Your Majesty threatened him with elephants and said that you would transport the seat of the Caliphate to Ghazna on their backs. In reply to your Majesty he has written down the passage [beginning with the two

[1] The usual formula for the heading of letters and other documents.

[2] Surahs 2, 3, 29 and 32 of the Koran begin with the initial Arabic letters *alif*, *lam*, *mim* in a formula whose true significance remains as yet unexplained.

Arabic particles A LAM]: "Didst thou not see how thy Lord dealt with the men of the elephant?" (Kor. 105, v. 1.)[1]

Mahmūd swooned and for long failed to return to consciousness. He then shed copious tears, bemoaned his conduct (as was to be expected from that monarch's piety) and begged for the Caliph's forgiveness—but the whole story is a long one. Upon Abu Bakr Qūhistānī he bestowed a robe of honour of great value and conceded him the privilege of being seated among the courtiers. Thus by this single utterance he attained to a high position.

I have heard a similar story to the effect that in the time of the Sāmānid dynasty[2] the Amir Bu 'Alī Sīmjūr[3] who was [stationed] at Nishapur, used to claim that he was army-commander and governor of Khurasan. Yet he never visited the [Samanid] capital, and as it was at the end of the period of the Samanids and of their florescence and they had not the power to bring him in by force, they were of necessity content with his acknowledgment of them in the [Friday]

[1] The legend is that in the year of the Prophet's birth, Prince Abraha of the Yemen, acting on behalf of the Negus of Abyssinia, built a church at San'a with the intention of diverting pilgrims to it from the Ka'ba at Mecca, which he planned to destroy. With this purpose he sent an army accompanied by two elephants, which, however, refused to budge when directed against the sanctuary. The army then turned towards the Yemen, but on the way Allah dispatched over it a vast flight of birds, each holding a pebble in its bill and two in its feet. These pebbles, which were "bigger than a lentil but smaller than a pea", they dropped on the retreating men, killing every one.

[2] They ruled mainly in Transoxiana, where Bukhara and Samarqand became flourishing centres of the arts and of learning, and in Khurasan, although for a period they had at least nominal control over most of Iran. The dynasty lasted from A.H. 261 to 389 (A.D. 874–999).

[3] He was governor of Khurasan for the Samanids and died in A.H. 386 (A.D. 996). *Cf.* further, Defrémery, *Hist. des Samanides*, pp. 260 f.

Bidding Prayer, his insertion of their name on the coinage and the payment of tribute.

Now 'Abd al-Jabbār Khūjānī, the Khatīb[1] of Khūjān[2] was a fine preacher, a man of culture, an energetic and clever scribe of sound discretion, and a person competent in affairs of all kinds. Him the Amir Bu 'Alī brought from Khujan and presented with the secretaryship of his personal court, granting him complete powers and, in view of his competence, transacting no business without first consulting him.

The secretary at the Amir of Khurasan's court[3] was Ahmad ibn Rāfi' al-Ya'qūbī, an accomplished person of high dignity to whose jurisdiction was allotted the district of Transoxiana. He had a liking for 'Abd al-Jabbar, not by reason of their ever having broken bread with each other or having met, but because through the kinship of their learning they had formed a friendship in the course of their correspondence with each other. One day the [Samanid] Amir of Khurasan said to his amirs, "If 'Abd al-Jabbar Khūjanī were not Bu 'Alī Simjūr's secretary we could bring Bu 'Alī into our grasp, for all the mischief caused by him is due to the sagacity and cunning of 'Abd al-Jabbar. A letter must be written to Bu 'Alī to this effect: 'If you own obedience to us and submit to our authority, it is your duty, when this letter reaches you, immediately to sever 'Abd al-Jabbar's head from his body, place it in a sack and dispatch it to the palace here by the hand of the messenger who brings this. Thereby we shall know that you acknowledge our authority,

[1] A mosque official responsible for services and, more technically, for the sermon and Bidding Prayer.

[2] A district of Nishapur.

[3] *i.e.* the Samanid court, that of the rightful ruler.

for we know that all your actions are undertaken by his counsel. Should you disregard this, truly I, who am the Amir of Khurasan, will come in person—[and then] prepare for war'."

Having formed this plan they agreed that in no circumstances must the letter be written by the hand of Ahmad ibn Rāfi'. "He is the friend," they said, "of 'Abd al-Jabbar and he will undoubtedly send someone to reveal what is afoot, and 'Abd al-Jabbar will escape." The Amir of Khurasan summoned Ahmad, however, and ordered him to write a letter in the terms mentioned, but told him at the same time that when he had written the letter he was not to leave the palace for three whole days and nights. During that time, moreover, no one in his service, or in that of the amir, was to see him. The amir continued, " 'Abd al-Jabbar is your friend. If he does not fall into my hands, I shall know that you have warned him and that it is due to your disclosure".

Ahmad ibn Rāfi' had nothing to say in reply. He thought to himself, "I wish I had never become a scribe; a man who is my friend and is endowed with such learning and excellence would not then owe his death to my writing. I do not know what to do". There then occurred to his mind the passage, "That they should be slain or be crucified" (Koran 5, v. 37). He thought to himself that although 'Abd al-Jabbar might not understand the allusion or arrive at the hidden meaning of the words, it was nevertheless his own duty as a friend to make an effort on his behalf.

When he had written the letter, he set down the address. Then at one edge of the paper he wrote with a fine pen the letter *alif* and at the other edge the letter *nun*, the two forming *An* [That], the first word of the Koranic verse mentioned.

That done, he laid the letter before the amir and, without anyone's heeding the address, it was read, sealed and handed over to the amir's personal racing cameleer. No special information was given him about the circumstances of the matter, except that he was instructed to give the letter to the amir 'Ali Simjūr and to receive and bring back what was handed to him.

For three days Ahmad ibn Rāfi' was detained and then returned home with a heart overflowing with woe. The cameleer, for his part, having arrived at Nishapur, presented himself before the Amir Bu 'Ali and delivered the letter, which he, with due formality, received and kissed, with inquiries about the well-being of the Khurasani Amir. That ceremony over, he handed the letter to the khatib 'Abd al-Jabbar, who was seated in his presence, and bade him remove the seal and inform him of the Amir's command.

As 'Abd al-Jabbar took the letter, before removing the seal, he examined the address, and there observed at one edge an *alif* and at the other a *nun*. Immediately there occurred to his mind the Koranic passage beginning with the word *An*, leading him to deduce that the letter dealt with the question of putting him to death. He laid it down with the seal still intact, and placing his hand to his nose as though it were bleeding, he remarked, "I will go and wash and then return".

Leaving Bu 'Ali's presence thus, with his hand to his nose, he passed through the door and was lost to sight. For a time they waited, and then Bu 'Ali ordered that he should be summoned; but although they sought for him everywhere he was nowhere to be found. It was asserted that he had not taken to horse and must therefore have gone on foot; yet he had not gone to his own house, and where he had gone was a mystery. Bu 'Ali ordered the summoning of another secretary, who read the letter in the courier's presence. When the substance of it was revealed, those present were left wondering who could have informed him of what was written there.

Although [inwardly] rejoicing at the way in which matters had fallen out, the Amir Bu 'Ali made a show of vexation while the courier was still present, and had criers sent about the town. For his part, 'Abd al-Jabbar sent a man secretly to inform him where he lay hidden. Bu 'Ali joyfully gave thanks to God and sent 'Abd al-Jabbar the order to remain where he was, and several days later bestowed a valuable robe of honour upon the courier, giving him at the same time a reply to the Amir's letter. In it he described what had taken place and asserted on oath that he had possessed no inkling of how it had come about—a fact to which the messenger would bear witness.

The story which the messenger related on his return astounded the Amir, who proposed sending Bu 'Ali a letter and a seal offering 'Abd al-Jabbar a free pardon on condition of his revealing the means by which he had discovered what was written in the original letter. Upon this, Ahmad ibn Rāfi' spoke. "If you will grant me immunity", said he, "I will tell you". "Say on", answered the Amir, who, after hearing him, absolved 'Abd al-Jabbar and asked for the return of his first letter so that he could inspect the secret message for himself. On its return he perceived that matters were as Ahmad ibn Rāfi' had said, but every one else remained puzzled to understand how it had been done.

Still another rule of secretaryship is this—that while you

are in close attendance on the court, you must anticipate the tasks to be performed, be quick of perception, of retentive memory, never forgetful of your duties and always inquisitive of what goes on. Furthermore, keep memoranda of what orders you are given and be vigilant of the manner in which persons employed in your bureau spend their time. Be fully aware also of the transactions of all tax-gatherers, investigate and make yourself acquainted at all points with the various taxation areas. If the knowledge is not immediately of use to you, the time will come when it will be so. Disclose the secrets so gained to no one, except when it becomes unavoidable.

Never pry openly into the doings of the vizier, and yet keep yourself informed covertly of all that occurs. Be proficient in accountancy, not neglecting, either, an interest in the control of affairs, in finance and the writing of business letters. All these are additional qualifications in a secretary. But the best of all qualities in a secretary is the practice of guarding his tongue, not revealing his patron's secrets, keeping his master informed of all that occurs and never being meddlesome.

It is a highly useful acquisition to become competent in penmanship and able to copy any variety of script that you see. But you should not inform all and sundry of your possessing it, if you desire to avoid the reputation of being capable of forgery and so lose the confidence of your patron. Once you gain that reputation, even when someone else commits a forgery it will be imputed to you, if the actual culprit is unknown.

Commit no forgery for a trivial object, but [reserve it] for the day when it will be of real service to you and the benefits substantial. Then too, if you practise it [rarely], no one will suspect you. Many are the talented and highly esteemed secretaries and wise viziers who have been destroyed because of forged writings. There is the story of Rabīʻ ibn al-Mutahhar al-Qasrī, a learned and highly esteemed secretary, who practised forgery while in the bureau of the Sahib [Isma'il ibn 'Abbad]. When information of this reached the ears of the latter, he was astonished but was unwilling to destroy the man, in view of his capabilities; on the other hand he was unable to reveal his discovery to him. He therefore considered how he was to deal with him.

In the meantime it chanced that the Sahib fell ill and many people came to visit him. On one occasion Rabīʻ ibn al-Mutahhar entered and, seating himself in the Sahib's presence, inquired in the usual way what illness was affecting him and what medicine he was taking. He replied that it was such-and-such a concoction. The visitor then asked what he was having as food and received the answer "*Muzawwar*"[1]. Realising that the Sahib had discovered what he was doing, he said, "Master, by your life and head[2] I swear I will not offend again". "If you repent of what you have done", said the Sahib, "I will not punish you, but grant you forgiveness".

This practice of forgery, then, is a grave matter; be on your guard concerning it.

I cannot do full justice in words to every craft and profession, otherwise my discourse would become over lengthy and I should fail in my purpose. Yet there are some which I cannot leave unmentioned and I will therefore say a little that may be to the point on each variety for your

[1] Meaning both "gruel" and "forgery".

[2] What the man who was swearing regarded as the most precious and inviolable object he knew.

information. If I say something on every category, you will be able (provided that you have listened with the ear of your mind) to make your own deductions, for from one lamp it is possible to kindle many.

If God grant you such grace that you advance beyond the degree of secretaryship to that of the vizierate, it becomes necessary for you to know the principles of that office also.

CHAPTER XL

Rules for the Vizierate

IF THE CHANCE befalls that you accede to the vizierate, become skilled in accountancy and acquire a good knowledge of how affairs are transacted. Behave honestly with your master, yielding him what is due to him in full equity. Do not covet everything for yourself; you will not be granted it. And even though at one time you may receive what you desire, it will at a later time be demanded back again, and what is allowed you in the beginning will not be allowed you in the end.

Take good heed, therefore, of what is your master's. If you consume any of it, do so holding on with two fingers, lest it should stick in your throat. Yet do not tie the tax-gatherers' hands completely, for if you begrudge the fire a little fat, your grill will remain uncooked, and unless you leave a farthing for others, you will not be able to enjoy your shilling. If you are avaricious, those who have been disappointed will not preserve silence nor allow the facts to remain hidden.

Further, just as you concede your patron what is rightfully his, it behoves you to deal equitably with the army and the people, and to practise no mean economies. Picking morsels from between your teeth and swallowing them does not provide satiety and by your petty economy you will both offend the army and turn the people into your master's enemies.

If you wish competently to perform your duties, exert yourself in the improvement of the land and in agriculture, reap the harvests therefrom and populate the unpeopled places in the country. Thus your resources will receive a tenfold increase without impoverishing humanity.

I have been told how one of the kings of Fars once conceived a dislike for his vizier and dismissed him. He told him to choose out some other place of abode for himself, which he would assign to him and to which he could remove his possessions and retainers for him to make his home there. The vizier replied that he desired no possessions and would resign all he had to his master. "Moreover", he continued, "I ask for no land which is in a state of cultivation to be granted me. Let your Majesty graciously concede me out of his territories some ruined village which I may hold. I will clothe myself in tattered garments and restore the place to prosperity, and there let me dwell."

The king ordered that the man was to be given as many ruined villages as he required. But although they went throughout the length and breadth of the king's realm, they found not a single span of uncultivated land to give to him. When they reported this to the king, the vizier spoke. "I myself knew", he said, "that in all your Majesty's country and in the territories which (under your sovereignty) I governed, there was no piece of land left uncultivated. Now that you have withdrawn the country from me, entrust it to someone who will return it to you, when you demand it, as I have returned it to you.''

When the true state of affairs had been made clear to his comprehension the king begged the pardon of the vizier whom he had dismissed, presented him with a robe of honour and restored the vizierate to him.

The point of the anecdote is this—that while you hold the office of vizier, you must be eager to build up and to do justice. In that way your word will always be effective and your life free from apprehension.

If the armed forces should rise up in revolt against you, the officers must at all costs be reduced to impotence, to prevent your master from being reduced to impotence. As for any wrong you will have committed [to cause the revolt] it will be not so much against the soldiers as against yourself and your master; your [false] economy may mean the failure of your career. Urge your master, therefore, to be well-disposed towards the bodyguard and the people; the king's continuance is dependent on his forces and the prosperity of the countryside on the peasantry.

Make it your constant endeavour to improve cultivation and to govern well; for, understand this truth, good government is secured by armed troops, armed troops are maintained with gold, gold is acquired through cultivation and cultivation sustained through payment of what is due to the peasantry by just dealing and fairness. Be just and equitable, therefore. Yet even if you are incorruptible and without any taint of dishonesty, stand in awe of your master, there being no one who has greater need than a vizier to fear his master.

If the king is young, do not presume upon his youth;

princes are like water-fowl in that young water-fowl need never be taught to swim, and it does not take young princes long to discover what is good or bad in your conduct. If the king is of mature age and in full possession of his faculties, he is necessarily one of two things—either a wise man or a fool. If he is wise, he will not reconcile himself to dishonesty on your part and will remove you from office in the most agreeable manner possible. If he is foolish and ignorant (which Heaven forfend!), he will dismiss you in the most ignominious way he knows. You may escape with your life from the wise man, but by no contriving is there any escape from the boor.

Next, wherever the king goes, accompany him; do not leave him alone, lest your enemies in your absence find the opportunity for slandering you and inducing him to alter his favourable opinion of you. Never remain uninformed of his opinions and so contrive that the people in close attendance upon him shall be your spies, informing you of every breath that he draws. That will enable you to consider your reply to his every utterance and prepare the antidote for every poison.

Furthermore, be careful to inform yourself of the activities of the kings in surrounding and nearby lands; it behoves you so to order matters that none of them, whether friend or enemy of your master, can drink a draught of water without your agent's informing you of the fact. Thus you will be as well informed about other countries as about your own master's.

I have been told that the Sahib Isma'il ibn 'Abbād, the famous vizier of Fakhr al-Dawlah, once absented himself from the bureau for two days. The agent reported the matter to Fakhr al-Dawlah, who sent a messenger to the

Sahib, saying, "I have had news of your trouble and am myself troubled by it. But its cause is unknown to me. If it chances that the seat of your anxiety lies within the kingdom, reveal it to me so that I for my part may use my endeavours to set matters right. If you have suffered any slight from me, let me know of it that I may ask your forgiveness." The Sahib replied, "Heaven forbid that your Majesty should suffer any anxiety on my account or that there should be any unsoundness in the empire. Indeed the affairs of the empire are in perfect order and your Majesty may engage yourself in diversion, for any present uneasiness will soon pass away."

On the third day the Sahib came to the royal palace and resumed his place in his usual tranquil spirit. When Fakhr al-Dawlah inquired the reason for his having suffered anxiety, he replied, "My agents had written me from Kashghar to say that on such-and-such a day the Khaqan had had a conversation with a certain military commander but that they had been unable to discover what had been said. The bread would not descend in my gullet for the anxiety of wondering why the Khaqan of Turkestan at Kashghar should utter words of which I here should be ignorant. But to-day a message has arrived disclosing what was said in that conversation, and my mind is now at ease."

And so it behoves you to possess intelligence concerning the activities of all princes and to expatiate on them to your master, that he may be fully informed concerning friend and enemy alike—and so realise the degree of your efficiency and vigilance.

Whenever you make an appointment to an office, let the person appointed be suited for it; do not, through avarice, place the world in the hands of ignorant and tyrannous men, nor assign to great office men of few possessions and humble means. Buzurjmihr,[1] when asked how it was that, although he was at the heart of the Sasanian dynasty's affairs, those monarchs fell to their ruin, replied, "Because in important and serious affairs they relied upon the aid of minor officials, with the result that their career ended as it did."

Never grant office to impecunious or impoverished men, especially if it is important office, because they will not concern themselves with provision for you until they have provided for themselves. Those, on the other hand, who have means and possessions of their own, will not immediately busy themselves on their own account and your interests will the sooner receive attention. It is like the irrigation of fields and gardens. If the canal supplying the field or garden is moist and well-soaked, it conveys water quickly to field and garden; but if the earth in the canal is dry, and water has not for a long time passed through it, then, when water is admitted, until it is itself saturated with moisture it will not deliver water to the field or garden. The impecunious tax-gatherer resembles the dry canal, in first satisfying his own needs and then turning to yours.

Next, maintain your authority with great firmness, allowing to no one the audacity to contravene your commands. I have been told, in this connection, the story of Abu'l-Faḍl Bal'amī[2], who bestowed on Sahl Khujandī the governorship of Samarqand, endorsing the patent of authority for that office and conferring upon him a robe of honour. On the day that he proposed to depart, Sahl betook himself to the palace to make his farewell and receive his orders.

[1] See p. 110.

[2] Muhammad ibn 'Ubaid Allah Bal'ami, most notable of the viziers of the Samanid dynasty, which for long held sway in North Persia. He died in 329/940.

During the ceremonial of leave-taking he refused to say openly something that he wished to say and begged for a private audience. The minister therefore ordered the room to be cleared, and Sahl then said, "May your Excellency live for ever! When I arrive at my post, orders will of course issue from here. Will your Excellency give your servant some indication of which orders are to be executed and which need not be, so that I may know how to act in accordance with your Excellency's desires?"

To this Abu'l-Fadl Bal'amī replied, "You have said well, Sahl. I know that you have been considering this for some time and I too must give it consideration; in a matter of this kind an immediate reply cannot be given. Postpone departure for a few days."

Sahl Khujandī thereupon returned home. But the governorship of Samarqand was then immediately given to Sulaiman ibn Yahyā al-Chāghānī, who was dispatched with a robe of honour and a patent of authority. As for Sahl, he was given the order not to emerge from his house for a year. And for a whole year he remained under arrest in his own house.

At the conclusion of that period his master summoned him into his presence and asked, "When have you seen us do our work by means of two kinds of command, the one true and the other spurious? We teach the great ones of the earth by the sword to be obedient; what folly have you observed in us that we should teach our subordinates to evade their obedience to us by instructing them not to carry out our command? When we desire something to be done, we order it so; for that which we do not desire to be done we issue no order. We have no apprehension or fear of anyone, nor are we powerless to execute our will. What you imagined about us is the characteristic of feeble men, and, since you conceived of us as incompetent in our transaction of affairs, we regarded you as incompetent for office. We accordingly prevented you from proceeding to your post lest you might go with the idea that a man might have the temerity not to act in accordance with our command.''

It behoves you, therefore, as long as you remain in office, to refrain from endorsing any spurious order. Should a provincial governor fail to execute your orders, inflict such condign punishment on him that for your whole life long you will have made your signature effective. In any event no one will act upon your signed instructions after you are gone, any more than the signed instructions of past viziers are acted upon now.

The orders, then, of both kings and viziers must be unequivocal and their commands decisive, if their authority is to remain firmly established and their interests to prosper.

Next, drink no intoxicant liquor; out of such drinking there arise carelessness, laxity and injustice—Allah protect us from a wine-bibbing vizier and a wanton governor! If it is the king who indulges in wine, decay soon pervades the realm. Therefore keep a watch upon yourself and conform to what I have told you; the vizier is the custodian of the realm and it would be a very ugly matter if the custodian should need another to have custody of him.

Now, if the chance befalls that your career passes beyond the vizierate to the command of the army, it becomes necessary for you to observe the conditions attaching to that office, in order that improvement may daily become apparent.

CHAPTER XLI

The Art of Controlling an Armed Force

MY SON, IF YOU come to have control of the army, deal generously both with your troops and the people, doing good for your own part and desiring it on your master's part. Be ever alert and acquire full knowledge of the art of leading troops and setting up battle-array. On the day when battle is to take place, appoint to the right and left of the line commanders who have been tried in war and possess experience of the world; station your most valorous commander and the choicest troops on the flank, where they are the main support of the force.

However weak the enemy may be, attribute no weakness to him and take as great precautions with him as you would with a powerful foe. Make no such display of valour in battle as will throw your forces to the winds; but, also, do not be so pusillanimous that by your cowardice you overthrow your own army. Never neglect to send out spies and to inform yourself of the dispositions of the enemy; let there be no neglect either by day or night in putting out sentinels.

On the day of battle, when the two armies confront each other, be of cheerful countenance and say to your own army, "Who may these be? What roots have they? Let us at once destroy them!" Do not launch your army all together. Send it forward standard by standard [of foot] and troop by troop of horse, assigning each separate commander and captain to his position, telling such a one to go to such-and-such a position with his men. Keep in front of you those that are to bear the brunt of the fighting and pay special regard to anyone who fights valiantly, overthrows or wounds one of the enemy, captures a horseman, seizes a horse or performs any other laudable deed. Reward such a man for his services by presentation of a robe of honour and increasing his pay; do not spare money at such a time. And in general do not be mean-spirited, that you may swiftly attain your object; for each of your troopers, seeing your open-handedness, will have his appetite for battle aroused and none will falter, and thus victory will be won as you desire.

If your objective is gained by the attack you launch, well and good. But do not then act with haste; remain in your place without further exerting yourself. Should the battle bear heavily on your commanders, so that danger threatens, then, when the fighting reaches you, act as the occasion demands and refuse to let the thought of defeat enter your mind. Fight to the death; he that reconciles his heart with death and can detach his mind from thought of life will not by any trivial means be dislodged from his position.

When you have won the victory, do not pursue too far after the defeated foeman, because many misunderstandings happen on the return and it becomes impossible to know how matters stand. That great amir, my father (Allah compassionate him!), never went in pursuit of a defeated enemy. He used to say that when defeated men become desperate they will renounce life and make a stand. If the enemy counter-attacks it is better not to persist against him, lest any mistake occur.

When you go to war, you will inevitably see with the eyes in your head the outward aspect of the situation and the way into the battle. But with the eye of the mind you must likewise have regard to the way by which you are to emerge, for it may be different from what you desire. Further, there is this one matter which you must not forget (even though I have spoken of it elsewhere, I repeat it): if, in the course of the battle your situation becomes difficult, let us suppose, and if one pace to the rear of you there is an easier position, beware against taking that one pace. If you retreat by a single span, you will be overthrown. Exert yourself always to advance from your position and never give way a single pace.

It is a matter of necessity that your troops should at all times be under an oath (sworn by your life and head) of loyalty to you, and you, for your part, must be generous towards your troops. If you cannot make lavish provision beforehand of robes of honour and presents, at all events allow yourself no niggardliness in promises, and take not a mouthful of bread or a cup of wine except in company with your troops; for what a trifle of food will accomplish cannot be accomplished by gold or silver or robes of honour. Keep your troops always contented and if you wish them not to grudge their lives on your behalf do not grudge them food.

Although all happenings are bound up with the destiny decreed by Allah, yet do you fulfil the obligation of planning in the manner most appropriate; what is destined will come about independently of you.

Therefore, if it should come about that God (May he be exalted!) has compassion upon you and bears you into the kingship, have a care for the rules of kingship and be noble of spirit after the fashion which I shall now describe.

CHAPTER XLII

The Conduct of Kingship

IF YOU BECOME king some day, my son, be God-fearing; keep eye and hand away from other Muslims' women-folk and let your robe be unspotted, for the unspotted robe means unspotted religion. In every undertaking let your own opinion be wisdom's servitor, and, in every task you propose, first consult with wisdom, for wisdom is the king's prime minister. As long as you see any possibility of leisurely action avoid haste; and, whenever you propose to enter upon an undertaking, first ascertain the way by which you will emerge from it—before you have considered the end, do not consider the beginning.

Be circumspect; where an undertaking can succeed only with the exercise of circumspection, embark upon it only circumspectly. Never consent to injustice and scrutinize every deed and word with the eye of discrimination, so that you may be able to distinguish the true from the false in all matters. If a king fails to keep the eye of discrimination and wisdom open, the way of truth and falsehood will not be revealed to him.

Be ever one that speaks the truth, but speak rarely and laugh rarely, so that those subject to your sovereignty may not become emboldened against you. It has been said that the worst auguries for a king are audacity in his subjects, disobedience amongst his retainers and the failure of his rewards to reach those who have earned them.

Expose yourself to the general gaze only rarely, and so prevent yourself from becoming a spectacle commonplace in the eyes of your troops and people, taking heed not to esteem yourself too poorly. Be merciful towards God's creatures, but be merciless against them that exercise no mercy; maintain stern discipline, more especially with your vizier, towards whom you should in no circumstances show yourself mild-mannered. Never be completely dependent upon his counsel. Hearken to what he has to say about persons or about the course to be taken in any affair, but do not make an immediate reply. Say, "Let us consider the matter, after which we will issue appropriate commands". Then make inquiry into the circumstances of the case to ascertain if it is your welfare he is seeking or his own benefit, and when all is known to you give him such reply as you think proper. Thus he will be unable to regard you as being governed by his views.

Whether you are young or elderly, have an old man as your vizier and do not grant the vizierate to a young man. The poet says:

Let armies be led by a man who is old,
For youth remains youth no matter how bold.

Moreover, it is inexpedient for an old man to take a young one as administrator and controller of affairs. If you are young and your vizier likewise young, the fire of your youth will be added to his and between the two fires the kingdom will be destroyed.

Next, it is essential that the vizier should be of imposing appearance as well as elderly or of mature years. He should also be well-formed, strongly built and of corpulent person;

a thin, diminutive man with a black beard lacks impressiveness. Yet the vizier must have a beard, and a large one. There is a story that the Sultan Tughril Beg[1] once wished to appoint to the vizierate some Khurasanī savant and selected the Sage of Fārāb, who had a beard down to his navel, very long and broad. This man therefore was summoned and the Sultan's message was delivered to him, as follows: "We have nominated you to be vizier to us and you will take control of our affairs, seeing that we know of nobody more fitted to the charge than yourself". The sage replied, "Say to our lord the Sultan, 'May you live a thousand years! The vizierate is an office in which many qualities are useful. Of all these qualities your servant possesses none but a beard. Let my lord not be misled by the beard, and let him bestow this function upon someone else'."

Whoever it is upon whom you bestow the vizierate, grant him full powers in his office to ensure that progress in the affairs of your kingdom shall not be hindered. Be generous towards his kinsmen and adherents to the extent that there shall be no parsimony in any provision made for them or in any largesse granted them. But never appoint to office the vizier's kinsmen and adherents (the whole of the fat tail may not be given to the cat at once), for he will not in any circumstances render a true account of his adherents' dealings nor condemn his kinsmen to penalties for the benefit of your revenues. There is the further reason that those related to the vizier, relying upon their kinship with him, can make exactions from fellow-Muslims so great that no stranger would dare to do one-hundredth part as much.

[1] Probably the Great Seljuq Sultan of that name is intended. He had control in North Persia and had himself proclaimed Sultan in Baghdad itself in A.D. 1055. He died in 1063.

Have no compassion upon robbers and never allow a pardon for them, nor grant any forgiveness to the shedder of blood. It behoves you to exercise caution where he is concerned, for if he deserves retaliatory punishment and you pardon him, you will be associated with him on the Day of Resurrection for the crime of bloodshed and will be held accountable for it. Yet be merciful towards your own henchmen, for the chieftain is like the shepherd, with the lesser men as his flock; if the shepherd is without compassion for his own sheep and fails to guard them from wild beasts, they will soon perish. Albeit, do not place reliance upon every person for whom you have made provision merely because you have done so.

Assign to every man a task and grudge no man employment, for the earnings which men thereby make they add to their own allotted portions and thus exist without lack of anything, while you are relieved of anxiety about them. Adherents are maintained for the purpose of working, yet when you make an appointment be careful to allot it to the man adapted to it and not one lacking the needful capacity. Do not, for example, give the position of wine-butler to the man fitted only for household work, nor the treasuryship to a man fitted to be wine-butler, nor the office of chamberlain to him that is suitable to be treasurer. Not every duty can be assigned to every man; as the Arabic proverb says, "Every task has its man and every occasion its speech".

By acting according to this rule you will avoid having the tongues of cavillers extended against you and no injury will be done to your interests. Obviously, if you assign a servant to a duty about which he is ignorant, he will never in his own interest admit to his lack of knowledge, although undertaking the work, which will consequently be badly done. Give the work, therefore, to one who is expert in it and thus avoid annoyance. As the poet says:

This gift on thy behalf of God I ask:
That you appoint men fitted for their task.

Accordingly, if you have an interest in a particular person's career and you wish to enhance his importance, you may assign him benefits and advancement without (unnecessarily) appointing him to an office, thus not providing the world with evidence of your folly.

In the course of your kingship, never permit your commands to be treated with indifference. The king's solace and pleasure lie in giving commands; in other respects the king is like his subjects, and the difference between them is that the king issues commands while the subjects obey. I have been told how in the reign of your grandfather, Sultan Mahmūd, there was a certain provincial governor named Abu'l-Faraj Bustī, to whom he had assigned the governorship of Nasā and Bāward.[1] At Nasā he pounced upon a particular man, from whom he exacted a large quantity of treasure and whose lands he sequestrated, afterwards flinging him into prison. The man, however, discovered means of escape from the prison and made his way to Ghazna, where he found entrance into the presence of the Sultan and demanded justice. The Sultan's order was that the Chancery should write a letter on the man's behalf, and this he received, presenting it to the governor on his arrival at Nasā.

The governor, considering with himself how the man

[1] Neighbouring cities in Khurasan.

could ever again have the means to go to Ghazna and see the Sultan, refused to return him his estates and took no action to comply with the letter. The injured man once again set out upon the road to Ghazna and, on his arrival there, went daily to the gate of the Sultan's palace until at last, one day seeing the Sultan emerging from the garden, he raised a cry and made great lament about the governor's conduct. Again the Sultan ordered that a letter be written for him; but he said, in reply, "I received a letter once and returned, but it had no effect at Nasā".

It chanced that the Sultan was at that moment preoccupied over some other matter and replied to the man, "My duty is to issue commands. If he has not carried my letter into effect, what am I to do? Go, cast dust upon your head." To this the man said, "O king! It is *your* servant who refuses to obey your command. Is it for *me* to throw dust upon my head?" At that Sultan Mahmud answered, "No, master. I spoke in error. It is for me to throw dust upon my head." And promptly he assigned two of his own palace attendants to accompany the man to Nasā and bring into their presence the viceroy of those regions. About his neck they suspended the royal letter, hanged him upon the scaffold and made proclamation that such was the punishment of any man who failed to execute the sovereign's command.

Thereafter no man had the audacity to neglect the sovereign's behest; his words had their full effect and men's lives again became secure.

Moreover, my son, when your maternal uncle, the martyred Sultan Mas'ūd, sat upon the throne, although he was well acquainted with the paths of valour and martial prowess he knew nothing of the art of government, and he preferred occupying himself in dalliance with his slave-girls to ruling as king. When his troops and viceroys perceived what his preoccupation was, they began to tread the path of disobedience, so that the people's interests suffered and both bodyguard and peasantry were stirred to insubordination. At last one day an old woman arrived from Ribāt Farāwa with a petition asserting that wrong had been done to her and lodging a complaint against the governors of the province. Sultan Mas'ūd commanded that she should be given a letter. However, the governor concerned paid no attention to it, thinking to himself that the old woman would never again be able to go to Ghazna. Nevertheless she did return to Ghazna and, presenting herself at the court for the redress of wrongs, demanded justice. The Sultan once more ordered that she should be given a letter, but to this the old woman objected that she had once before taken a letter, without effect.

"What am I to do?" asked Mas'ūd. To which she replied, "Your course of action here is simple. Maintain your authority in such fashion that your instructions will be acted upon, or else resign your authority and let another possess it, leaving you to occupy yourself with your pleasures. Thus mankind will cease to be held fettered in the miseries of tyranny." Mas'ūd was shamed into procuring justice for the old woman and the governor was hanged at the gate of Farawa. Thereafter Mas'ūd awoke from the sleep of indifference and no man dared to fall short in the fulfilment of his commands.

Where, therefore, the king's command is ineffectual, the difference between him and the ordinary run of men is nonexistent and he must realize that the welfare of his kingdom lies in the effectiveness of his authority. If there is no effective authority, ruin overwhelms the state, and effective authority cannot be maintained except by strict control. Therefore, there must be no weakness if commands are to be effective.

Further, it is inexpedient for the king to place soldiery in authority over the people, else the realm will fail to retain its population. The welfare of the people must be as carefully guarded by him as that of the bodyguard, for the king resembles the sun in that he cannot shine upon one man and not upon another. Moreover, in the same way that the people's submissiveness is secured by the soldiery, so the maintenance of the soldiery is made possible by the people. And it is through the people that the country is made prosperous, for the revenues are earned by the people, who remain settled and prosperous if given what is rightfully theirs. Therefore let there be no place in your heart for extortion; the dynasty of kings who recognize rights endures long and becomes old, but the dynasty of extortioners swiftly perishes, because fair treatment means prosperity and extortion means a depopulated land. Since prosperity needs an extended time for its perfecting, it long endures; and, since desolation may be brought about swiftly, it implies brief endurance. The sages say that the well-spring of thriving conditions and of gladness in the world is a just king, while the source of desolation and misery is a king who is an oppressor.

Do not tolerate suffering among mankind, nor remain constantly secluded in your private quarters. If you turn in abhorrence from your soldiers and people, they in their turn will conceive an abhorrence for you. Let there be no falling short in your good treatment of either your troops or your people; to permit any shortcoming will mean the profit of your enemies.

As for your bodyguard, do not let it consist entirely of a single race. If a prince's bodyguard is all from one race, he is ever the prisoner of his bodyguard and tamely submissive, for the reason that the members of one race will be in alliance together, rendering it impossible to use them in holding each other in check. If they are of all races, one is held in check by another, and no single group, through apprehension of the other, is able to show disaffection. Thus your control of your army will remain effective. Your grandfather, Sultan Mahmūd, had four thousand Turks as palace guards and four thousand Hindu rāwuts; he constantly overawed the Hindus by means of the Turks and the Turks by means of the Hindus, with the result that both races submitted to him through the fear of each for the other.

Then, also, you should frequently invite the chiefs of your soldiery to food and wine; treat them generously in respect of robes of honour and gifts of various kinds, and make it a practice to indulge them with expectations and encouragement. Yet if you wish to make a gift to any one of them, and it is a small one, do not announce it audibly in public. Declare it secretly to someone who will be your messenger, thus saving yourself from committing a petty action unworthy the high dignity of kings. You will, further, thereby save yourself the reputation of pettiness amongst your people.

For eight years I was at Ghazna as intimate companion of the Sultan Maudūd, whom in all that time I never saw commit three particular acts. One was that he never announced any gift of less than two hundred dinars in public, except through a messenger; another was that he never laughed in such fashion as to display his teeth; and the third was that when in anger he refrained from insulting language. This was most excellent behaviour. I have heard that the kings of Byzantium have a similar practice, but they also have another custom which is not in fashion amongst the kings of the Arabs and Persians. It is that if the king once strikes a man with his own hand, no other person dare strike him thereafter; as long as he lives it is said of him that the king struck him with his own hands, so that any other person who strikes him must be a king.

We now return to our original topic. I can tell you nothing further on the subject of open-handedness except that you should be lavish with money. In brief, never be petty-spirited; if you cannot resist your own disposition, at least follow my advice in not displaying your meanness of spirit in public. If you do not cultivate the habit of open-handedness, the whole world will be hostile to you. Although men may not immediately be in a position to comment, yet they will not sacrifice themselves on your account if an enemy should make his appearance; and your friends will become your enemies.

Strive against becoming intoxicated with the wine of kingship and permit no shortcoming in your fostering of these six qualities: awesomeness, justice, generosity, respect for the law, gravity and truthfulness. If any one of these is lacking in a king, he is near to intoxication with kingship, and no king who becomes intoxicated with kingship regains sobriety except with its disappearance.

During your reign as king do not neglect to inform yourself of the position of other kings in the world. The ideal at which you must aim is that no king shall be able to draw a breath without your being aware of it. I was told by my father, the late amir, how Fakhr al-Dawlah fled from his brother 'Aḍud al-Dawlah[1] and was unable to settle in any place until he came for safe protection to the palace of my grandfather, Qābūs son of Washmgīr [Shams al-Ma'ālī]. He granted him protection, provided him with generous entertainment and gave him my aunt to wife, spending immense sums of money on the wedding, on the grounds that my grandmother was the maternal aunt of Fakhr al-Dawlah, who, like my own father, was also the grandson of Hasani Fīrūzān.

Some time later, 'Adud al-Dawlah sent an envoy to Shams al-Ma'ālī with a message to this effect: "Adud al-Dawlah sends many greetings and declares he knows that his brother, the Amir 'Ali [*i.e.* Fakhr al-Dawlah], has arrived there. Now you are aware that fraternal affection exists between you and me and that our two houses are one, whereas this brother of mine is my enemy. It is incumbent on you to seize and send him to me. As a reward for that service I will transfer to you any region of my country which you name, and our friendship will be further strengthened. If you are unwilling to incur this possibility of ill repute, give him poison; by that means my purpose will be achieved and no suspicion will fall upon you; moreover, any lands you desire will accrue to you."

To this Shams al-Ma'ālī replied, "Allah be glorified! What compels so great a nobleman as yourself to address such a proposal to a man like me? I could not commit such an act, for ill fame would cling to me until Resurrection."

"Your Highness", urged the envoy, "do not forfeit 'Adud al-Dawlah for the sake of the Amir 'Ali. Our king is

[1] One of the Dailamite (South Caspian) dynasty of robber princes who ruled over a large part of Persia and Iraq. He died in A.D. 977.

more attached to you than to his own brother. I declare on my oath that on the day when he charged me with my mission and dispatched me on my journey, he said in the course of his speech, 'God knows that I have a great affection for Shams al-Ma'ālī. [I am aware that] on Saturday, the such-and-such a day of such-and-such a month, he went to the hammam and in the middle chamber his foot slipped, so that he fell. I was distressed by this occurrence and asked myself whether it was possible that senility could have overtaken a man in his forty-seventh year and that his powers have failed!' "

The envoy's purpose in this speech was as though to say: "See how well informed my master is concerning your every doing", and it had in fact been his instruction from 'Adud al-Dawlah.

Shams al-Ma'ālī replied, "Long may he live! I am indebted to him for the kindly interest he displays; but inform him that I also in my turn have been anxious on his account. It was on such-and-such a day of the month of so-and-so, the day following being that on which he bade you farewell. That night he drank wine in such-and-such an apartment and slept in such-and-such a place in the company of Nushtagīn the cup-bearer. At midnight he rose and went into the women's quarters, where he ascended to the roof and entered the room of Khaizurān the woman lute-player, with whom he had intercourse. On his way back, while descending from the roof, his foot slipped and he fell down two stairs of the staircase. It was then that I too became anxious on his account. I asked myself whether deterioration had begun in his brain at the age of forty-two. Why should a man, and a king, at the age of forty-two drink so much wine as to make him incapable of descending from the roof? Why at midnight should he leave his bed so rapidly as to bring about this mishap?"

In such fashion he gave the envoy to understand that he in his turn was informed of what occurred in the other's country.

Then, in the same measure that you are informed of affairs in the world generally and of the doings of its princes, it is your duty to be acquainted with your own country and the conditions prevailing amongst your people and bodyguard. If you are ignorant of conditions in your own State, you will be even more ignorant of conditions in foreign States.

You will remember that in the reign of the Sultan Maudūd ibn Mas'ūd, your cousin on your mother's side, I came to Ghazna. He treated me with the highest regard and generosity, and, after having for a time observed and tested me, he made me his intimate boon companion. It is an appointment which involves the holder's never being absent from the royal presence, and it was consequently my duty always to be in attendance at the Sultan's table and when wine was being drunk, whether any other courtier was there or not.

At dawn early one day he was taking his morning glass of wine and at the same time giving audience to his bodyguard, with people entering, making their bow and turning aside again. Now his vizier was the Great Chamberlain, Ahmad ibn Hasan Maimandī, whom he detained to drink wine with him. After a certain time the Court overseer entered and handed to the eunuch 'Ali ibn Rabī', a letter, which he submitted to the Sultan. Taking a draught of wine the Sultan read the letter, turned to the vizier and said, "Have that agent beaten five hundred blows of the stick, to teach him that in future he must make his reports in detail. In this letter he says that last night in Ghazna sumach-broth was being prepared in twelve thousand houses. Since I am unaware in which houses and which streets that was, one might assert anything one wished''.

The Chamberlain replied, ''Long live your Majesty! He makes his statement in this fashion in order to lighten the general report. If he were to set out everything in full, it would make a book which could not be read in a day. Thus, when he said 'sumach-broth', other dishes too were included. I beg your Majesty to forgive him and spare him this punishment, so that I may instruct him that in future he is not to present his report in the form of a summary, but to mention each house and householder by name, stating that such-and-such persons ate such-and-such dishes at such-and-such places in such-and-such a quarter.''

''This time'', said the Sultan, ''I forgive him, but hereafter it must be as the Chamberlain has said.''

So, therefore, it is your duty not to be ignorant of conditions in your realm, of the circumstances of your people or those of your soldiers. More particularly you must be vigilant concerning the doings of your vizier. He should not be able to swallow a drink of water without your knowing it, for you have entrusted your life and possessions to him. If you are neglectful of him, you are neglectful of your own life and possessions, and not merely of the conduct and activities of your vizier.

As for the rulers of the various parts of the world who are your fellow-sovereigns, if you are on terms of friendship with them do not let it be half-friendship; but if you are at enmity with them let it be overtly, so that you can openly display your hostility. Do not be at secret enmity with your equal. I have heard how Alexander, setting out on one occasion to do battle with an enemy, was told that the foeman was a careless man against whom a night-attack should be launched. Alexander replied, "He is no king who gains victory by stealth".

During your kingship let your actions be habitually on a noble scale. Since the king is greater than other men, his conduct whether in deed or speech must be imposing; only so may he acquire wide repute. In illustration it may be asked how if Pharaoh (Curses upon him!) had not uttered magniloquent words, the Creator would have reported his having said, "I am your supreme master" (Koran 79, v. 24)? Until the Resurrection, men will read this verse and speak of him as of someone great, though he was evil and accursed and the intention of the verse was other than laudatory. Further, maintain your sign manual as something of importance. Do not affix it to anything trivial, but only to such things as patents for high office or some great fief which you may assign. Once you have affixed your sign manual to a document, do not contradict yourself except with obvious justification; self-contradiction is always unworthy and especially so in a prince.

These are the requirements for kingship. It is a rarely-acquired position and not everyone attains to it, but I speak of it because it is demanded by this work. If some other career falls to your lot, such as agriculture or one of the crafts practised in the bazaar, whatever it be, you must keep its laws to ensure that your work shall prosper.

CHAPTER XLIII

Agriculture and Craftsmanship

IF YOU BECOME a cultivator of the land, make yourself familiar with the due seasons for performing the tasks demanded by agriculture, never letting the time for an essential operation pass by without your having performed it. Indeed it is better to sow ten days before the proper time than two days after it. Keep the implements used in cultivation and tilling in good repair and ready; give orders that good oxen should be bought and well fed, always keeping a yoke of oxen well rested and apart from the others, so that if some disease befalls one of your oxen you will not be behindhand with your work and the time for sowing will not pass you by.

At times other than those for sowing and harvesting, do not fail to keep the ground broken up and make preparation this year for next year's sowing. Always sow on land which covers itself [with crops]; land which cannot cover itself will not cover you. It is necessary always to be engaged in improving the land in order to make agriculture profitable.

If you are a craftsman in the bazaar, whatever your craft, let your work be quick and worthy of praise, so that you may acquire many patrons; and whatever the work you do, let it be better than that of your fellow-craftsmen. Be content with modest profit, for while you sell at eleven a single article which costs you ten, you may sell two at ten-and-a-half apiece. Do not drive customers away by importuning and over-insistence; thus you will gain a livelihood from the practice of your craft and more people will transact business with you. In the course of selling an article exert yourself to say "My friend", "My dear Sir" or "My brother", and to make a show of humility, and with all your strength restrain yourself from harsh and foul language. By your gentleness the customer will be shamed from bargaining and you will gain your object.

By use of such methods as these you will win many customers, undoubtedly become the envy of your fellow-craftsmen and be known and distinguished throughout the bazaar.

Make honesty your practice both in buying and selling, and beware of avarice even though exercising economy. Be generous to them beneath you [in the craft] and submissive to them who are of greater skill. Do not bear hardly upon the powerless and never seek to gain an advantage over children or women in your bargaining, nor demand exorbitant prices from foreigners. Yet do not be bashful in the course of trade, for frequently your moderation may bring you loss; but take into partnership a modest man who shall not be over-sharp in bargaining. Deal kindly with the deserving and with traders act like a trader, keeping true scales and weights.

With your own family never have two hearts or two purses, and never deal dishonestly with your partners. Whatever the craft you engage in, do nothing fraudulent, letting your work be of one quality whether for the expert or the uninstructed and being scrupulous therein.

If there is occasion for the granting of a loan, recognize it as an opportunity. Swear no lying oath, offer no usury and do not be extortionate in bargaining. If a friend owes you money and you know that he is without means, do not constantly be importuning him for payment; be kind-hearted, in order yourself to receive kindness and for God to bless your buying and selling.

The craftsman who conducts himself as I have set forth will be the noblest of his craft; but each group of craftsmen, according to the various crafts, has its own code of honourable conduct.

CHAPTER XLIV

Knight-errantry, the Sufi Path and the Codes of the Craftsmen

MY SON, IF YOU make knight-errantry your career, you must first understand what it is and whence it arises. Realise, then, that there are three human qualities to the lack of which no man will confess. Whether he be a sage or a fool every man is happy in possessing these three gifts of God, even though, if the truth be told, God has bestowed them upon very few persons and all who possess them are especially favoured of God.

Of this trio the first is wisdom, the second truth and the third virtue. Properly regarded, no man lays claim to wisdom, virtue and truth unjustifiably, for there is no person existing devoid of these three qualities. Yet the bluntness of men's understanding and the obscuring of their original path keep the door of these qualities closed against the majority of humankind.

The Almighty, then, created human beings of all manner of different constituents, so that you are equally correct whether you call man the macrocosm or the microcosm. The reason is that each constituent of the body, whether deriving from the elements, the heavens, the stars, essence, matter, form, spirit or mind, is itself an independent world. These constituents are assembled in their various degrees, retaining their individuality and not being compounded; men thus being associations and collections of these worlds. These collections God combined by means of links, there being no affinity between the various constituents—links of the kind which, in the larger universe, you see holding together heavens and elements. Although diverse in their essence they are joined together; as, for example, fire and water (which are opposed to each other in all respects) or earth and water (which are similarly opposed).

Now the intermediary between fire and water is earth, its link with fire being dryness and with water coldness. Water's link with earth is coldness and with air softness, air's link with water being softness and with fire heat. Fire's link with the aether is essentiality, the aether being linked (through its glow) with the sun, which is monarch of the stars and of the heavens. The sun is linked to matter by essentiality, through its reception of influences from the glow of matter, the nature of the sun deriving from the quintessence.

Between matter and spirit links were formed by sublime emanation, and between the humours and the elements by the material of food and nurture. Should the humours fail to receive strength from such material, which is the link associating them, they perish. And you may draw a similar analogy for the association of the humours with the heavens, of the heavens with matter, of matter with spirit and of spirit with mind.

Next, all obscurity and heaviness in the human body is the result of the compounding of the humours, whereas form, appearance, life, strength and mobility accrue from the heavens. The five physical senses—hearing, smell, taste, touch and sight—derive from matter, whereas the spiritual senses—such as memory, thought, imagination, speech and foresight—derive from the spirit. But for what is noblest in the human being no origin is discoverable and no direction with regard to its source can be given. It consists of virtue, knowledge, sincerity, nobility or the like, the material of all of which is mind.

Wisdom is derived by effluence from the Universal Mind into the body. Thus, this body of ours is animated by the soul, the soul by spirit and spirit by mind. Every person whose body you behold in movement must inevitably possess a soul; every one in whom you behold a soul capable of speech is inevitably possessed of spirit and every one in whom you behold appetitive spirit is inevitably possessed of mind—all these are present in every human being.

Nevertheless, when sickness forms a veil between body and soul the link weakens from its normal state and matter from the soul does not pass in entirety into the body—that is, the five senses [are affected]. Also, when folly, dullness and ignorance form a veil in any person between soul and mind, the matter of mind fails to reach the spirit—that is, thought, foresight, virtue and truth [are affected]. Truly, therefore, no person exists who is deprived of wisdom and virtue; but if the passage of the spiritual matter is barred to the Sublime Effluence, you find pretension for which there exists no substance.

No one in the world, therefore, exists who does not claim virtue. Yet it behoves you, my son, to be different from the rest in pretending to nothing which you cannot substantiate, and in keeping the spiritual passage open to the Sublime Effluence through instruction and exposition, whereby you may become possessed of every real quality without any pretence.

You may know, my son, that the philosophers have formed an image—in words and not physically—of virtue and wisdom. To that image they have attributed body, soul, senses and ideas, in human fashion declaring that the body is "nobility", the soul truth, the senses knowledge and the ideas attributes. This image they apportion out amongst mankind. Some receive body and nothing besides, others body and soul, still others body, soul and senses, and others again body, soul, senses and ideas.

The group whose allotted portion is body are the guild of knights-errant[1] and soldiery, who have the valour suited to their circumstances and to whose virtue is given the name of "nobility". The group that acquired body and soul are first the possessors of exoteric and esoteric knowledge and then faqīrs[2] of the Sufi[3] persuasion; their virtue is called fear of God and gnosis. The group that acquired body, soul and senses consists of the philosophers, prophets and saints, whose virtue is named knowledge and exaltation, while the last group—consisting of those to whom there came body, soul, senses and ideas, is that of "spiritual" men and the apostles.

[1] This is as near as can be got to a formal translation. Those intended are men of the Robin Hood type, popular heroes who benefit the poor at the expense of the rich, whom they rob.

[2] *i.e.* men who have taken a vow of poverty. "Dervish" is a synonym.

[3] The Muslim form of mysticism.

Now, therefore, exert your utmost endeavour, my son, to make all the advance of which you are capable and which lies within your scope. The sages declare that "nobility" consists of three things—fulfilment of your every promise, adherence to the truth both in word and deed and the habit of endurance. Under these three heads is ranged every attribute included in "nobility".

If you find this difficult of comprehension, my son, I concede that it is so. I will therefore reveal to you how these three qualities are applied to the various groups in the measure of their position and importance. Know then, my son, that the noblest of all men is he that is endowed with a variety of good characteristics. To begin with, it behoves him to be brave and manly. Then he must exercise patience in every action, be pure in his sexual life and in his thinking. He must never desire other men's loss for his own benefit; on the contrary he must regard as proper the incurrence of loss for himself in order to benefit his friends. Let him never oppress the weak or let his hand be stretched out extortionately against captives of war; he must grant aid to them who are deprived of means and he must repel harm from any who suffer wrong.

As he speaks the truth, let him listen to it, granting justice of his own accord. To that table at which he has eaten bread and salt let him never bring harm. It behoves him never to requite good with evil, always to hold hypocrisy a disgrace and not to regard hardship as a misfortune.

Truly regarded, all these virtues I have recounted are connected with the three things I have spoken of. It is related by tradition that a group of knights-errant were one day seated together in the mountains when a man approached and after greeting them said, "I am an envoy to you from the knights-errant of the city. They send you greetings and request that you will hear three questions which I will put to you. If you can answer, they will consent to own themselves your inferiors, but, if you cannot, they demand that you acknowledge their superiority."

"Speak on", said they.

Whereupon he asked, "What is 'nobility'[1] and what distinguishes 'ignoble' conduct from 'nobility'? Lastly, suppose a knight-errant to be seated at the roadside as a man comes by. Suppose, further, that a little while later another man comes by, with a sword in his hand for the purpose of slaying the first man, and demands of the knight-errant whether he has seen a man of such-and-such a description passing. What reply should he give? If he says that such a man did pass that way, that constitutes a direction. If he says the man did not pass that way, it is a lie. Neither of these is a worthy answer, and in the code of knight-errantry both would be regarded as 'ignoble'."

When they had listened to these queries, the mountain knights-errant looked at each other. Now there was amongst them a man named Abu'l-Fadl and he undertook to give the replies. On their asking him to speak on and let them see what he would reply, he said, "The root principle of 'nobility' is to perform everything you promise; the distinction between 'nobility' and 'ignoble' conduct lies in endurance; and the response to be made by the knight-errant seated on the roadside is that he must immediately take a step onwards, seat himself again and then say, 'While I have been sitting *here* nobody has passed'. Thus he will have spoken the truth."

When you have comprehended these words the nature of

[1] The Persian word used also means "knight-errantry".

"nobility" will be plain to you. It is proper to look for such "nobility" as I have described as existing in knights-errant amongst soldiers also, for the acme of knight-errantry lies in the soldier's profession. In the soldier, generosity, hospitality, open-handedness, gratitude, chastity and the condition of being abundantly armed should be present in a higher degree than in the rest of mankind, but while a cavilling tongue, regard for self, obedience and submission to command are merits in a soldier, they are faults in a knight-errant.

There is also a "nobility" proper to the men of the bazaar, but as I have dealt with that subject in the chapter on craftsmanship, there is no need to repeat it.

Now for the group which, from the image of virtue, received body and soul. I have said of those men that they are the possessors of knowledge and religion and the faqīrs of the Sufi persuasion, whose virtue we have called fear of God and gnosis. This group possess "nobility" in a greater measure than other men, for the reason that, "nobility" being the body of the image and truth its soul, they possess the soul—that is, truth. Consequently, so far as spiritual culture is concerned, they are such persons as are possessed of knowledge of religion—for example, doctors of religious law.

Their virtue lies in their possession of the qualities now to be described. They must be God-fearing in speech; both in speech and conduct scrupulously honest, steadfast in the faith, far removed from dissimulation, without trace of meanness, zealous in the faith, never to be suspected of envy, never guilty of hypocrisy, never for selfish purposes tearing aside the veil shrouding the inviolability of others, never issuing legal decisions which are wicked or otiose (and thereby barring men from presumptuous indulgence in oaths and divorce). Yet by their decisions they must not bear too hardly upon men. If an unfortunate man by inadvertence breaks the law and the matter can be set right [by money], let the interpreter of the law not be mean but give a lesson in unselfishness. Yet let him not make a display of his piety but thrive to gain himself an honourable reputation.

Let the learned doctor not rebuke the sinner for his sin, especially before other men. If he desires to admonish a person, let him do so out of sight of other persons; to give people advice in public is to insult and wrong them. Let him not be over-hasty, where a man's life is concerned, to give a decision in favour of the penalty of death, even though he may know that the man deserves it. One can make reparation for a sentence passed in error except only where capital punishment is concerned, for a dead man cannot be brought to life again.

Out of sectarian zeal let him condemn no man as an unbeliever; unbelief is hostility to the faith, and not hostility to any particular sect. Further, let him never denounce any book or piece of knowledge which is unfamiliar to him—not everything which may be unknown to him is heresy. Let him provide no encouragement for the common man to transgress, nor cause any man to despair of God's mercy.

The legist or the man of religion who possesses these qualities, is both a virtuous and a "noble" man.

The rules of virtue and "nobility" on the Sufi Path have been set forth by bygone masters in their dissertations, in particular by our master Abu'l-Qāsim al-Qushairī[1] (God

[1] Passed the earlier years of his life at Nishapur, but later migrated to Baghdad. He died in A.D. 1074. His work was designed to revive interest in Sufism, when it was at a low ebb.

compassionate him!) in his "Dissertations on the Rules of Sufism", by the Shaikh and Imam Abu'l-Hasan Maqdisī in the "Exposition of Purity", by Abu Mansūr of Damascus in the "Grandeur of God" and by 'Ali Wāhidi[1] in his "Exposition concerning the Unveiling of Sight". I cannot retail the whole system of this Path in this book in such fashion as it has been retailed by the learned in other works, for my object in this book is to give you counsel and seek after your welfare. Yet I will fulfil my duty of calling them to your attention, so that if ever you are thrown into the society of members of this persuasion, you may not be burdensome to them nor they to you.

I propose to expound the rules of "nobility" prevailing in this community, because no community endures such hardship as this in living its life sincerely and honourably, for the reason that its members regard themselves as superior to the rest of mankind. I have heard it said that the first man to reveal the principles of this Way of Life was Uzair [Ezra] the Prophet. He reached such a height in his career that the Jews came to declare that he was the son of God. I have also heard it said that in the time of the Apostle (God's blessings upon him!) there were twelve men, called "Companions of the Porch", with whom he frequently sat in private conclave and with whom he was intimate. It is for this reason that the code of conduct of this persuasion and the system of "nobility" of this society is more difficult than that of any other society.

Etiquette and "nobility" in this body are of two kinds, the first being appropriated to dervishes of the Sufi Order and the second to supporters. I shall give an account of both kinds.

[1] Another native of Nishapur and a noted commentator on the Koran. He died in A.D. 1075.

Understand then that the whole of dervishism lies in being rid of property—ridding oneself of possessions and independence being the essence of Sufism. I have been told the story of how on one occasion two Sufis were travelling together, one utterly bare of worldly goods and the other in possession of five dinars. The penniless one went along entirely free of concern, asked for no companion, and, whatever the nature of the place they reached, whether safe or dangerous, sat or slept and rested without fear of anyone. The other man, who had five dinars, kept him company but was in constant apprehension.

They at last arrived at a well, situated in a dangerous spot which was the haunt of robbers and highwaymen. There the possessionless dervish took a drink from the well, laid down his head and fell asleep; but the owner of the five dinars dared not sleep. He kept softly repeating to himself, "What shall I do? What shall I do? If only I were safe from accidents!" Suddenly the possessionless dervish awoke and, hearing him, said, "O, so-and-so, what has happened to you that you keep saying, 'What shall I do?' 'What shall I do?' " He answered, "My brother, I have five dinars with me and this is a dangerous place. You went to sleep, but I can neither go to sleep nor depart from here."

Thereupon the penniless Sufi said, "Give me the five dinars and I will arrange matters for you". On the other's handing over the money, he took it and threw it into the well, saying, "Now you are relieved from troubling about what you are to do. Lie down and go to sleep in security. Pennilessness is a brazen fortress."

In the agreed view of the initiated, therefore, the reality of Sufism lies in three things: ridding oneself of possessions, self-surrender and belief. Provided you possess any one of these three you are inaccessible to misfortune, and if in your whole person you are without taint of self-indulgence, the essence of this Way of Life is yours. The dervish, therefore, must practise self-surrender and never stand in opposition to his brother except on behalf of another brother. His one constant source of grief must be his brother's failure to be better than he is himself.

It behoves him to put self out of his thoughts, never to foster personal ambition, to lay aside self-seeking, to fix his regard upon conviction concerning the truth and upon poverty, to see nothing with the eye of duplicity and to cease looking [upon the world] with apprehension or [thought of] being opposed. None will stand in opposition to the views of him that is convinced of the truth and is without fear, for the essence of verity is the negation of ambiguity and the essence of conviction concerning the truth is the negation of its reverse. Understand, my son, that if a man were to step out upon the waters with the conviction of truth, the waters would become firm beneath his foot. Further, if a man relates to you stories of some of the miracles of the saints—stories or ideas remote from the path of reason and such that appear impossible to you—you will not deny them once you have gained a knowledge of the truth of phenomena. Upon conviction about the truth there lies a mark which can be perceived by your heart neither through reason nor a blind adherence to forms, but only through God's grace and bounty and your own physical composition.

The dervish, then, is he that looks upon things with the eye of conviction of the truth, makes no declaration of loneliness [*i.e.* of being cut off from the society of men], keeps his external conduct at one with his inward feelng and never permits his heart to be devoid of conviction of God's unity. In his thinking it behoves him to exercise calmness and deliberation, so that he may avoid being consumed in the fire of thought. Those who follow this Path see in thinking a fire, the water to counter which is relaxation. They have therefore created entertainment, dancing and music as conducive to relaxation, any dervish who is averse to music and singing being ever burnt up in the fire of thought.

Yet it is impossible for him that is without thought of declaring God's unity to indulge in music and singing, for darkness [*i.e.* absence of fire] is but increased by darkness. Shaikh Akhī Zingānī[1] towards the end of his life forbade music, saying, "Music is water, which should be where fire is not. Pouring water on fire merely brings darkness and mud. Suppose that in a company of fifty persons, one is attacked by fire; it would be contrary to the fitness of things to cast the other forty-nine persons into darkness for the sake of that one. Tranquillity is as little to be expected in that one person as conviction of the truth in the others".

If a man is a dervish who is not possessed of esoteric learning and spiritual knowledge, then it behoves him to acquire exoteric learning so that he may be equipped with one at least of the two aspects.

The qualities, then, demanded of the dervish are—that he should be trustworthy, polite in speech, clear of imperfection, in a state to have his sins forgiven, of obvious piety, clean in his person and immaculate in his sexual conduct.

The dervish must be equipped with the necessary utensils whether for the road or for settled life. These are such articles as a staff, a water-pot for ablutions, a loin-cloth,

[1] A Persian gnostic who died in A.D. 1058.

shoes, a prayer-mat, a cowl, a comb, a tooth-brush, a needle and nail-scissors. He should be independent of others' help for tailoring and the washing of clothes. In these two operations he should serve his brethren. He must have a liking for travel but should not go alone, seeing that misfortunes happen through solitariness.

When a dervish enters a convent, let him not be an impediment to acts of piety, that is, let him not discourage approaches made to him. First, [on entrance] he must remove the shoe from his right foot—the left foot being the one first to be covered with a shoe. He should not enter a company with his waist-girdle tied about him, and it is his duty to take his seat in the corner allotted to him. Before seating himself, he must ask leave and, by leave also, he must utter a short prayer. Whenever he comes in or goes out he must make salutation, although if he omits to do so it may pass. There must be no oversight, however, with respect to the morning ceremony of wine-drinking.

His converse with people must be pleasant but he should avoid the society of persons who are suspect. If he is not familiar with lofty Sufi diction, he should utter no words from its vocabulary. He should enter no dwelling or convent until he is made welcome, nor force his society upon any man, but he should carefully respect other men's right of privacy, such respect being a prescribed religious duty, whereas sociability is not.

All his actions must depend upon the decision and consent of the company. If it expresses disapproval of him, even though he is blameless, he must not oppose it but ask pardon, offer amends, suffer the humiliation and make no harsh criticism of the society. He should rarely be absent from his prayer-mat and never of his own accord visit the bazaar.

Whenever he wishes to arise, desiring to perform some such personal task as putting on or taking off clothes, he must ask leave of the company or of the eldest in the company.

The dervish should not sit cross-legged upon his prayer-mat, nor mend his patched dervish-robe secretly and out of sight of others, nor eat in secret even as much as a single almond, for that is accounted bad behaviour. When in the society of others he should not indulge in over-much talk. If they throw open their robes, he must do likewise, and similarly if they remove them. So far as lies within his power he must never rend another dervish's robe.[1] When it comes to the partitioning of food, he must not propose to undertake the task, with which are connected a number of rites not within the power of everyone to execute. Yet he should seize any opportunity of pouring water for ablutions.

He may not set his foot on another's prayer-mat, nor hasten through the midst of the company, nor pass in front of a large company, nor sit in the place allotted to another, nor annoy any person. During the performance of music or the ceremony of robe-rending, while the Elder is engaged in observance of the rite it behoves the dervish not to rise from his place nor to utter any word. Nor must he perform a purposeless dance, nor turn his back upon anyone while he dances. When he has rent the garment upon his own person, he must not immediately shed it, nor clothe himself in the presence of the Elder.

If another dervish either praises or blames him, he must thank him for his words and lay something before him as

[1] "It is a custom of the Sufis to rend their garments, and they have commonly done this in great assemblies where eminent Shaykhs were present." [*The Kashf al-Mahjūb,* the oldest Persian treatise on Sufism, by 'Alī al-Hujwīrī, translated by R. A. Nicholson (London, 1936), p. 417.]

a gift. If another dervish offers him a dervish-robe, he may not refuse it but must accept it, add [a patch] to it and then hand it back. If he does another dervish a service, whether it be to stitch or wash a garment for him, he must not hand the article back without thanks. If he commits an act which causes annoyance to another dervish, he must quickly make amends, but if it brings pleasure to the other he must [himself] render thanks.

The dervish must of his own accord grant what is due from him to others, but should not demand, so far as it is possible for him, what is due from others to him. (Nevertheless, the dervishes of Isfahan both demand and give [without demand] what is due, those of Khurasan neither demand nor give, those of Tabaristan demand but do not give, those of Pars give but do not demand—and I have been told that it was in Pars that the practice of Sufism was first invented.)

The dervish should regard the hardship of his life as a boon. (For his journeying he should adopt a gentle pace.) At meal-times he should not absent himself from table, so that the company may not be kept waiting for him, and he should not before the others stretch out his hand towards the food nor withdraw from food except in company with the others. He should not expect more than his share nor, except by leave, should he express a preference for a particular morsel for himself, to the loss of someone else. If by reason of illness he is unable to partake of food, he must make his excuses before the table is laid; once at table he must say nothing. If he is keeping a voluntary fast, he must inform nobody of it, but [when at table] must break his fast in agreement with the others.

He must exercise care when going to stool and should keep his clothes short. For ceremonial lustration he should not at one time use the 'Iraqi method and at another the Khwarazmian. After lustration, and while his feet are wet, he should not seat himself upon the prayer-mat nor slip his feet into his shoes, nor place them on the ground even though it be clean. By [not] doing these things he will prevent himself from invalidating his purification.

That, then, is the code of the "nobility" and the etiquette of Sufism. The code of the uninitiated adherent is that he must express no disapproval of the esoteric talk of Sufis, must never demand an explanation of it, must regard their faults as virtues (even, to take an extreme example, to the extent of recognising their [apparent] misbelief as true faith), must atone for any speech disapproved by them, must maintain himself unspotted in their presence, must seat himself respectfully in his own place, must show respect to any dervish-robe of theirs which falls to him (by kissing it, laying it upon his head, preventing it from falling to the ground and not using it for any unworthy purpose).

The uninitiated adherent of Sufism should at all times do what is correct. If he sees the Sufis taking off their robes, he must do so too; if they have taken them off in an access of conviviality, he must buy them back with an invitation or with food, must remove and kiss them, lay them upon his head and restore them to their owners. If the robes have fallen off in the course of a quarrel, he must in no circumstances interfere, but leave all to the Elder. By all possible means he must avoid concerning himself in a quarrel between Sufis, and, if one should occur in his presence, he must remain still, uttering no word and leaving them to arrange matters to their satisfaction.

In the presence of Sufis let him not play God's advocate, saying, "It is time for worship", or "Let us rise for worship''. He should not urge them to religious duties, for they have no need of any other person's urging to be pious. When he is amongst them let him not laugh to excess, nor yet be gloomy in spirit or sour-visaged; if one is a person of that kind, they call for his shoes that he may depart.

If at any time he should procure a sweetmeat, even in the smallest quantity, he should carry it to them with apologies and say, ''I did not wish to commit a blunder, even though this is so very little. But Sufis have the first right.'' A reference to the subject occurs in this quatrain of mine:

O thou whose beauty is beyond compare,
A Sufi I, as all men are aware.
In sweetness rich your lips are sugar-plums,
And sweetness is the Sufi's chiefest care.

If you act in this fashion you will fulfil the whole duty of uninitiated adherents of Sufism and attain to what is their ''nobility'', for the code of duty and ''nobility'' of novices and the uninitiated is such as I have described.

Now for the group who received as their allotted portion of the image of virtue, body, soul and senses; that is to say, ''nobility'', truth and knowledge. That group is constituted by the prophets, for every person in whom there exists this combination of three qualities is of necessity an apostle or the percipient executor of the will of an apostle, seeing that both the physical and the spiritual virtues exist in him, the physical virtues being truth and knowledge and the spiritual one gnosis.

If it is an enigma to you why gnosis has been translated on to a higher plane than that of knowledge, you must understand that *shinākhtan* [''Gnosis''] is the Persian equivalent of the Arabic *ma'rifah* [''Knowledge''] and that its true significance is "transference of something out of the realm of the unknown into that of the known". Further, the Persian equivalent of the Arabic *'ilm* ["Recognition"] is *dānish*, the true significance of which is the perfect comprehension of known and unknown as being such, to the end that you may understand the gradations of good and evil.

Understand further that knowledge of anything implies cognition of five qualities in it: quiddity, quality, quantity, reason and purpose. Quiddity implies your saying, "I recognise what (or who) so-and-so is", and that is knowledge. In that sense the beasts are associated with man, because they recognise their food and young in the same way as man. When increased knowledge came to man, he learnt to associate with quiddity the qualities indicating quality, quantity, reason and purpose. Do you not observe how, when you light a fire in a place where cattle pasture, they will not move away before they have put their heads into it and suffered the torment of the fire and been burnt? The reason is that they know the fire only in its quiddity and not in its quality, whereas man knows both quiddity and quality.

This, then, is proof of the claim that gnosis is on a higher plane than knowledge, and, on the same line of reasoning, he that is possessed of gnosis in its perfection has the qualities requisite for prophethood. The argument for this is that the prophets have as great a degree of eminence and distinction surpassing ours as we have over those of the animals, on the grounds that animals have knowledge of quiddity and no more and [ordinary] men have knowledge of quality and quantity in addition, whereas prophets have knowledge of quality, quantity, reason and purpose. The animal knows merely that the fire burns, whereas man knows the reason for which fire burns when it is lit.

Now the acme of humaneness is virtue; that is, that in which there exists the acme of ''nobility'', the acme of ''nobility'' being that in which there exists the acme of knowledge. This is prophethood, and the acme of prophethood is spirituality, because, in the scale of humanity there is no degree higher than that of prophethood.

As for the group who receive (as their allotted portion of the image of virtue) body, soul, senses and ideas, it cannot consist of any but prophets. The man who has received the whole of the image of virtue cannot be described in terms other than those of Spiritual Purity. He passes beyond ordinary conception, and recognition of him comes about in his dealings with men rather than in his utterances. The experience of the man endowed with this spiritual purity is peculiar to himself, as also is his knowledge. His purity has no precedent and the object he has in view is without trace of egotism or self-seeking. He is untainted by misanthropy and unspotted by selfishness; being detached from material cause his subsistence lies in his dying to self. The description of him is that he is pure in attribute; he beholds himself from a position outside himself and looks into his essence with the eye of ''eyelessness''.

It is proper, therefore, to regard the plane of this group as an elevated one and as occupying a position appropriated to philosophical speculation.

Now, my son, whatever you become, be provident and wedded to ''nobility'', and thereby become the world's chosen one. If, whatever be the society to which you belong, your desire is to tread the path of knight-errantry, then do not cling [slavishly] to the prescriptions of the law, but keep three things ever closely controlled: your eye against seeing what is not meant to be seen, your tongue against uttering what should not be said, and your hand against taking what is not yours to take. But, on behalf of your friends keep three things open: the door of your house, a place at your table and the fastenings of your purse, to the full extent of your powers.

Never utter a lie; ignoble men betray themselves by their lying and the whole essence of ignoble conduct lies in falsehood. Should a man throw himself upon your chivalry, then, even if he has slain the one dearest to you and though he be your greatest enemy, once he has surrendered to you, admitted his helplessness and entrusted himself to your chivalry rather than that of any other man, though your life is likely to be imperilled by your act, let it go. Have no fear; fight for your life on his behalf and thus achieve "nobility".

Guard against becoming obsessed with desire to avenge some past injury, or planning treachery. Treachery can play no part in the code of "nobility". This subject, my son, is one that can be pursued to great lengths, and if I were to expatiate on what constitutes "nobility" in each organisation, with the how and wherefore of such codes, my discourse would be over-long. But let me speak briefly, promising that what I say is the cutting-edge of the subject.

Understand, then, that it is the height of "nobility" to recognise that what is yours is yours and to destroy any particle of covetousness for what is other people's. If you possess wealth, rather let others have a share of it than be rapacious of their goods, and do not take away what you yourself have bestowed. If you can do men a kindness, do so; but if you cannot do good, then at least refrain from doing injury to others. The greatest of men in the world is he that lives in the manner I have described, for he will inherit both this world and the next.

You will have realised, my son, that in various passages in this book I have spoken of contentment. Yet I will repeat myself here again to say, "If you do not wish to be constantly unhappy, be content and never envious; so may your life ever be pleasant, for the root of vexation lies in envy".

Understand also that celestial influences, both good and bad, are ever reaching downwards towards men. My teacher used to say, "Man must ever stand with braced shoulders and open mouth confronting the heavens; if they send a hard blow it can be taken by the shoulders and, if a dainty morsel, by the mouth." Thus God declares [Koran 7, v. 141] "Take what I bring you and number yourself among the grateful". The influence of the heavens can only determine one of the two [good or evil].

Once you have decided upon your course and made contentment your habit, as a man unfettered you will be in thrall to no one. Never allow rapacity to find a place in your heart but acquiesce in the fortune which chance has allotted to you, whether it be good or bad. Consider that the whole of mankind, in whatever station, is subject to one Master and all men are the descendants of Adam. Yet one man is inferior to another by reason of his desires and rapacity. Once a man has cast rapacity out of his heart and adopted contentment as his way of life, he will cease to make demands upon the rest of his mortal fellows. Indeed, he who makes least demand upon his fellows, is he who finds most honour in the world, whereas the meanest and most despicable of mankind is he that is filled with greed and avarice.

It is because of such greed and covetousness that men turn themselves into the bondsmen of their own kind. There is an anecdote concerning Shiblī[1] which tells how he once entered a mosque to say a short prayer and rest for a while. There was a school attached to the mosque and boys came in to eat, it being then the hour for their meal. It chanced that two boys seated themselves near Shiblī, one the son of a wealthy man and the other a poor man's son. The one had in his basket some halwa[2], while the other had only dry bread in his, and as the rich boy was eating the sweetmeat the poor man's son kept begging from him, until at last he said, "If you want me to give you some halwa, you must be my dog". At this the other said, "I am your dog". "Now", said the rich boy, "bark!". The unhappy poor boy thereupon bent double and barked like a dog, and was given a piece of halwa.

Shiblī, who was a spectator of all this, burst into tears, and on his disciples' demanding the reason for his weeping, he replied, "See to what a state greed reduces men. If that boy had been content with his own bare piece of bread and had had no desire for the other's halwa, he would never have needed to become the other's dog".

Thus, then, whether you be saint or sinner, exercise contentment and let your actions be worthy of approbation. So will you become the greatest person in the world and the one with fewest fears.

Consider, my son, that I have in this book composed forty-four chapters, each upon some topic of which I had knowledge. To the best of my ability I have described what I had in mind for your benefit and given you all I possessed in the way of counsel and beneficial advice. The one exception is the subject of wisdom, for I can in no fashion tell you that

[1] A well-known Sufi saint of Baghdad, where he died in A.D. 946.
[2] A sweet cake made of a variety of ingredients.

you are under an obligation to be intelligent and wise. One cannot become intelligent by compulsion.

Now there are two forms of intelligence, the one innate and the other acquired (and each has its special designation in Persian). The acquired form can be learnt, but innate intelligence is the gift of God and cannot be learnt by instruction from a teacher. If it so happens that God endows you with innate intelligence, undertake the labour of learning also that which may be acquired, adding the acquired to the natural so that the degree of perfection is attained and you become the prodigy of your age.

Should there be no innate intelligence, however, neither I nor you can do anything in the matter. But in that event there must be no deficiency in the acquired form of intelligence. You must learn to the full extent of which you are capable to ensure that, although you may not be numbered amongst the wise, you are, on the other hand, not reckoned amongst ignorant fools. Thereby you will become endowed with one kind of intelligence at least; for, as the proverb says, "Where there is no father, nothing is better than a mother".

Should it, therefore, be your desire to become a man of wisdom, acquire philosophy, because it is possible to learn wisdom through philosophy. As Aristotle said, when asked whence wisdom drew its strength, "Every man's strength is derived from his food, and the food of wisdom is derived from philosophy".

Understand now, my son, that I have given you some description of every kind of science, accomplishment and craft known to me, and these I have combined with statements of my own practices to form a book in forty-four chapters for your benefit. Consider, my son, that from youth to old age it has been my habit to behave as I have described and I have spent the space of the sixty-three years of my existence in such courses. I began my book in the year 475 [of the Hijrah, A.D. 1082–3] and if God grants me life henceforward, I shall continue to behave as I have done in the past for the remainder of my life. What I regard as fitting for myself I approve for you, but if you consider other qualities or practices to be preferable, adopt them. Otherwise, listen to these counsels of mine with the ear of your heart and apply them in practice. If you neither listen to them nor approve of them, there is no compulsion upon you to do so. The person whom God has created to be felicitous will hear and approve of them and will apply them in practice; for everything that I have uttered is an indicator to this world and the next—to them that are destined for bliss.

May God Almighty vouchsafe mercy to me and you and extend to you my happiness in both worlds by his favour, grace and magnanimity.

Praise be to God, Lord of all worlds!

INDEX